Community Buildin Twenty-First Century

The School of American Research gratefully acknowledges the co-sponsorship of the Society for Applied Anthropology in developing this volume.

Publication of the Advanced Seminar Series
is made possible by generous support from
The Brown Foundation, Inc., of Houston, Texas.

**School of American Research
Advanced Seminar Series**

George J. Gumerman
General Editor

Community Building in the Twenty-First Century

Contributors

Julie Adkins
Department of Anthropology, Southern Methodist University

Marietta L. Baba
Department of Anthropology, Michigan State University

Linda A. Bennett
Department of Anthropology and College of Arts and Sciences,
University of Memphis

Noel J. Chrisman
School of Nursing, University of Washington

Stanley E. Hyland
School of Urban Affairs and Public Policy, University of Memphis

Robert V. Kemper
Department of Anthropology, Southern Methodist University

Anthony Oliver-Smith
Department of Anthropology, University of Florida

Michelle Owens
Department of Anthropology, University of Memphis

Jean J. Schensul
Institute for Community Research, Hartford, Connecticut

John van Willigen
Department of Anthropology, University of Kentucky

Community Building in the Twenty-First Century

Edited by Stanley E. Hyland

School of American Research Press

Santa Fe

School of American Research Press

Post Office Box 2188
Santa Fe, New Mexico 87504-2188

Director: James F. Brooks
Executive Editor: Catherine Cocks
Manuscript Editor: Kate Talbot
Design and Production: Cynthia Dyer
Proofreader: Amanda A. Morgan
Indexer: Jan Wright
Printer: Maple-Vail Book Manufacturing Group

Library of Congress Cataloging-in-Publication Data:

Community building in the twenty-first century / edited by Stanley E. Hyland– 1st ed.
    p. cm. – (School of American Research advanced seminar series)
  Includes bibliographical references and index.
  ISBN 1-930618-61-1 (cloth : alk. paper) – ISBN 1-930618-62-x (pbk. : alk. paper)
  1. Community. 2. Community development. I. Hyland, Stanley, Ph. D II. Series.

HM756.C63 2005
307--DC22

                    2005010893

Cover illustration: *Norwalk Fabric, An American Experience* © 2004 by Rita I. Phillips. Quilt made with paper piecing, appliqué, ink drawing directly on fabric, embroidery, photo transfer to fabric, three-dimensional attached American flag, 50 5 " x 65.5 ". Used by permission of the artist.

Contents

Figures and Table

Acknowledgments

This book occurred because of an idea to collaborate around a critical societal issue that was growing in national and international significance—community and community building. In 1999 the School of American Research, long noted for its commitment to scholarship, and the Society for Applied Anthropology, long noted for its commitment to addressing human problems through scholarship, began a long-standing relationship. More specifically, Douglas Schwartz, then president of the School of American Research, and Linda Bennett, then president of the Society for Applied Anthropology, and Tom May, executive director, saw an opportunity to return to a question that, historically, was held deeply but was also generating much interdisciplinary and policy debate in forging a path to resolving conflicts brought about by global structural inequalities, scarce resources, and ethnocentrism. Research on the topics of community and community building had grown exponentially in the preceding decade—so much so that scholars and practitioners were talking past each other.

Their wisdom to grapple with a rethinking of the growing literature and its applications led them to invite a group of engaged scholars involved in community development work over the past three decades to begin this task. The work of these scholars over a three-year period has been challenging. Each brought a different focus and set of methods to the table. Each challenged the others' frameworks. Each worked diligently in light of the others' scholarship. Along the way, several distinguished scholars were brought into the mix. I would like to acknowledge Mary Catherine Bateson for her invocation at the 2001

SfAA meetings in Merida and her emphasis on communities of inclusion and diversity and, similarly, Jodi Kretzmann for his forceful articulation of the processes of community building through the mapping of community assets. Equally important has been the facilitation provided by Nancy Owens Lewis and Linda Bennett, as well as the critical feedback by the SAR/SfAA reviewers and the SAR Press editor, Catherine Cocks. I particularly want to acknowledge the assistance of Kristen Maurette, a graduate student, and my wife, Keife, who worked with me through every critical step of this effort.

Stan Hyland

Dedication

To the practicing anthropologists who continue to commit themselves to community-building efforts throughout the world.

Community Building in the Twenty-First Century

1

Introduction

Stanley E. Hyland and Linda A. Bennett

Community Building in the Twenty-First Century is a plenary seminar-publication project initiated in 1999 by the School of American Research (SAR) and the Society for Applied Anthropology (SfAA). In light of the growing interest in community and community building, SAR President Douglas Schwartz asked a group of scholars affiliated with the SfAA to revisit the question of the community's role in the twenty-first century. The request was linked to a plenary session at the society's 2001 annual meetings held in Merida, Mexico, in the Yucatan, where Robert Redfield studied and extensively wrote on the "little community" fifty years earlier.

THE DEFINITION OF *COMMUNITY*

Community was specifically chosen as the topic for the opening collaborative program because, as a unit of study, it has been social scientists' focal point for research and action since the rise of industrial capitalism (Nisbet 1966). For anthropologists and sociologists, the concept of community has changed in use and application over the past four generations. Since Redfield's (1955) classic study of the little community, most anthropologists have used the local community (village, town, neighborhood) as a basic unit of study and analysis in their field research (Arensberg 1961; Arensberg and Kimball 1965). Both archaeologists and sociocultural anthropologists have adopted the concept of community as a cornerstone of their analyses. In fact, Redfield (1955:3) noted, the local community "has been the very predominant form of human living throughout the history of mankind."

Building on Redfield's research and The Chicago School of Urban Sociology's ecological studies of communities in the 1920s and 1930s, urban sociologists and anthropologists in the 1960s expanded their work on residential ethnic communities to examine the processes of social order (Gans 1962a; Suttles 1968) and political mobilization (Kornblum 1974) in a variety of residential settings such as inner-city neighborhoods, suburbs, and retirement communities (Gans 1967; Hannerz 1969; and Jacobs 1974). During this period, they increasingly applied the concept of community to occupational groups, special interest groups, lifestyle groups, imagined communities, and power configurations as these affect decision making (Jacobs 1974; Anderson 1983; Pilcher 1972; Johnson 1971; Cavan 1972; Hunter 1953; Hawley and Svara 1972; Hawley and Wirt 1974).

The conventional wisdom of the post-World War II period was that the systematic study of the community had developed around the general focus of shared living based on common locality (Warren 2004:54; Keller 2003). Therefore, *community* was typically defined as a group of interconnected people located in bounded geosocial space, sharing a common origin, and supported by an economic, religious, social, political, and physical infrastructure—that is, connected to resources (Gallaher and Padfield 1980). In terms of our understanding of culture and globalization, community was the point of intersection between the individual and the larger society and culture (Warren 2004). Community was perceived as a unit that was larger than families, social networks, and groups but smaller than a society's most complex components, such as the city, state, or multinational corporation. Community was also the location of production, socialization, participation, norms, and mechanisms of social control.

By the end of the twentieth century, the definition of *community* had expanded. Etzioni (1993), in his book *Spirit of Community*, elaborated on the significance of communities as beacons of moral voices that lay claim to their members. Carl Moore (1996:28), a scholar and an activist who participated in the SAR-sponsored advanced seminar "Rethinking Communities in the Year 2000," wrote in *The Chronicle of Community* that certain agreed-upon factors can be used to construct a working definition of *community:* "A community is the means by which people live together. Communities enable people to protect themselves and to acquire the resources that provide for their needs. Communities provide intellectual, moral, and social values that give purpose to survival. Community members share an identity, speak a common language, agree upon role definitions, share common values, assume some permanent membership status, and understand the social boundaries within which they operate."

Anthropologist R. Helperin (1998:5), based on her extensive field research in an inner-city Cincinnati neighborhood, succinctly stated that community "is not just a place, although place is very important, but a series of day to day, ongoing, often invisible practices. These practices are connected to but not confined to place."

Susanne Keller's book (2003:8) titled *Community: Pursuing the Dream, Living the Reality* affirms Moore's multidimensional definition. Of significance to our book, she argues that, for the term *community* to be useful, we must move away from all-encompassing generalizations and misconceptions based on exclusivity. We must emphasize its dynamic quality, that is, its evolution over time through the examination of context.

LOCAL COMMUNITIES UNDER ASSAULT

Early community studies by anthropologists such as Goodenough (1961), Arensberg (1961), and Arensberg and Kimball (1965) contributed to an understanding of the persistence of community life patterns through cooperation in the context of globalization and increasing outside threats to local control. In the post-World War II period, numerous community studies emphasized the living dynamics of peasant communities (Roberts 1978) and urban villages and subcultures (Gutkind 1973; Hannerz 1969; Mangin 1970). During the 1960s, however, community studies increasingly focused on the overwhelmingly negative impacts of macro changes on the life patterns of localized communities. This trend led to a growing anthropological concern for uprooted rural families who faced problems of adaptation to urban areas (Gmelch and Zenner 1996; Foster and Kemper 1996; Southall 1973). Addressing the causes of the migration streams, in 1965 Art Gallaher and Douglas Schwartz initiated a discussion of classic anthropological and sociological questions about the demise of the local community—why and how do local communities function through time?

Broadening this discussion, in 1976 Art Gallaher and Harland Padfield led an advanced seminar at the School of American Research in Santa Fe, New Mexico, to examine the dynamics of dying communities. They argued that too little critical analysis had focused on the "need to develop a conceptual and theoretical framework for examining the decline and dissolution of community" (Gallaher and Padfield 1980:xi). In contrast to a plethora of studies on community development, very few social scientists were addressing concerns regarding the decline and demise of local communities.

Gallaher and Padfield began with the paradox that community is a critical sociocultural adaptation used by all human groups but that it needs to be nurtured with resources. Otherwise, the local community will decline and die. They note that "all associational forms share what we believe to be the most basic of all purposes—the development of collective solutions to meet the needs of group survival. If these needs cannot be met in a specific case, the psychological sense of community diminishes, and a community begins to die" (Gallaher and Padfield 1980:2). Their thesis was that both the resources and the decision-making prerogatives for allocating those resources must be present.

The cross-cultural case studies published in Gallaher and Padfield's *The Dying Community* illustrate the growing influence of global forces on local groups and demonstrate the necessity of controlling resources at the local level. Since publication of this book, outside change factors have transformed the nature of local community life at an accelerated pace. These factors include growing economic inequality, natural disasters, human degradation of the environment, global diseases, public policy and the shifting of economic resources (capital), and concomitantly increasing economic disparity among groups. As the twentieth century came to a close, the centralization created by information technology (the digital divide), global transportation, and marketing had blurred the boundaries defining local community identity and action.

THE GROWING DISCOURSE

As global forces have taken an increasing toll on local communities, social scientists have begun to focus their research on how local community-based groups react to these macro forces. Responses range from adaptation, social networking, organizing, and coalition building, to various types of resistance. Social scientists, policy makers, planners, developers, marketers, and activists are now expanding their discussion of and applications for community, with respect to change, development, building, and the commodification of community (Warren 2004).

By the year 2000 the international and national discourse about community had assumed great significance. The discourse was largely attributed to the publication of three widely read books, notably, Putnam's *Bowling Alone* (2000), which advances the notion of social capital; Keller's *Community* (2003), which revisits the question of how a sense of community takes hold; and Kretzmann and McKnight's (1993) *Building Communities from the Inside Out*, which advocates an asset-based approach to community building.

Putnam's work on social capital and community generated a national debate on its application to the restoration of a civic society in which ideologies of rugged individualism and capitalism are associated with a widening economic gap between the rich and the poor, as well as decreasing participation in political and social associations. Putnam notes, "Over the last three decades or so, the gap between haves and have-nots has grown steadily and alarmingly.... At the same time, Americans of all classes and races, and in all sections of the country, have become increasingly disconnected from their communities and from one another" (Saegert, Thompson, and Warren 2001:xv). Central to his work and the chapters in this book is the concept of social capital, the idea that resources such as skills, knowledge, reciprocity, norms, and values facilitate community members' working together to make substantial improvements in the entire community's living conditions. Parenthetically, as each contributor to this book points out, anthropologists have been describing social capital and its link to community development in their ethnographies of local populations for decades. Irrespective of this, social capital by Putnam's definition is an essential dimension of community building.

In Kreztmann and McKnight's work with social capital and community assets, they targeted the community-activist practitioner concerned with revitalizing largely forgotten areas. Their work advocated new tools and skills employed at the local community level to empower local community members and build social capital. Kretzmann and McKnight's work is notable among the new approaches that extend the earlier discussion by Schwartz and Gallaher to address dying (troubled) communities, not by studying them but by developing tools for rebuilding them. At that time, applied anthropologists such as Steven L. and Jean J. Schensul (1978) were pursuing similar paths in developing advocacy anthropology and participatory action research that engaged community partners in the research and outcome process. All this research has resonated through the foundation, government, and community activist worlds, which continually seek new approaches to revitalization.

THE PURPOSE OF THE BOOK

In light of the growing international and national policies focusing on strengthening communities through new approaches and tools, this book is an effort to pull together disparate areas of community and community-building studies and link them to the development of a new conceptual framework for future anthropological work. Specifically, *Community Building in the Twenty-First Century* aims to stretch our understanding of community and community building, especially stock definitions based on traditional social and physical features. We emphasize the human processes of relationship building by which people live and work together in place and time (Moore 1996). The chapters in this book examine how old definitions of place associated with community are linked with the creation of newer ones in the context of change. In turn, new definitions of place and community are used to reconstitute relationships and institutions that integrate and anchor, to varying degrees, new and old institutions and people.

Furthermore, this work aspires to scrutinize the limitations of customary approaches to community development, which have come to dominate the liberal welfare state in advanced industrial states. Typically, such approaches stress a deficiency-oriented understanding of low-income people and neighborhoods and recommend outside expert intervention. Kretzmann (2001), in his address at the 2001 SfAA meeting in Merida, noted that "government policies supported by problem-focused social science research, as well as philanthropic relief and relentless violence-seeking spotlight of the mass media, have combined to obscure the internal resources of struggling communities and reinforce an 'outside in' set of problem-solving assumptions and strategies." Kretzmann's presentation (2001) further described the six major community-building observations that challenge all future research and practice:

1. The focus on local communities is now a national and even an international phenomenon. From the developing world through the former Soviet Union and Eastern Europe, to Western Europe and North America, policy makers are rediscovering the importance of the local forms of civil society and social capital.

2. Why is this happening? A growing body of evidence suggests that many of the outcomes we value most highly—food, health, strong families, a clean environment, a vibrant economy, safe and secure communities—are actually produced, to a significant degree, by strong and active local communities.

3. What obstacles stand in the way of community building? There are many, but one major difficulty is the inclination of our most powerful institutions (for example, universities, private and public funders, and media) to focus relentlessly on the needs, problems, and deficiencies of struggling communities while ignoring their assets.

4. What is the alternative to deficiency-focused policies and strategies? Vital communities recognize and mobilize their own unique combination of five categories of community assets: the skills of local residents, the power of local voluntary associations, the resources of local institutions, their natural and built physical resources, and their local economic power.

5. Communities are inventing powerful strategies to engage all five kinds of assets, but mobilizing the first two is often the greatest challenge. Capacity inventories and gift interviews are

tools to invite even the most marginalized citizens to contribute to the community. Also, mapping and mobilizing local associations (block clubs, sports teams, choirs) add power and depth to community-building efforts.

6. Providing effective support from the outside (for example, the government or a funder) remains a challenge. But creative community-building supporters are finding ways to move from a "charity" to an "investment" strategy and to create important "citizen space" in which local communities can act.

The chapters in this volume address Kreztmann's community-building observations from various geographic contexts, research perspectives, and literatures—resettlements, rural villages, inner-city neighborhoods; voluntary associations and faith-based organizations; multinational corporations and virtual communities; and community health. All the contributors take issue with past approaches that emphasized the effectiveness of top-down and expert-oriented practices focusing on local deficiencies.

Each chapter in this book emphasizes community assets as a critical factor in community building. At the same time, each considers the various political, economic, and social factors that divide a community and cannot be resolved simply by an optimistic view that people will come together around assets and resources. In chapter 5, Hyland and Owens discuss the inner-city tensions between drug dealers and community activists debating whose vision for the neighborhood should win out. In chapter 8, Jean Schensul suggests an example from her fieldwork in a small rural community where past firings intimidated teachers from challenging corrupt local practices. In chapter 6, Baba describes a series of cultural and political factors that undermine community building in corporations. The documentation, analysis, and confrontation of divisive internal factors within a community-building framework are critical to all future work.

Broadening the scope of community development approaches, each chapter in this book recognizes the importance of strengthening human relationships to build communities based on the mobilization of local assets and collaborative approaches, in contrast to processes that encourage the status quo or even demise of communities. One cannot talk about community and community building without, first, acknowledging the existing relationships within the community and examining the myriad other relationships that develop, either consequently or intentionally, and, second, considering the various political, economic, and cultural factors that are divisive in all the processes involved in building and sustaining community.

As globalization and technology expand their influence on communities and bring even the most disparate communities in contact with one another and the world at large, it becomes more complex and also more important for social scientists to attend to these elements. Researchers and practitioners are challenged to develop theories, methods, and tools that will help not only to sustain and grow communities in the face of these global and technological changes, but also to make governmental, social, and business attitudes and policies more responsive to community values and needs.

The contributors to this book are scholars who have spent the past three decades engaged in the field of community development and who possess an expressed sense of social justice. They also reflect a theoretical and political heterodoxy in their approaches to community building for the twenty-first century. Some contributors assume or state directly that community building must be rooted in participatory democracy; others strongly advocate that community development efforts be appropriate to the particular group in question. These positions raise the question of community-building efforts in political settings that dictate nondemocratic solutions. Chapters 3 and 4 offer critiques of corporate capitalism in local community-building efforts; chapter 6 describes community-building efforts to strengthen productivity in corporate capitalism. This book builds the case that community building is not a process that is limited to one approach, one location, one function, or one theory, nor one politics. Community building is a complex, difficult effort with still unresolved conflicts. Each chapter reflects a unique interplay of politics and research. In fact, we argue that there is more diversity of research and application than is captured in the book and that this book is one step in building a more comprehensive knowledge base on community building for the twenty-first century.

THE RATIONALE FOR SELECTIONS AND ORDER

When considering what to include in this compilation, we decided to select anthropologists whose current work is based on a breadth of experience and effort that comes only with years of research and practice. We also considered their involvement in and contributions to the Society of Applied Anthropology. Finally, we wanted the totality of the compilation to illustrate the wide-ranging types of community that exist in society, as well as the characteristics and challenges both shared by and unique to these communities. Although we believe that our selections meet these criteria and effectively illustrate the variety of communities that exist, we want to emphasize that the compilation is not exhaustive. There are many other communities—rural, homeless, educational, occupational, utopian, gay and lesbian, science fiction, and so on—whose study would be very beneficial in the expansion of literature and creation of knowledge in our field. Our hope is that all applied and practicing anthropologists, especially those up-and-coming, use this compilation as a springboard to research such communities.

With respect to the order, we start with van Willigen's chapter because it provides the historical overview and sets the context for traditional anthropological study of community. Oliver-Smith in chapter 3 and Kemper and Adkins in chapter 4 follow naturally with their place-based examinations of community. Next is the work of Hyland and Owens in chapter 5; their community-rebuilding efforts and examination of an inner-city neighborhood are linked to new information technologies. In chapter 6, Baba extends the work to the application of information technologies and non-place-based studies of multinational corporations. Chrisman's chapter 7 focuses on community in a topical context, that of health systems. This approach would be well applied to other topics of anthropological interest, such as education, environment, and tourism. Finally, we end with Jean Schensul's chapter 8. Schensul simultaneously integrates many components of the other chapters and forecasts future challenges to anthropologists, as well as proposing the tools necessary to meet them. The concluding chapter 9 presents a final overview of implications for those engaged in community building and sets the stage for future engaged scholarship and community building.

MAJOR GOALS

In advancing the purpose of this effort, the book is organized around four major goals. First, we show how not attending to the elements of relationships, both intentionally and unintentionally, can undermine and destroy community and community building. Second, we explore the dynamic approaches and methods currently used by anthropologists and other social scientists to strengthen community-based efforts. The approaches and methods discussed in this book not only use cultural, material, informational, and intellectual resources that foster and develop relationships and partnerships, but also use strong existing relationships and partnerships to develop and expand these various resources. The contributors offer some of the incredible possibilities that culture, social capital, information technology, computer/asset mapping, networking, partnerships, participation, research, and so forth, present in establishing, improving, and sustaining community when good relationships in and with the community are at the foundation. Third, we propose a conceptual framework for future engagement and action that leads to building communities with the capacity to become self-sustaining and self-renewing. Our own work with inner-city Memphis yielded this framework, and the community-building experiences recounted by the other contributors support its substance. Finally, we offer suggestions and direction for future engagement and community building.

THEMES

All the contributors discuss community and their community-building efforts in very distinct contexts; nonetheless, their work converges around several common themes. Attending to existing community relationships, revitalizing or creating community identity and meaning, and encouraging participation and partnerships are integral, cohesive components of community building. Therefore, operationalizing these components are prevalent themes in all the chapters.

Attending to the Elements of Relationships in Communities

The concept of relationships is easily grasped because it is universally shared at the most basic, personal level—individually. It is also recognized as a concept integral to each and every level of association and communication that takes place within the broad spectrum of society. Nonetheless, in the same ways we forget, neglect, and undermine the foundational elements of positive personal relationships—mutual trust and respect; shared and connected meanings, goals, and visions; shared participation; shared power and resources (mutual control and investment); and shared knowledge and tools—we can readily forget, neglect, and undermine these in our organizational and institutional relationships within the broader contexts of community and society. Although defining each of these essential elements separately might seem easy, it quickly becomes apparent that, in doing so, each meaning somehow becomes diluted. It is in their cohesive functioning with one another that these elements become fully operational and are best understood.

All the contributors in this volume, explicitly or implicitly, begin their chapters by stressing the importance of understanding relationship building from the bottom-up perspective of the individual or small group. Authors then link this relationship building to the power of local voluntary associations such as the community institutions described by van Willigen; the faith-based organizations described by Kemper and Adkins; the local public, private, and nonprofit organizations described by Oliver-Smith, Hyland and Owens, Schensul, and Chrisman; and the government and large-scale intermediaries, even large corporations, as described by Baba. In each chapter, the discussion of trust, shared values, and social bonds in the pursuit of some commonality, in the context of some outside assault, is critical to the conceptual framework. In turn, all the authors examine how trust, social bonds, and resources are linked to survival, and they discuss growth and increased productivity in terms of defined values such as ethnicity, heritage, identity, and place.

Revitalizing or Creating Meaning and Identity in Community

Each chapter also identifies a set of competencies among human beings. In the course of reconstructing the history of their community, members often find new meaning to that community. Such reconstructions can help create a new or revitalized identity for the community. Typically, revitalizing or creating new communities requires significant vision into the future, with new insights and strong enthusiasm. A very important factor in strengthening a community is an increase in internal social networking to invigorate the social and civic fabric of the community. Internal social networking contributes to the development of ongoing strategies for more participation that is open and inclusive. Collectively, these chapters demonstrate that a sense of meaningful connectedness among community members is essential for social, physical, and economic endurance and advancement, especially during times of upheaval.

Anthony Oliver-Smith's chapter 3 is an on-point example of how ethnicity, heritage, identity, and place are crucial to the survival of communities displaced by natural or technological disaster, political conflict and violence, and large-scale national and international development projects. By describing the displacement of such communities in Peru, China, and Zimbabwe, he illustrates how uprooted communities draw on the constructs of space, time, and people to re-create the elements of their community, if only in symbols and themes. Oliver-Smith advocates a balance between material resources and cultural resources (collective memory, history, rituals, symbols, and traditions) to successfully reconstruct individuals, families, and communities. Policies that focus only on the material and tend to be donor-designed around budget and efficiency undermine trust, self-esteem, integrity, and identity. In fact, Oliver-Smith shows how these negative effects compound the problems of displacement by intensifying original societal hostilities and thwarting the rebuilding of social networks, ultimately creating dependency. In spite of the tragedy of displacement, Oliver-Smith shows how each community resisted the resettlement in one way or another, invigorating community members to maintain their interconnections and work together for their collective survival.

Robert Kemper and Julie Adkins, in chapter 4, show the ways in which US communities, when threatened by economic decline and/or social injustices such as poverty, unfair labor practices, inequality, and restricted civil liberties, attempt to assert themselves through local, regional, and national faith-based organizations. Congregations (or parachurch agencies) are, for many, institutions of trust that sustain traditional rituals and ceremonies. As such, they can provide valuable services for new and immigrant communities, as well as for established populations. Kemper and Adkins trace the history of faith-based organizations out of their congregational and parachurch roots, from the nineteenth-century Social Gospel Movement, to the Great Migration and European Immigration period, through post-WWII, and into the present. This history illustrates how faith-based organizations have moved from providing charitable services to promoting community development. In the process, they have concentrated more on the cultural resources (opportunities) necessary to the collective self-determination of specific communities and on building relationships vital to community transformation in the face of external social and economic forces (threats).

In chapter 6, Marietta Baba takes a slightly different approach to the discussion of relation building, culture, common values, and shared meanings, by looking at work communities affected by global economies. She examines the emergence of global distribution as an organizing principle of work communities, and the achievements and shortcomings of information technology that supports professional relationships and their distributed communication and collaboration. By adopting Bronfenbrenner's ecological framework designed for research on human development, Baba gives a better picture of how individuals converge to form a work community and provides a framework that incorporates both micro- and macro-level settings and influences in investigating the context of a globally distributed work group. In her discussion of a fourteen-month-long case study of a globally distributed work team, Baba finds that, ultimately, information technology is necessary but not sufficient for effective performance and collaboration of geographically separated and culturally diverse work groups. Most notably, Baba states that a commonality of mutual understanding, shared goals, and mutual respect for individuals' knowledge and experiences is essential if geographically separated and culturally different work groups are to trust one another and collaborate successfully. To disregard these basic elements, intentionally or not, is to set up work groups, indeed any community, for failure.

Establishing and Encouraging Participation and Partnerships in Community

The relationship building thus far described is more than just an outcome; it is an ongoing process. Increasing the connection to external groups through community members' development of ongoing strategies for collaboration and partnership helps to strengthen and expand community relations by bringing new social, economic, and political resources into the community. Such bridging of community groups is essential for balancing and maintaining a community's assets, needs, and control throughout stabilization and growth processes. Resources generated through internal and external networking can be distributed in such a way that survival, growth, and reconstruction can take place. Additionally, articulation and negotiation can resolve inter-community conflicts. Another essential result of such networking is expanded information, which, in turn, is helpful for effective engagement in policy development and reformation.

Kretzmann and McKnight (1993), with their asset-based approach of community building and development, have been at the forefront of the idea of using existing relationships and resources to expand a community's participation and networking. This approach focuses on a community's social capital and includes developing a community assets map. The value of social capital and community assets articulated in this approach constitutes an important dynamic in each of these chapters. John van Willigen explores the idea of community assets historically in chapter 2 and finds that, although early perspectives on community assets differed with respect to context and political views, they still valued community assets in some of the same ways as Kretzmann and McKnight.

To illustrate the merits of an asset-based community development approach, van Willigen describes the work he did on the Tohono O'Odham Community development project. The primary value of the approach, he states, is that community is evaluated according to capacities instead of deficiencies. By using the assets and knowledge of individuals, associations, and institutions that already exist, problem solving begins in spite of limited resources, and the potential for long-term success is greater. Because the community needs, circumstances, and goals are primary and community members trust the existing social institutions, van Willigen shows, community members are more likely to participate and become invested in the development process. He notes that this increases the community's capacity for problem solving and self-direction.

The other part of the community assets–based approach is the allocation of resources. Van Willigen states that resource allocation should be tied directly to the community's felt needs and should enhance the community's capacity to define and achieve collective goals in the long run. He stresses that any approach that does not respect the community's history of physical and social assets will misapply resources and ultimately reduce a community to a state of dependency.

Kemper and Adkins also provide useful examples of an asset-based approach, articulated through faith-based organizations. The evolution of faith-based organizations into strong corporations with an incredible network of partners and resources has increased communities' political and economic power. Because faith-based community development builds on relationships within the community and then expands these relationships to include external individuals, associations, and institutions, the local community's values are sustained. Ultimately, the bottom-up approach favored by many faith-based organizations keeps community relationships, needs, goals, and participation at the heart of the process of community building, a process that Kemper and Adkins appropriately characterize as social capital development.

In Noel Chrisman's discussion (chapter 7) of applied anthropology's role for the purposes of public and community health in community building, he shows the significance of social capital in community collaboration and participation by identifying the basic principles of applied anthropology and stressing their importance in public and community health policies. The basic principles include the following:

- Proposals and procedures must be consistent with the community's culture, values, and beliefs.
- Collaboration with the community is necessary in identifying its wants and needs.
- The participation of community members is integral to realistic planning, delivery, and evaluation of a project.
- Collaboration with existing organizations and their leaders is a must.
- The design and implementation of projects must make sense to the community.
- Anthropologists must respect the people with whom they work.

- Anthropologists must be agents for change by working *with* people, not *on* them.

Chrisman is quick to point out that missing from these principles is the importance of creating partnerships at the macro level: "While we engage in community building, our challenge will be to develop and maintain relationships with political and economic institutions whose money and influence can promote (or inhibit) community growth." His ensuing discussion and practical illustrations of these principles also demonstrate the primary value of social capital with respect to public health in the community-building process.

Using Anthropological Skills, Methods, and Tools in Community Building

Social capital development, or the assets-based approach, is offering numerous possibilities in community building with the development of anthropological methods and advances in information technology. In addition to discussing assets-based approaches, van Willigen acknowledges the critical importance of tools and methodologies that anthropologists can bring to the table of community building. In his own work, he advanced a methodological system of rating internal and external community-development resources according to specific characteristics that advance the community's assets/capacity and ultimately lead to sustained community building and development.

The succeeding chapters by Hyland and Owens, Schensul, and Chrisman propose several other tools for strengthening communities: ethnography and storytelling, mapping, community assets, capacity building, social network analysis, participatory action research, needs assessment, and resource mobilization. Social liaisons are particularly critical tools for advancing community interests. Leadership training of community members in a way that is meaningful to the objectives they hold for the community is essential. In research, approaches such as participatory action research and community mapping involve community residents in setting out the objectives, design, and procedures. Similarly, assessment approaches such as evaluation and risk assessments can involve residents in ways that enhance community-building efforts.

Hyland and Owens explore many of these tools in chapter 5, which addresses the timely issue of the role of information in building communities. Hyland and Owens examine the possibility of bridging the digital divide in inner-city neighborhoods and rural villages through the use of computer mapping as a tool for community building. Their chapter draws on the lessons learned from a number of inner-city community-organizing efforts and their applicability to future computer-mapping efforts. Hyland and Owens postulate that " information has become as essential to the creation and maintenance of wealth as the control of capital, land, and natural resources." They propose computer mapping as one way to bridge the digital divide within the context of community and community building: "computer mapping can be used to layer resource information including physical, economic, and social variables," a valuable tool for community-based organizations. Hyland and Owens review three major approaches using community mapping: intermediate data providers, global and local participatory mapping, and computer assets mapping and community building.

Like Baba's analysis of virtual communities, in spite of the unlimited possibilities, they found many challenges to using computer mapping successfully. There was the very real question as to whether the diffusion model of computer mapping is sufficient to bridge the divide. Characteristically, neighborhood leaders seldom view computer mapping as a major priority. As a result, Hyland and Owens examine how to reframe the issues in the community's interest, drawing on three themes of community organizing and community mobilization: the mobilization of multiple stakeholders around critical issues that threaten the community, the power to make decisions that affect the control of community infrastructure such as land and housing, and the ability to generate wealth and social capital through local change within the community. Primary in each of these themes is asset mapping (a la Kreztmann and McKnight)—the inventory of all the gifts and skills of individuals and organizations in and around the targeted area illustrated on a map. Citing several experiences in Memphis, where engaged anthropologists used asset mapping as a part of computer mapping, Hyland and Owens found that it is possible, under specific conditions, to achieve community building through sustained computer mapping.

Jean Schensul considers yet another tool that, together, social scientists, community researchers, and cultural workers can use to strengthen their communities. She describes the ways in which research can be used in community building, specifically, in communities marginalized by the lack of research-related infrastructure and limited involvement in science-related policy, usually as a result of economic distress and/or social injustices.

Schensul proposes that the use of research theory, methods, and results can strengthen five common structural elements essential to a community's survival. These structural elements follow the themes previously discussed. First, a community must be able to survive under the stress of its specific crisis, specifically, through the reconstruction of infrastructure, relationships, cultural traditions, and economic and property development. Second, a community's cultural conservation and development must be promoted through storytelling, rituals, and institutions; these serve to maintain and preserve, and sometimes recreate, the collective identity, meaning, and goals in new places and circumstances. Third, a community must be able to expand resources, and information—both access to it and control of it—is a key factor that enables this. Fourth, a community must be able to negotiate sociopolitical change. "Research can help local communities gain information to improve their understanding of the structure of power, economy, and social policy. Fully informed, they can prepare effective responses and enhance their capacity for dialogue and negotiation." Fifth, to use information and technology for local development and penetration of the world market, a community must gain computer and Internet literacy.

Schensul's chapter 8 suggests that community research partnerships are central to enhancing the strategies that meet these structural needs. She describes four approaches to community-based research that increase the capacity of local communities to gain local knowledge and expertise through the use of scientific research and to use that knowledge to participate with those experts who have decision-making power. These approaches include conducting participatory action research, building formative research partnerships, testing and evaluating theory-driven community interventions, and conserving, documenting, and representing culture. Such approaches offer communities "opportunities to access new information related to survival issues."

Schensul states that "methods training, by itself or through collaborative projects, diffuses collective research technology for assessing, analyzing, recording, and re- and co-constructing components of cultural identity and social issues." In addition, people and organizations become united around common problems and issues related to power and resources. Schensul explains that "research partnerships with activist-oriented community agencies and residents use science technology more effectively as a tool for advocacy, mobilizing disenfranchised people to find a voice in claiming more equitable distribution of scarce resources."

In chapter 7, Chrisman also emphasizes anthropological tools and methods in community building—ethnography and participatory action research (PAR)—but in the arena of public and community health. Because of changing views of population health and new conceptions of public health practices, especially regarding chronic diseases that are closely linked with the ways in which people live or are related to social determinants of health, the 1988 Institute of Medicine recommended balancing its concern about disease with equal consideration of working more broadly on health and community. The ensuing mandates compelled community mobilization, which, in turn, requires particular anthropological skills of assessment, community mobilization, and evaluation. Chrisman explains that traditional, top-down public health initiatives are unsuccessful because they are set in multiethnic communities and are explicitly based on coalitions or community governing groups yet have little regard for the issues and nuances of community. When the funding stops, there is no local organization to carry on the endeavor. Consequently, Chrisman describes a trend in public and community health toward recognizing "that macro social forces have powerful effects on the public's health," in contrast to most existing public health programs, which focus on the micro level.

In the face of these forces, Chrisman discusses the value of community-based participatory research. He also discusses the special attention placed on community involvement and control, partnerships among diverse community organizations, and cultural sensitivity and competencies—all of which require anthropological theoretical and methodological abilities.

Chrisman identifies two sets of tools that are necessary to address these social determinants of health: the conceptual focus on culture and on community and the methodological skills in ethnography and participatory action research—or the rapid assessment process. With these tools, he states, anthropologists can expand public health practitioners' views and methodologies, which are limited by the very nature of their disciplines. Chrisman states that the medical model of research has focused on populations and isolated variables, not on communities and cultural contexts and patterns. In addition, anthropological methodologies aid public health researchers in designing prevention and control programs. They offer a significant set of techniques to gather data for community assessment and mobilization and for evaluation. He states that these methods and the resulting qualitative and quantitative data are more successful in examining chronic diseases correlated to lifestyles and in answering the questions that quantitative analysis cannot. Also, they are more capable methods at *both* the micro and macro levels.

A CONCEPTUAL FRAMEWORK FOR FUTURE WORK

The contributors to this book suggest a sequential model for sustaining existing communities: (1) recognize existing community relationships and connections, (2) identify unambiguous needs, (3) establish realistic, meaningful objectives, (4) formulate a skills and assets inventory, (5) develop cooperative relationships, (6) connect to helpful outside resources, (7) build trust through shared experience, (8) express identity through symbols and rituals, (9) advance group identity, (10) engage in collective problem solving and enrichment, (11) acknowledge concrete accomplishments, (12) celebrate achievements, and (13) redefine needs and objectives.

To sustain a community, we assert, the first step is to identify community relationships and connections already engaged in articulating current needs. The needs of a given community change through time. Identified needs that are vague, too far-ranging, or not agreed on by community members undermine the staying power necessary to resolve them. Community members must concur on practical, relevant objectives that can be addressed in a reasonable time. To decide on a strategy, community members and outside experts together must formulate an inventory of existing skills and assets in the community. This activity enlists greater support and investment by more community members, furthering the identification of available resources that can help advance the entire enterprise.

Without strong, cooperative community relationships and significant connections to outside resources, all efforts will lose momentum. Mutual internal and external relationships nurture trust through cooperative experience.

Shared symbols and rituals that express these relationships help to solidify and advance group identity. In turn, a solid group identity encourages community members and outside experts to act collectively in solving problems and enriching community life.

These critical, meaningful social and cultural processes must be translated into concrete accomplishments recognizable to community members. Celebrating achievements and honoring major contributors in a public forum help to sustain community zeal. After publicly acknowledging that goals have been reached, the community is ready to take another look at its needs, assets, and objectives, and a new cycle of community building can begin.

This approach to community building suggests certain outcomes. Our idea of a successful result is a self-sustaining, self-renewing community. Community members become actively involved in collective problem solving and enrichment. A successful outcome manifests in improved lives, greater equity, stronger relationships within the community and with members of related communities, and expanded networks, institutions, and assets. Working together, people can enjoy new standards and expectations.

2

Community Assets and the
Community-Building Process

Historic Perspectives

John van Willigen

Community-building practice of the twenty-first century can gain much from an understanding of how the concept of community assets has been used in various action settings in the past. This chapter compares examples of scholars/practitioners' writings about community assets in community-building practice from the present and the past. Intertwined with these examples are reflections on my experiences with what these days would be called "community building." My conclusion is that, to be effective, community building must include processes that incorporate community assets.

It is clear that community assets are crucial to community building and have been recognized as such since the 1950s. My view is that this is not a new idea, although it has been expressed differently through time. The specific disciplinary, ideological, and contextual situation of the scholar/practitioner no doubt results in different emphasis and focus. The most constructive path through this variation is to look for the common themes and to compile from the diversity a more richly nuanced conception of community assets, rather than attempt to find the "best" version. We can start the process with an important aspect of the topic, community itself.

Anthropologists have been concerned with community in their research and action practices since the beginning of the discipline. The intensity and conceptual clarity with which anthropologists have dealt with community has varied through time. In the period following World War II until the end of the 1960s, anthropologists' concern for community was especially intense. Many of the most frequently cited theoretical (Redfield 1955), methodological (Arensberg 1954; Arensberg and Kimball 1965), empirical (Banfield and Banfield 1958; Dollard 1937; Miner 1939, 1949), and practical studies date from the late 1930s to the 1960s. The emergence of the community study method (Arensberg 1954) encouraged much of this intensity. Both anthropologists and sociologists were actively involved in what could be thought of as the "community study movement."

Within anthropology, community study appears as a transition away from the use of "whole cultures" as the unit of analysis in the study of communities, marking the shift from historicism to functionalism. Community studies focused on the culture and practices of people in named localities. The majority of the studies concentrated on rural places, often villages that were small and dense enough to allow some sort of interaction. The approach was also apparent in urban research in the framework of either a "neighborhood as village" (for example, Whyte 1943; Gans 1962a) or a social network (for example, Bott 1957). The concern with social space is evident in one very widely cited definition of that time, which stated that community is "the maximal group of persons who normally reside together in face to face association" (Murdock 1949:79).

The community studies thread in anthropology and sociology was closely associated with a mode of social intervention called "community development practice" that emerged during roughly the same time. Community development had a special technical meaning. In the language of today, one would have to stress its participatory and community-building aspects; it did not just make physical improvements to the community. Projects not based on the community's "felt needs" and not involving participatory community-building processes might be called "community development," but community development practitioners viewed these as inauthentic, defective, and probably harmful.

Classical community-development practice emerged from several historic threads, including indirect rule and mass education in British colonial administration. Early special use of the term *community development* replaced the term *mass education* at a conference on administration in Africa organized by the British Colonial Office (Mezirow 1963:9). Similar ideas were expressed in US government-sponsored development through organizations such as the International Cooperation Administration (ICA) (Mezirow 1963). In addition, within the United States, there have been community development activities in the US Department of Agriculture/Land-Grant University–based Cooperative Extension Service, as well as in what was called "community organization practice" within social work. Another important thread is the work of Saul D. Alinsky and the Industrial Areas Foundation. Expressed through various community organizations, such as Chicago's Woodlawn Organization, and in a series of books (Alinsky 1946, 1971), Alinsky's strategy was more confrontational than that advocated by those operating through the Cooperative Extension Service.

The classic evolved statement on community-development social practice, to me, is *The Community Development Process: The Rediscovery of Local Initiative* (Biddle and Biddle 1965). From this conceptual high point, the community development (CD) approach went into a decline. What seem to have displaced it are modes of practice such as action research, participatory action research, cultural action (Freirean method), and the various specialized, participatory research methods (van Willigen 2002). The CD approach is still evident in journals, professional associations, and projects.

The CD literature addressed the idea of community assets in the community-building process, an idea central to CD ideology. In comparing the use of community assets in selected early CD literature produced by anthropologists with usages in contemporary community-asset-based development practice, I consider the similarities and differences in what constitute community assets. Also, I explore the various rationales for the reliance on community assets. This literature consists of practical statements (proto-theories) about how to conduct the community development process. No literature on the topic (that I am aware of) is strongly empirical. The writers did not intend to produce theory, yet their practical advice in these statements constitutes a theory about effective development. Mostly, this theory is expressed in statements about how a practitioner should act if a certain kind of effect is desired. None of this is empirically tested in the usual sense. Much of it is lived through, derived from experience, resulting in a mid-level inductive theory of development practice.

THE PROBLEM OF COMMUNITY ASSETS

Perhaps the most important and widely cited contemporary source on community assets in community development is Kretzmann and McKnight's (1993) *Building Communities from the Inside Out: A Path toward Finding and Mobilizing a Community's Assets.* Along with community leaders with whom they worked, Kretzmann and McKnight developed the idea of asset-based community development. This practical manual introduces their idea to community leaders and practitioners alike and guides community members in their "own community building context" to meet their own "challenges."

My comparison of contemporary, asset-based community development with classic community development is based on early texts that were widely read in the past and are probably representative of classical community-development thinking, and which I used as a community development administrator. When I started this chapter, I was attempting to improve my understanding of the Kretzmann and McKnight model by comparing it with earlier approaches developed by anthropologists whose focus was on what could be construed as community assets. I came to see my analytical task as being more concerned with understanding the role of community assets in community development generally.

EARLY PERSPECTIVES ON COMMUNITY ASSETS

The starting point in my discussion of earlier conceptions of community assets is Ward Goodenough's *Cooperation in Change: An Anthropological Approach to Community Development* (1963) and David Brokensha and Peter Hodge's *Community Development: An Interpretation* (1969). While none of the authors of the earlier texts used the term *community assets,* they seemed to recognize the value of community assets in the development process in ways similar to Kretzmann and McKnight.

A short biographical note might clarify this. My first encounter

with Goodenough's book was in the context of a community development seminar at the Department of Anthropology, University of
Arizona, in the 1960s. This two-semester seminar, along with an internship, composed the University of Arizona's M.A. program in anthropology and community development. The faculty included
anthropologist Edward H. Spicer and sociologist Courtney Clelard.
For me, the seminar was a good introduction to community development. It also resulted in my getting a lead for an administrative position in community development with what was called the "Papago
Tribe of Arizona," now the Tohono O'Odham Nation.

I spent about two years as director of the Tohono O'Odham
Community Development Program, working with a staff of community-level workers who provided various services to the communities that
selected these. At the peak, there were seventeen workers. This program used a classic community-development approach, emphasizing
community participation in determining felt needs and what is now
often called "community building." As my Tohono O'Odham colleagues explained their role to the community in O'Odham Neok
(their language), I would suddenly hear "CD approach" in *Milgahn*
(English) in their circumspect and breathless way of speaking.[1]
Communities were greatly concerned about increasing their organizational strength so that they could better develop and implement plans
in a sustained way. Various projects addressed their felt needs: building
a community meeting hall, installing community water systems, putting
waterproof roofs on many houses. We organized these activities so that
project identification, planning, and implementation involved high
levels of community participation that resulted in community building.

The definition of community development used in the Tohono
O'Odham Community Development Program proposals and widely
cited in contemporary sources unambiguously stressed the importance
of community assets: "Community development is a process of social
action in which the people of a community organize themselves for
planning and action; define their common and individual needs and
problems; make group and individual plans to meet their needs and
solve their problems; execute the plans with a maximum reliance upon
community resources; and supplement these resources when necessary
with services and materials from government and non-government

agencies outside the community" (International Cooperation Administration 1955:1).[2] What drove the concern about use of community assets was the goal of sustainable development. In this era, sustainable development meant continuing beyond the period when a project or program was active. It did not address environmental concerns. The approach was often communicated with the iconic, heavily loaded phrase "project versus process," or "process approach." A process approach is consistent with the ICA definition. Project approaches ignored capacity development and felt needs, and goals were externally defined. Putting in a water system in a community was one thing, but having the community-appointed water committee design the water system and teach people how to use and maintain it, with labor contributed by the community, was another.

I used Goodenough extensively during those times, keeping the book on my desk and often using it in planning community development training for the people with whom I worked. These experiences are discussed in a chapter titled "Community Development" published in *Applied Anthropology: An Introduction* (van Willigen 1993).

Goodenough (1963:11) wrote his book to help "people engaged in developing 'underdeveloped' communities" deal with the "human problems" encountered in that kind of work. He planned the volume during a Cornell University project "training people for development work," held during the summer of 1952.[3] It was published along with two interesting case books edited by Edward H. Spicer (1952) and Benjamin Paul (1955), which should be replicated. Many ideas in the book continue to be valuable, but it sounds paternalistic now. One can see the tremendous transformation that has taken place in thinking about the development process and the role of the professional developer.

Like Kretzmann and McKnight, Goodenough intended his volume as an alternative to the development models in use at the time. The book actually represented informed, modernization-oriented, community development action. It did not use ideas that resemble contemporary participatory development practice, but I think that its sentiments may be consistent with these ideas. For the most part, Goodenough discusses approaches in which people outside the community defined needs. In Goodenough's case, the goal was "cooperation-in-change" (CIC). Expressed in simple terms, cooperation-in-change occurred when the development professional acted in a way that was sensitive to local culture. CIC recognized the necessity of understanding the local community and addressing felt needs instead of those defined by the developer. With the correct approach, communities cooperate rather than resist.

The goal of the CIC approach was primarily "to mobilize the community to do something toward the achievement of its own wants," as well as secure cooperation in the "programs for change" among the persons and groups involved, "each with different purposes and values and each with different customs and traditions" (Goodenough 1963:37).

One of the ideas that can be construed as parallel to the idea of community assets is that of community institutions and their role in the development process. I do not think that this was the core idea in CIC, but it was still very important. Reference to "community assets" in Goodenough is ambiguous, yet it is very clear in much of the classic community-development literature. During the 1950s and 1960s, community development practitioners apparently emphasized community assets.

Also, considerable discussion revolved around the question, what is a community? The concept of community was subject to extensive debate and refinement. Redfield's (1960) "little community" appears to have figured prominently in these early discussions. His conception emphasized "distinctiveness, smallness, homogeneity, and all providing self-sufficiency" (Brokensha and Hodge 1969:5). Arensberg and Kimball (1965:2–3) focused on the community as a structure in process when they defined it "as a process involving social structure and cultural behavior in interdependent subsidiary systems (institutions)." Goodenough's conception solved many problems. He defined community as "any social entity in a client relationship with a development agent or agency" (Goodenough 1963:16).

THE IMPACT OF PUBLIC DISCUSSIONS ABOUT POVERTY AND THE NEED FOR EXTERNAL ASSETS ON COMMUNITIES

Public discussions about the poverty and needs of social groups (communities, groups of people, countries, and regions) affect how others depict these social groups. Depictions, in turn, affect how the social groups regard themselves. Often, depictions are used to produce "understandings" of the cause for the condition of need.

Kretzmann and McKnight's conception of community relates to their concerns about how communities are depicted. Their work focuses on the troubled neighborhoods of American cities. They argue that much development effort concentrates on community "needs, deficiencies and problems" rather than on "capacities and assets." This policy is ineffective and possibly destructive.

Externally defined needs become the essentialized depiction of the community. Negative images "are not regarded as part of the truth; they are regarded as the whole truth" (Kretzmann and McKnight 1993:2). Community members may accept the negative image and become too discouraged to do anything about their problems. In some ways, the extra-community service providers benefit from their clients' negative self-image and reduced capacity to solve their own problems. Certain development anthropology literature also reflects this line of thinking.

Arturo Escobar's (1995) *Encountering Development: The Making and Unmaking of the Third World* explores the process in which externally defined needs shape the conception of a community. He develops his idea under the rubric of "the problematization of poverty," which addresses the issue at a macro level. He posits that public discussions (what he terms the "discursive regime") and development policies create a set of ideas and expectations (a cultural construction) that a part of the world not only is poor but even *should* be poor. This "naturalization" of poverty convinces people of capitalist development as the solution, reinforcing the hegemony of capitalism. This conception also promotes a shift from local efficacy to the privileging of the expert, resulting in a cycle of dependence.

People outside a community, even with good intentions, often depict the community in terms of its needs. As a consequence, the community loses a sense of self-efficacy. Its negative self-image parallels and, in many ways, supports the interests of extra-community "experts." Edward H. Spicer (1970) identified the concept of "patrons of poverty" while working with the Pascua community of Yacqui people of greater Tucson in the late 1960s. Because patrons tended to control access to the community, the community came to regard the patrons as the only ones who could help the community.

Communities have histories of experience with development

assets. These histories not only shape the community in a physical sense but also transform its capacity to define and achieve goals. Misapplication of development resources can impair a community's problem-solving capacity. Fred Gearing (1960, 1970) expressed the idea of structural paralysis in his writings about the Mesquakie, a community of Native Americans.[4] Sol Tax, in working with the Mesquakie, developed (with Gearing and others) what came to be called "action anthropology." Action anthropology is a value-explicit approach to doing anthropological research and community development. Starting in the late 1940s, Sol Tax (1958) and his associates made use of the structural paralysis concept.

In the context of this project, Gearing (1970) was able to identify a functioning Mesquakie social structure. He raised questions about how well the structure worked. Based on his fieldwork in the Tama, Iowa, community, Gearing recognized that the social organization no longer worked well, so participation of the community members in these structures was neither satisfying nor rewarding. This "structural paralysis" was, according to Gearing (1970:96), the most significant problem the Mesquakie faced: "a state of chronic disarticulation in the community-wide webs of influence and authority which form a small community." According to Gearing, the cause was the nature of the historical relations between the Mesquakie and the federal government. By generating conditions of dependency, the federal government slowly preempted Mesquakie responsibility for the day-to-day management of its community affairs (Gearing 1970:96). Gearing's argument shows the "culture history" of what Kretzmann and McKnight assert. He believed that Mesquakie activities could be classified into two categories: the clan ceremonials, the annual powwow, and various other activities that could be characterized by a certain competence and assertiveness, and "school affairs, matters of health, and law and order," which were characterized by "mutual hostility, fear, ignorance, self-pity and a feeling of incompetence" (Gearing 1970:96). It is in this latter area that the term *structural paralysis* applies.

Gearing consistently argued that the conditions of culture contact generated Mesquakie problems. Structural paralysis was causally linked to the nature of the relationship between the whites and the Mesquakie. Gearing also identified problems that grew out of the different conceptions the Mesquakie and whites had of each other. Gearing viewed the Mesquakie problem primarily in terms of white beliefs concerning the nature of the Mesquakie; Mesquakie self-conceptions, especially as these related to actions by whites; and the dynamic interrelations between these elements. The approach used by Gearing emphasizes the differences between Mesquakie and whites. The Mesquakie perceived whites as in a "becoming" process, described as "a ceaseless effort to make the real self coincide with that ideal self" (Gearing 1960:296). In contrast, according to Gearing (296), the Mesquakie do not have such tendencies: "The Mesquakie individual does not seem to create such an ideal self; he does not see himself as becoming at all; he is."

Through enculturation, the Mesquakie individual is committed to harmonious relations with his fellow Mesquakie. The white, however, is much more independent of group pressure. The Mesquakie's harmonious relations produce a behavior that whites interpret as laziness and unreliability; the Mesquakie perceive the whites as selfish and aggressive. The interpretation of Mesquakie behavior as laziness provides a basis for whites' belief that the Mesquakie are a "burden on honest, hard-working taxpayers" (Gearing 1960:296). Whites consider the Mesquakie to be "temporary"; that is, they are in an inevitable, unstoppable process of acculturation that will result in assimilation. The white imputation of impermanence has certain effects on the Mesquakie: They tend to resist change. They view their life positively and want to continue living as Mesquakie. And further, they are threatened by the changes proffered by the whites acting out the view of the Mesquakie as temporary. As Gearing (1960:297) notes, "they want their lands to remain in protected status. They are instantly opposed to any suggested changes—in their school system, in their trust status, and in the jurisdiction of their law and order. They oppose the idea of change, irrespective of the substantive details that never really get discussed. They do this because they fear failure—generically."

The fear of failure is simple to understand. In a white-dominated world, the game is white, as are the rules. For the Mesquakie, success is more frequent when the Mesquakie are in control. Yet, the kinds of activities in which the Mesquakie can successfully engage are limited. The Mesquakie have an especially difficult time with activities requiring hierarchal organization of authority. As discussed above, they mistrust authority and invest much effort in social control to resist its accumulation in the organizations of which they are a part. For this reason, Gearing explained, the Powwow Association of the Mesquakie was an important community asset (to put it in Kretzmann and McKnight terms).

Therefore, not only the development project is important, but also the *process*. This view is consistent with the "process versus project" viewpoint expressed in early community development work. The project approach focused on physical transformations of the community without reference to the implications of the process involved in accomplishing the project. An effective process strengthens community organization and increases the community's capacity to be effective in subsequent actions.

COMMUNITY ASSETS–FOCUSED APPROACHES

A community-assets approach has many advantages. Using community assets as the starting point, problem solving can occur in spite of limited availability of assets. Also, the community becomes more effective in problem solving and self-direction. The community becomes invested in the development process, which increases the likelihood of success. Kretzmann and McKnight (1993:5) assert that "all historic evidence indicates that significant community development takes place only when local community people are committed to investing themselves and their resources in the effort." This is also an important theme in classic community-development writing.

What do Kretzmann and McKnight mean by *community assets*? There are three major categories of assets: individuals, associations, and institutions. Individual assets include capacities, skills, gifts, and assets of lower-income people and their neighborhoods. These exist in vast array and are little used in development. In the process of asset-based community development, "problem people" are relabeled as "asset people." Associations are "vastly underestimated" assets that, in development, are stretched beyond their "original purpose" (Kretzmann and McKnight 1993:6). Institutional assets include businesses, schools, libraries, community colleges, hospitals, and parks. Kretzmann and McKnight's (1993:374) conception of assets is very broad: "It seems to us that the obvious necessity in this decade is for citizens to use every resource at their local command to create the future."

Obtaining resources for developing communities is difficult. Communities need to rely on their own resources. This does not imply that outside assets are not part of the process, but outside assets are more effective when the community is fully mobilized. With the local assets approach, the community mobilizes more, and when this occurs, outside assets have a bigger impact. The process requires identifying all local assets and re-creating linkages to them to increase effectiveness. A weakness in the community-assets perspective of Kretzmann and McKnight is that they conceptualize community assets narrowly. As I will discuss below, there are other asset classes that are important. These are community institutions and local knowledge.

COMMUNITY INSTITUTIONS AS ASSETS

Development practitioners were encouraged to obtain information about the community within which they were working. This research agenda included community institutions. As Goodenough (1963:45) states, the development professional should have an understanding of the "community's particular resources, customs, institutions, beliefs, and needs."

What are community institutions? Community institutions are "publicly valued procedures and arrangements" for getting things done (Goodenough 1963:344). This consists of "recipes, stockpiles, materials and social arrangements and schedules to which people are committed" (344). Goodenough states that he draws upon Malinowski's analysis of institutions for his discussion (Malinowski 1944:52–54).

The concept of institution was a core idea in the functionalist theory of Bronislaw Malinowski. His concept incorporated community assets. Malinowski (1945:50) defined *institution* as "a group of people united for the pursuit of a simple or complex activity; always in possession of a material endowment and a technical outfit; organized in a definite legal or customary charter, linguistically formulated in myth, legend, rule, and maxim; and trained or prepared for the carrying out of its task." His functionalist theory helped anthropologists overcome the limitations of other theoretical viewpoints, including diffusionism and evolutionism. Of course, it is subject to its own set of problems:

functionalist theory tends to overstate social coherence, takes an ahistorical and uncritical perspective, and treats persons as socioculturally bound rule followers.

The cooperation-in-change approach emphasizes the importance of development workers focusing on community institutions in project planning, as well as on felt needs. The basic principle is that work to solve community problems should be done through the community's established institutions. As expressed by Goodenough (1963:347), "for development agents it is a safe rule that insofar as it is possible to solve a client community's problems by utilizing its established institutions, the solution is more likely to make sense to the community's members and not strike them as threatening. It is also more likely to be one that they can put into operation with minimal initial difficulty, and, more often than not, with fewer compensatory adjustments later." In addition, communities turn to community institutions when faced with problems (Goodenough 1963:346). The advantages of this approach are that projects make more sense to the community, are less threatening, increase the likelihood of initial progress, and cause less subsequent disruption. He goes on to say that "applications of existing institutions to new problems, however, even when it results in serious dislocations, gives people a sense of continuity with the past" (Goodenough 1963:346).

The idea of institution is at the core of another value-explicit approach developed within anthropology, research, and development anthropology. Community institutions form the starting point in the development process (Holmberg 1958). The development specialists, in determining the various institutional contexts of the community and then in collaboration with the community's organization, work to transform these institutions with the goal of improving welfare.

KNOWLEDGE AS AN ASSET

Brokensha and Hodge (1969:52) expressed the idea of community knowledge as an asset when they wrote that "native wisdom, the know-how which comes from intimate and long acquaintance with local environment and climate, has too often been ignored by community-development workers coming from outside the community with their imagined superior technical knowledge."

Widely used in development circles, *community knowledge* refers to knowledge and practices enmeshed in a local community, in contrast to expert knowledge, which is the technical information brought in by technically trained outsiders such as agronomists, sanitarians, physicians, or foresters. Community knowledge is sometimes referred to as "indigenous knowledge" (IK) or "indigenous technical knowledge" (ITK). The latter labels seem confining in that *indigenous* implies only knowledge that is locally generated. Another term is "traditional knowledge," but this label suggests that the knowledge is unchanging.

Within development practice, privileging the knowledge of technically trained persons from outside the community shifted to valuing community knowledge. For example, in agricultural development, "instead of starting with the knowledge, problems, analysis and priorities of scientists, it starts with the knowledge, problems, analysis and priorities of farmers and farm families" (Chambers, Pacey, and Thrupp 1989:xix). Emphasizing the expert is consistent with a top-down approach.

Anthropologists have always been concerned with local knowledge, but explicit concern for this emerged little more than two decades ago in the development arena. This concern involved a reconceptualization of local knowledge, going against the widely held view that local knowledge was uniform, static, and invalid. More and more, researchers realized that local knowledge systems were very much like the expert systems—dynamic, experimentally based, and valuable for understanding how things worked. Increasingly, local knowledge assumed a role in the development process, and researchers began to emphasize the fundamental similarities in the sciences of all the people of the world.

Success in development programs often requires paying attention to local knowledge. For a number of reasons, local knowledge-based developments are usually more sustainable. Basing a project on local knowledge can mean using locally available, lower-cost resources instead of more costly materials from outside. Usually, the community can better understand local knowledge-based projects and therefore more easily manage them. Local knowledge-based projects can be more easily adapted to local circumstances. Emphasizing local knowledge in project planning can increase the likelihood that the project will address local needs and circumstances. It may also decrease the potential to create dependency on the part of the community. The use of a local knowledge-based approach is necessary to achieve participatory development.

To this point, we have considered how the meanings associated with the source of assets influences a community, and we have made some distinctions about various types of assets. To provide a more nuanced view of development assets, I will discuss a way of evaluating development resources to explore aspects beyond the basic internal and external dichotomy considered here.

In our community development work among the Tohono O'Odham, we were concerned about the impact of development assets on the community's potential for solving problems in the long run, that is, to make decisions and act in concert. Sometimes, outside development resources seemed to create dependency (van Willigen 1973). The Tohono O'Odham Community Development Program was interested in solving problems identified by the community, so at community meetings we asked what these were. Among other things, community members identified housing, drinking water, sanitation, and community facilities as important needs. My administrative co-workers and I were concerned that resources could have a negative impact on the community, independent of their intended purpose. In that setting, I defined resources as "any goods or services that can be used to achieve a community goal."

While emphasizing community resources, one of my tasks as an administrator was to obtain whatever resources were necessary for communities to achieve their goals (that is, felt needs). At biweekly CD worker meetings held in various parts of the three Tohono O'Odham reservations, I also planned training focused on new sources of development resources. For example, a representative of the University of Arizona Cooperative Extension Service would make a presentation on the county-based, cost-sharing programs of the US Soil Conservation Service.

Even though community development workers and their communities made a strong commitment to felt needs and community assets, their response to these values was very complex. A strong opportunistic thread ran through everything. These communities were very poor. Family incomes were much lower than other poor Americans'; that is, the financial community-asset base was very low. Communities would mobilize to take new resources from outside the community if the resources were consistent with their goals. During the many discussions of community needs, members would reorder priorities in response to opportunities and ignore priorities for which there were no resources. Suddenly, new objectives would be established in response to resources. Because the resource allocation system was effective, agencies would proffer resources to the program in response and advocate partnering to increase impact. As a result, the community would use many inside and outside resources.

I analyzed the thirty-one resources that had been used in the program in terms of characteristics that I thought related, on one hand, to the abstract goal of avoiding dependency and, on the other, to community building. I conceptualized resources as those organizations that provided resources and were already present in the communities. Some examples included NGOs such as Save the Children, government programs such as the Bureau of Indian Affairs Housing Improvement Program, community-based organizations such as the Stockmen's Associations, and charities such as St. Vincent de Paul. I did not examine the skills and knowledge of persons and families, even though these are important. The identified resources were rated in terms of six variables, each of which I thought related to the dependency generation/community-building issue:

> 1. *The location of the institution providing the resource.* This variable was especially important. I thought that the community had more control over internal resources because it better understood the procedures associated with internal resources. This increased the chances that development would be more culturally appropriate. "Community use of intra community resources is a demonstration of community competence, in that a community's organizational capacity is made obvious as it increasingly meets the needs of its members" (van Willigen 1973:3).
>
> *Location* means social or even political location. An example of a resource located within the community is the Stockmen's Associations. The membership of these groups was entirely Tohono O'Odham, and their program was almost entirely defined locally. Ironically, the community saw the Stockmen's

Associations as quintessentially local, even though the Bureau of Indian Affairs originally organized these many years ago.

2. *The focus of the resource's application.* Does the resource focus on the individual or the community? We felt that "resources which focus on individual goals tend to weaken community organization in bypassing the community to serve an individual. This accentuates the community organization's impotence"(van Willigen 1973:3). A common problem was that the Bureau of Indian Affairs would allocate resources that addressed its own conception of needs, distributing materials directly to individuals without community input or participation. Sometimes it would rationalize this in statements like "we help those who help themselves." When housing resources periodically became available, they would go to the person who could get them first—a person with a relative in the agency and inside information as to availability. Interestingly, the bureau's housing program eventually allocated assets through community workers based on community priorities because it recognized that this way worked better. The bureau ranked projects according to community perceptions of need rather than "first come first served."

3. *Goal orientation of the resource.* How many (or few) constraints were attached to a resource? "The more general the goal orientation of a resource, the greater is the community's opportunity and need to plan (van Willigen 1973:3)." A general orientation would increase the chances that community priorities receive greater consideration in planning. In these settings, we thought, communities would have more control.

4. *Duration of the resource.* We thought that resources without deadlines attached to them would allow greater community participation in the process. This was consistent with our goals of community building.

5. *Linkage of a resource with a community's organization.* Some resources required the establishment of organizations within the community to decide on and manage projects. An example of this was the creation of numerous Save the Children committees.

They would recruit children to be sponsored by donors, care for and allocate the community share of sponsorship funds, and define and manage projects.

6. *Formation of new roles within the community.* In some cases, resource-providing organizations required that the community form community-based groups in order to qualify for the research.

The program did foster a "community first" mentality, which encouraged us to find resources with properties we thought worked best and to guide resource providers toward doing things in a better way. The approach worked well. Formerly resistant communities developed real programs that they themselves controlled. The point of this is that development assets, whether within or outside the community, can be evaluated in terms of how they contribute to community building.

CONCLUSION

When I compared contemporary ideas about community-asset-based development with classic community development from the 1950s and 1960s, I was struck by a broad similarity in conception. Kretzmann and McKnight's (1993) scheme, however useful, comprised a selected subset of the total range of community assets to discuss, leaving important content areas such as local knowledge and community institutions largely unaddressed. The considerably disparate emphases in these views can be best attributed to the contextual differences in which the approaches are applied and, perhaps, changing political fashions. In a graduate seminar I led on community action and practice, discussants felt that Kretzmann and McKnight's asset-based community development framework was more or less ahistorical from the perspective of anthropologists. Gearing's ideas about structural paralysis would be an example of useful historic perspective. In Gearing's case, a set of historical relationships resulted in the loss of community assets. Histories need not be always negative. My own work with older people in rural Kentucky (van Willigen 1989) and India (van Willigen and Chadha 1999) attests to the important dimension of the history of social relationships in the community. This research made very clear that caring and cooperative relationships in the past were carried forward to provide a caring environment in the present. Reciprocal relations are durable. Again, when we think of community assets, we must include a community's history.

While the community-assets views of Kretzmann and McKnight differ from classical community development, both have fundamentally similar orientations concerning the implications of how assets are mobilized for community-building goals. A historical reading reveals differences in the way community development and community building are discussed. Nevertheless, what are called the community building approach and the community development approach have a very strong family relationship. In my opinion, this is mostly a matter of changing focus. The term *community development* seems to be most concerned with the "improvement" aspect of the process, which is understandable, given how the process developed. Classic community development involved community building virtually by definition. As I stated, if community building did not occur, the process was viewed as inauthentic and defective. The two perspectives share many concepts and values. The differences can be attributed to different disciplines working in different kinds of communities. I think that the various conceptions of assets can be used to construct a more nuanced general theory of community development practice. This writing suggests that one kind of research that needs to be done should involve inquiry into and reflection on the effects of development resources on human communities.

Community institutions, local knowledge, physical infrastructure, and history—these important assets enable a community to reach its goals and meet its needs while increasing its potential for problem solving. The source of a development asset or resource influences the outcome of the development process as much as the resource or asset itself. Use of internal resources can ensure that the development effort is culturally appropriate. By solving its own problems, the community demonstrates to itself, and thereby strengthens, its own capacity for development. In addition, internal resources can be mobilized more quickly. External resources can overwhelm local communities, leading to disorganization and increased dependency (structural paralysis). Little empirical research has compared the use of inside resources with that of outside resources. We need to conduct critical and reflective studies on how these two types of resources affect community building and development.

The use of community assets has important consequences for several aspects of the community development process that can be dealt with as research questions: What are the positive and/or negative self-images community members have about themselves as a consequence of using assets from internal sources and assets from external sources? How do external sources affect the community's capacity to develop plans and act on them (that is, community building)? What is the relationship between the resource allocation process and the cultural and social appropriateness of the development plans? How does the use of community assets influence the cost, efficiency, and effectiveness of the development process? How does the use of external assets cause distortions in local social organization?

Notes

1. Milgahn is a cognate of American and apparently translates as "white man." With humorous intent, my last name had become van Milgahn.

2. The ICA, created in 1955, was a US government agency within the Department of State. It became the Agency for International Development.

3. The project involved John Adair, Solon T. Kimball, Henry F. Dobyns, Alexander H. Leighton, Tom Sasaki, and Edward H. Spicer and is described in Bunker and Adair (1959).

4. The Mesquakie are also known as the Fox.

3

Communities after Catastrophe

Reconstructing the Material,
Reconstituting the Social

Anthony Oliver-Smith

DISPLACEMENT IN THE LATE TWENTIETH AND EARLY TWENTY-FIRST CENTURIES

The twentieth century saw enormous numbers of people set in motion against their will. For example, in 1999, civil and international conflicts produced twenty-one million refugees who fled across international borders to escape violence. Uncounted in these numbers are millions of peoples uprooted by environmental upheaval and by natural and technological disasters, from sudden-onset earthquakes and hurricanes to slow-onset contamination by insecticides or groundwater pollution. In 1999 these internally displaced people numbered twenty-five million. That is a rough total of fifty-six million people uprooted in 1999 alone. To put those numbers in comparative perspective, fifty-six million is the equivalent of the population of Italy, the twenty-third largest country in the world. It is more than half the population of Mexico and twenty million more than the entire population of Central America.

In the present century, whole communities continue to be displaced, uprooted, and set adrift. The World Bank has calculated that publicly and privately funded development projects—ranging in scale from the Three Gorges Dam in China (1.3 million to be uprooted) to roadway or building construction (uprooting sections of urban communities)—displace approximately ten million people a year. In addition, all these people suffer violation of their basic human and environmental rights: they have been uprooted against their will, and their communities have been destroyed, often before their eyes, either by human hands or by a nature made harmful by human organization and structure. Forces such as ethnic nationalism, global climatic change increasing storm activity and sea levels, and globalized forms of development such as tourism, hydropower, and urban renewal promise more of the same for the century we are just beginning.

RADICAL CHANGE AND THE REINVENTION OF COMMUNITY

In 1970, in an effort to characterize the conditions and challenges facing humanity in the late twentieth century, the psychiatrist and psychohistorian Robert J. Lifton coined the term "Protean Man" after the shape-changing figure of Greek mythology. Lifton (1970:43) was describing a consciousness that had become separated from "the vital and nourishing symbols of...cultural traditions—symbols revolving around family, idea systems, religions and the life cycle in general" and, I would add, community. Consciousness that is freed (or torn) from these traditional anchors of identity must engage in a continual process of radical reinvention of the self, drawing upon the kaleidoscope of imagery available in modern culture. Lifton (1970:43–44) stresses that such a psychological style is "by no means pathological as such, and in fact may be one of the functional patterns necessary to life in our times." He does not address the possible pathologies of our times. He does, however, consider something he calls "psychohistorical dislocation," referring to the forces of rapid economic and political change that often involve an uprooting from family and community far from familiar landmarks. These forces have, in many senses, dislocated all of us, obliging us to adopt the consciousness of the constant radical reinvention of the self. Because human beings are social creatures, the reinvention of the self is intimately linked to the reinvention of community as humankind's principal form of social living.

MATERIAL AND SOCIAL DESTRUCTION

The causes of this massive dislocation, as well as the uprooting process itself, are nothing less than catastrophic for both the individual and the community. These forces—natural and technological disasters, political conflict, and large-scale development projects—are what I call "totalizing phenomena" in their capacity to affect virtually every domain of human life. Moreover, these forces all too often trigger and compound one another. For example, natural disasters have been known to trigger social conflict. War has frequently compounded displacement from violence by making the home environment toxic through the use of chemical defoliants and other ecologically destructive agents.

Millions of people face the partial or total destruction of the material and social expressions of community. In all three forms of displacement, the communities have some concrete material existence. In the majority of cases, this existence conforms to the traditional understanding of community as a site of residence and as a context of shared understanding. In disasters and wars, the material destruction may occur suddenly and massively. Mortality may also be high. In some cases, the physical community may have to be abandoned to the elements or to invaders. Because more people exist in vulnerable circumstances and are exposed to a greater variety of hazards, natural disasters inflict widely varying forms of destruction, from loss of productive resources to total destruction. Technological disasters can uproot communities by sudden destruction, as in the gas explosion of Guadalajara, Mexico (Macias and Calderon Aragon 1994), or by saturation of the environment with toxic substances, as in Bhopal or in Valdez, Alaska (Rajan 1999, 2002; Dyer 2002). Development projects produce material destruction that is more gradual but is frequently as devastating. The inundation of a community to create a reservoir constitutes as thorough a form of material destruction as a saturation bombing or an earthquake of 8.0 Richter scale magnitude. Development-induced resettlement does not usually cause immediate mortality, but higher morbidity and mortality rates do characterize populations that have been resettled by development projects (Cernea 1997).

Removing people from their known environments separates them from the material and cultural resource base on which they have depended for life as individuals and as communities. Moreover, a sense of place plays an important part in individual and collective identity formation, in the way time and history are encoded and contextualized, and in interpersonal, community, and intercultural relations (Altman and Low 1992; Malkki 1992; Rodman 1992; Escobar 2000). "Geographical experience begins in places, reaches out to others through spaces, and creates landscapes or regions for human existence" (Tilley 1994:15). Resistance to resettlement reveals how important a sense of place is for the creation of an "environment of trust" that links space, kin relations, local communities, cosmology, and tradition (Giddens 1990:102 as cited in Rodman 1992:648). Removal from one of the most basic physical dimensions of life can mean removal from life itself. Disrupting individual or community identity and stability in place, resulting in resettlement in a strange landscape, can baffle and silence people in the same way a strange language can (Basso 1988 as cited in Rodman 1992:647). Culture loses its ontological grounding, and people must struggle to construct a life world that clearly articulates their continuity and identity as a people again. The human need for environments of trust is fundamental to the sense of order and predictability implied by culture.

The psychological and sociocultural centrality of place in the formation of community as physical space varies cross-culturally. Liisa Malkki (1992:30–31) cautions against the application of what she refers to as a western "sedentarist metaphysic." This "incarcerates the native" in an ecological or territorial identity; the uprooting of peoples becomes "not only normal, [but] it is also perceived as a moral and spiritual need." Her work with Hutu refugees in Tanzania reveals that the true Hutu nation was imagined as a deterritorialized moral community formed by refugees and the land expanse called Burundi, as merely a state (Malkki 1992:35). Hansen's work with Angolan refugees in Zambia demonstrates a far greater sense of dislocation among refugees settled in camps than among those self-settled among co-ethnics in villages. In effect, the people who fled across the border but settled with co-ethnics never felt themselves to be refugees (Hansen 1992). In other words, culture and community are variously "rooted" in places; uprooting occasions varying levels of stress, depending on the circumstances. As well as place, then, the separation or fragmentation of community that frequently accompanies uprooting is a prime source of socially based stress and suffering. Conversely, as Hansen's and Malkki's work shows, communities that can maintain their cultural identity and social fabric are more resilient in the face of dislocation.

Uprooted people generally face the daunting task of rebuilding not only personal lives but also those relationships, networks, and structures that support people as communities. In some cases, survivors resettle themselves individually or as families in new environments, facing the challenges of integration. In the developing world, these event/processes set people on the road, often breaking up families and communities. Hurricane Mitch, which devastated Honduras in 1998, forced many people to leave their families to seek work in Mexico, Guatemala, and the United States. Thousands who remained behind were still living in provisional shelters more than two years later (Stansbury et al, 2001). In other cases, competition for aid exacerbates existing social conflicts or reawakens old enmities. For communities devastated by war, social destruction takes the form of individuals traumatized and disabled by atrocities, and communities fragmented by the violence of hostile internal factions. People who occupy sites that communities have fled because of threat or actual violence may resist the return of original occupants and owners. In refugee camps, often in foreign countries with culturally different host populations, very disparate peoples who are antagonistic to each other may be grouped in the same settlement (Payne 1998). Historically, people dislocated by development projects have had little recourse other than isolated migration to other areas, usually urban slums. Those resettled by the development project itself face graft, incompetence, and inadequate resources that produce social disarticulation of varying degrees, as well as conflict with host populations (Cernea 1997; McCully 1996).

All these event/processes endanger not only physical and social security but also confidence in one's culture and the social fabric. Such disruption and uprooting suggest the ineffectiveness of human effort and the fragility of the implicit contract that life will be reasonably predictable, that it will make some sense. Increasingly, those threatened with development-induced resettlement are undertaking significant resistance movements, but initially, at least, people confronting the state and international capital may feel unable to defend themselves

(Oliver-Smith 2001). Self-esteem and a sense of personal and community integrity may be eroded unless reconstruction aid and efforts are organized so that people can demonstrate renewed capabilities. In all three forms of displacement, communities are fractured by contending interests and allegiances regarding the distribution of aid and reparations and by differential perceptions of loss that often intensify original societal tensions into outright conflict.

These trying circumstances, as well as the enormous variation that these millions of people in their diverse contexts represent, test the resilience of real communities, the validity of fundamental social-scientific constructions about community, and the politics and methods employed to assist them in recovery. For the millions of uprooted peoples who have suffered these event/processes and for those who would support and assist them, the task is to reconstruct self, family, and community in material structures and processes and in social and cultural expressions. Indeed, when we examine the process of social reconstruction, we address the basic elements of the nature of society and the creation and durability of the essential social bonds that sustain community. The core elements of post-catastrophe reconstruction express the fundamental principles of community building that were central to the broader discussions of the SAR/SfAA combined seminar and plenary. The detailed discussions generated in this joint effort demonstrated that, although the process differs in detail according to culture, the specific means people employ in the process of social reconstruction after catastrophe articulate the essential foundational features of community and community building explored in numerous contexts by the authors in this volume.

In general, the process of reconstruction has been approached as a material problem. The aid and assistance marshaled to help these unfortunate people have largely focused on material needs such as housing, nutrition, and health care. There is no denying that the often excruciating material needs of the displaced must be addressed. The question that is often unsatisfactorily answered, though, is *how* these should be addressed. Material aid is mainly donor-designed as a transfer process that compounds the social and psychological effects of destruction and displacement, by undermining self-esteem, compromising community integrity and identity, and creating patterns of dependency. Perhaps our most pressing need at this juncture is to achieve a greater balance between addressing the material needs of displaced communities and acting in a way that supports, rather than undermines, their struggle to reconstitute the social bases of their communities. We are beginning to make progress in conceptualizing this balance and putting in practice strategies that sustain and support social reconstitution, as well as material reconstruction, through greater community participation in both processes. As I shall show presently, communities themselves are our best guides in understanding this process.

THE DIALECTIC OF MATERIAL RECONSTRUCTION AND SOCIAL RECONSTITUTION

An inextricable tie exists between material and social reconstruction, but the connection implies much more than being materially sustained while reconstituting the community. To be sure, prolonged, severe material deprivation in certain circumstances has been shown to erode the basic identities and interactions upon which community is based (Dirks 1980). To what extent is some basic level of materiality a necessary precondition for social reconstitution? Conversely, to what extent does social reconstitution in some form of cooperative action undergird and enable material reconstruction? No community can survive without a material base. And after basic elements are re-established, they must be continually reproduced through cooperation (which is not always based on material interest) if the community is not to sink into prolonged dependency.

I would add, however, that these questions also challenge our methods and policies in dealing with such conditions. In effect, the material and social rebuilding processes must be mutually reinforcing; in some sense, they must be mutually constitutive. The built environment in which we live is a material instantiation of our social relations (Harvey 1996). It expresses and shapes our social relations. Nowhere does this relationship become more crucial than in the process of community reconstruction. Material reconstruction can support and express social reconstitution. Material reconstruction can confirm social reconstitution. It can also undermine the process severely, and very frequently has.

It is well known that the built environment can neither create nor re-create community. Also, we know from the experience of many millions—disaster victims, refugees, and people resettled by development projects and because of architects' and urban planners' failed designs—that the built environment can seriously work against or even prevent the emergence of community. The long, even rows of barrack-like structures built for the uprooted and resettled can aggravate the social tensions and conflict that often plague such displaced populations. Plans and structures are generally elaborated according to donor needs of efficiency and cost rather than the needs of the displaced to reconstitute community. The design, materials, and construction of such settlements often reflect elite constructions of the poor and the minority group more than any informed desire to assist. In the long run, the cost is greater because the settlements and houses are abandoned or destroyed and the social disarticulation these foster undermines productivity and self-sufficiency. To permit the development of community, the built environment must take a form that is both recognizable and appropriable in organization and substance in local cultural terms. If a planned settlement does not take a form that people can appropriate as their own, and add to and embellish, community recovery will be impeded and the settlement will fail.

Re-establishing Materiality

In material terms, the needs of individuals, households, communities, and the extra-local systems to which they belong, as well as the organized responses to these needs, are numerous, diverse, and interconnected. Needs in any uprooting crisis are urgent, and relatively adequate procedures have been developed to respond to these. A uniform standard has yet to be reached, though, despite the much debated Sphere Project (2000) guidelines for reaching such standards. Unfortunately, the procedures put in place to cope with emergency needs are rarely linked to key features of community organization. In the development of the longer-term rehabilitative system, these can very negatively impact the future viability of the community.

Homes and life-sustaining activities are the most deeply felt needs in establishing a long-term system for dealing with material necessity in the stress of uprooting and resettlement. Whether uprooted by sudden disaster, civil violence, or the bad (or absent) planning of development projects, resettled people are frequently housed in "temporary" quarters. However inadequate and inappropriate, these quarters become permanent in all too many cases. Donor-driven housing and settlement designs endanger the connection that people establish with their built environment, violate cultural norms of space and place, inhibit the reweaving of social networks, and discourage the re-emergence of community identity (Oliver-Smith 1991).

The other great need to be addressed at the material level is employment for the uprooted. From both a material and psychological standpoint, economics drives the process of reconstruction. Employment not only provides needed income for personal and household needs not provided for by aid, but also enables people to become actors instead of disaster victims, refugees, or "oustees," roles that are essentially passive. Uprooting causes many people to lose the means of production, whether it be land, tools, or access to other resources. Without these means, resumption of normal activities is impossible. There may be a difficult trade-off between reconstituting economic resources (especially land and property) and staying together for the social and cultural benefits. This is especially true in development-induced displacement when a project has opted for land replacement and the host population is dense. Settling a community on sufficient land may be difficult or even impossible. People may need to move far from extra-community networks in order to have sufficient land and avoid dispersal of the community (Koenig 2001). These choices create hard questions. Until people find employment, however, they must depend on external resources, and reconstruction remains incomplete.

Reconstituting Community

Before addressing this final and extremely complicated issue, we need to be clear about our understanding of community and the process of social reconstitution. I have no intention here to become entangled in the long, complex debate regarding the definition of community. For my purposes, the word *community* designates a group of interacting people who have something in common with one another, sharing similar understandings, values, life practices, histories, and identities within a certain framework of variation. A community also possesses an identity (Cohen, 1985) and is capable of acting on its behalf or on behalf of those who have a claim on that identity. Social reconstitution, therefore, is the regaining of that capacity at the minimum. The word *community* does not connote homogeneity and certainly does admit differences within and among communities. More than anything else, community is an outcome, a result of a shared past of varying lengths.

The displaced tend to fall into a mindset that has been called "the wished-for former state," that is, idealized images of the community before the displacement, whatever the cause. This longing is only natural for people who have been thrust into conditions of uncertainty and want. Almost anything is better than what they have. If we want to address the issues of social reconstitution, however, we must recognize communities for what they were, are, and can become. We must avoid idealizing the lost community and must recognize its tensions, strains, and inequalities, for these will surely surface in the process of reconstruction.

We must also bear in mind that many displaced people will never be able to draw on the cultural resources of community, because they resettle as individuals or as families in totally alien surroundings. Many of the displaced after Hurricane Mitch in Honduras wended their way north as illegal immigrants to find work in the United States. When no resettlement plan or project was provided to thousands displaced by many early dams, they ended up living in the desperate slums of large cities (Cernea 1997). A similar fate has awaited those internally displaced by the decade-long but recently intensified conflict in Colombia (Partridge 2001).

Even displaced communities that manage to resettle as a group face serious challenges to the reconstitution of community. The stresses of displacement and discontinuity, particularly over time, tend to exacerbate internal perceptions of difference that crisis-induced solidarity temporarily submerges (Oliver-Smith 1999). In disasters, the differential perception of whether aid should address basic needs or compensate for loss can generate serious social divisions along socioeconomic lines in stricken communities, impeding the reconstitution of community and the reconstruction of society (Oliver-Smith 1992). In development-induced displacement, the fragmentation of social groups by resettlement programs causes the disintegration of mutual assistance networks, frequently producing serious social disarticulation and undermining the reconstitution of community (Cernea 1997). In political upheaval, people may flee their communities under threat of violence, cross international borders, and settle as individuals or families in completely new environments, where they must adapt to a totally different society. Where violence is widespread, refugee camps maintained by asylum nations or the United Nations High Commission for Refugees may group together large numbers of people of different ethnic identities, religions, geographic origins, and languages, all of which form effective barriers to the constitution of community. In all three contexts, individuals traumatized by loss and suffering, often hideous, may be unable to reconnect, to re-enter the weave of the torn social fabric that was their community (Maynard 1997; Cernea 1997; Cernea and McDowell 2000).

The quality of the resettlement project itself can foster community life or deter the community from recovering. Such projects are really about reconstructing communities after they have been materially destroyed and socially traumatized to varying degrees. We should approach the goals of reconstructing and reconstituting community with a certain humility and realism about the limits of our abilities. Such humility and realism have not characterized, to any major extent, the planners and administrators of projects dealing with uprooted peoples to date. Usually, the goals of such undertakings stress efficiency and cost containment over restoration of community. As Chrisman notes in chapter 7 of this volume, top-down initiatives have a poor record of success because these lack any regard for local community resources. Planners tend to perceive the culture of uprooted people as an obstacle to success rather than as a resource.

Normally, communities do not construct themselves—they evolve. Even purposive communities, self-organized around a common ideology and highly homogeneous, do not have an impressive record of success or longevity. Reconstructing or reconstituting a community means attempting to replace, through administrative routine, an evolutionary process in which social, cultural, economic, and environmental interactions develop through trial and error. Also, through deep experiential knowledge, a population achieves a mutually sustaining social coherence and material sustenance over time. The systems that develop are not perfect, are often far from egalitarian, and do not conform to some imagined standard of efficiency. The kind of community that sustains individual and group life, never perfectly, is not a finely tuned mechanism or a well-balanced organism, but rather a complex, interactive, ongoing process composed of innumerable variables subject to the conscious and unconscious motives of its members. The idea that such a process could be the outcome of planning is ambitious, to say the least.

One of the best outcomes imaginable for resettlement projects is a system in which people can materially sustain themselves while beginning their own process of social reconstruction. The least we could hope is that resettlement projects not impede the process of community reconstitution. If the level of impoverishment experienced by most resettled peoples is any indicator, though, even adequate systems of material reproduction are beyond the will and capabilities of most contemporary policy makers and planners.

Notwithstanding these challenges, people can call upon many resources to reconstitute community, a fact that has been recognized for a long time but has begun to influence policy and practice only in the past decade. Moreover, resources of an essentially cultural nature, by aiding in the reconstitution of community, help the individual to heal as well (Maynard 1997:209; Oliver-Smith 1992). Community reconstitution and individual recuperation become mutually supportive processes in which the survival of community restores meaning to individual lives battered by circumstance. When those who would assist uprooted peoples understand the importance of these cultural resources, they support the process of community reconstruction and reconstitution. I would like to focus on the cultural or symbolic assets that enable communities to engage in the process of social reconstitution. In particular, I would like to suggest that such resources are mined from the history of the community.

The idea of a shared past becomes a key element in social reconstitution, as Schensul suggests in chapter 8 of this volume. For successful reconstitution of self and community, the displaced must master their grief. Loss of material possessions or personal or social relationships presents people with the difficult problem of how to hold on to what was significant in the past and invest it in the present and future without living in the lost past. Grief thus involves a negotiation between allegiance to the past and commitment to the present (Marris 1975). Rituals of mourning enable the bereaved to integrate the loss into their lives, to come to terms with it, and, through the grieving process, to resolve the conflicts between allegiance to the past and healthy reconstitution of life. People also must grieve for their communities, homes, social contexts, and culturally significant places and structures. Over the past fifty years, Wallace (1957), Fried (1963), Gans (1962a), and others have shown us that people grieve for a community as they do for a person.

Community can be recovered through the commemoration of its loss. The re-enactment of rituals, such as celebrating various secular and sacred holidays, can help to reconstitute the community's social existence. The evocation of symbols, such as objects, places, or people that provided anchors to community identity in the past, also contributes to social reconstitution, though these will most likely be reinterpreted and perhaps reformulated to fit present circumstances. Physical features that previously symbolized community identity can be reconstructed. The methodology of community mapping that Hyland and Owens explore in chapter 5 of this volume is a valuable tool that people can employ on their own behalf in recovery and reconstitution. Churches, chapels, shrines, images, plazas, town squares, informal gathering places, forests, rivers, springs, waterfalls, mountains, and a host of other physical features have important symbolic meanings for community. Other kinds of common property, such as burial grounds and community and religious shrines and centers, also serve as social resources, tangible evidence of a group identity. These also may include economic infrastructure that creates a local identity, for example, a periodic marketplace, a bus station, or a crossroads. It is important to reconstitute these resources as well (Koenig 2001).

To discuss the challenge presented by reconstitution of community, I will briefly examine three cases, one from each of the three major dislocating forces. These cases are not meant to be representative, but rather to illustrate some of the problems communities face and some of the resources people employ to overcome the loss of home and community.

DISASTER-INDUCED DISLOCATION: YUNGAY, PERU

The first example comes from my own fieldwork in the disaster-stricken city of Yungay in the north-central Andes of Peru (Oliver-Smith 1992). In May 1970 an earthquake devastated an area larger than Belgium, Holland, and Denmark combined, killing approximately sixty thousand people and destroying 86 percent of the buildings in the region. One of the central tragedies took place in the city of Yungay, which was located below, and with a spectacular view of, Peru's highest mountain, Huascaran, at 22,190 feet. The earthquake shook loose an enormous piece of Huascaran's peak, more than 800 m wide and 1.2 km long, which dropped a vertical mile before colliding with a glacier and quadrupling in volume. This gigantic mass of ice, rock, and mud careened down the slopes of the mountain to engulf and devour the city of Yungay, killing 95 percent of its inhabitants and leaving only four palm trees from the main plaza protruding through the surface of the avalanche.

Several months after the disaster, I began a study of recovery and social reconstitution in Yungay that was to last for ten years. The surviving Yungainos, grouped in a makeshift camp just north of the avalanche, faced the daunting task of constructing a new city and new material context and reconstituting a decimated community. For reasons of geologic safety, the government announced plans to resettle the survivors some 15 kilometers to the south in the town of Tingua, which was intended to become the provincial capital. To the Yungainos, this relocation was the final blow, the potential death knell of Yungaino existence and identity. What nature had started, the government would finish.

The Yungainos met this challenge by re-creating a sense of meaning and significance that would enable them to continue living whole lives as individuals and as a community. Three culturally constructed elements—space, time, and people—came together to form an "ethos" of Yungay's survival. The word *ethos*, not used much anymore in anthropology, refers to a single theme that dominates a culture. Space, time, and people are three themes that became woven into a continuum, expressed primarily in terms of community. The Yungainos were intent upon reconstructing their past, their story, to restore what Bellah and his colleagues (Bellah et al. 1985:152–55) so aptly termed "a community of memory" in *Habits of the Heart*.

In terms of space, the Yungainos drew upon their links to the environment, both natural and built. Although Huascaran was a potential danger and often cursed as "an assassin" and "a vile traitor," the mountain overlooking the buried city was inseparable from the Yungaino survivors' image and identity of their old city and the new city to be constructed. Aspects of the old Yungay became equally potent elements in the forging of community survival. The barracks city constructed for the survivors soon displayed various symbolic expressions of survival and persistence in multiple references to Huascaran and the use of old Yungay's street names for the narrow alleys between barracks. Such images and phrases were symbolic actualizations of the determination to reconstruct the community. This little chapel, that saint's shrine, the cross at the town's entrance, that little plaza in the barracks city, all named for their lost counterparts in old Yungay, were means by which survivors expressed and reconstituted the centrality of place in their endangered individual and community identities.

The four lone palm trees in the midst of the avalanche scar symbolized survival and became a site for ritual renewal of the ties that every survivor maintained with lost family members and community. A small chapel of palm fronds and lashed logs was erected against the partially exposed top of the steeple of Yungay's church. This little chapel, the palm trees (symbolic of all survivors), and the cemetery mound further down on the avalanche were the most important ceremonial locations in the disaster zone and soon became national monuments.

The cemetery, perched on top of a pre-Incaic temple mound, was the city's principle expression of its link with the past and the dead. The relationship between the living and the dead, between the past and the present, has always held great importance in traditional Latin American cultures. The disaster forged an even stronger link with the dead, integrating time into a total continuum with shared realities and allegiances for the living. Ordinary time had been cleaved in two by the disaster. Non-ordinary, time-symbolic, eternal time joined the living and the dead in a unified whole in which parallel existence is a reality the living must consider while conducting their lives and the life of the community. The disaster strengthened the bond of past, present, and future in the continuing commitment to reconstruct and reconstitute the community.

Specific people were woven symbolically into the sense of community survival. A policeman who oversaw the burial of the thousands of dismembered bodies and subsequently suffered an emotional breakdown became a symbol of fidelity, endurance, and courage in the struggle for survival. A woman who was hit by the avalanche and carried for several kilometers, emerging grievously wounded and bereft of her family, returned after convalescence in Lima to a role as a symbol of Yungay's survival.

How did they move from this dense cluster of symbols and rituals, essentially founded in the lost past of a destroyed community, to the reformulation of a meaning structure for a changed and distorted present and, further, to action that ensured their survival as a community? The catalyst for this process was the government's plan to remove the survivors from their site close to the buried city. The announcement of the resettlement plan galvanized the survivors into a single body, united around a single theme—the rebirth of Yungay in its place next to the avalanche. The conflicts of loss and grief were transformed into conflicts of interest between the survivors and the government. In effect, the conflict between the survivors and the government created a politics of identity reformulation. In the Yungainos' furious resistance to relocation, they were forging continuity for their community and molding new, meaningful identities and purposes for themselves. Their misery in the aftermath acquired a purpose, the defense of their homeland, their place in the world, and the survivors could newly affirm and heal themselves in enacting this purpose and making it known in the world. The Yungainos' struggle against relocation gave them opportunity and motive to voice and give substance to the continued existence of a community called Yungay and, in the process, helped them to recapture a sense of meaning, to return from despair and to re-engage life. The survivors' final victory over resettlement was evidence of their healing process, which persists to this day.

After the battle against relocation had been won and community survival guaranteed, the focus of interests and identities returned again to the individual and his or her reference group. The social life of Yungay began to reflect the varying patterns of allegiance and identification that correspond to the challenges facing individuals and community in the process of permanent reconstruction. The people of

Yungay fragmented and coalesced numerous times around specific problems crucial to the survival of the individual and community. In effect, the separation and coincidence of individual and community concerns at different times became crucial to the survival of both. In short, once the community was assured of survival, people could attend to individual interests again, and the interplay of consensus and contention that characterizes life in any community emerged.

Today, Yungay is clearly no longer the provisional refugee camp of the early 1970s. It is the established capital of its province and one of the major cities of the region. Thirty-five years of national, social, political, and infrastructural changes have led to increased integration of the entire region into national political and economic life. Despite the many years and changes since the disaster, however, Yungay's ordeal and its triumph over death remain at the core of local community identity.

DEVELOPMENT-INDUCED DISPLACEMENT: THE VILLAGES OF YONGJING, CHINA

The second example is drawn from a recent article by Jun Jing (1999) in the *American Ethnologist*, titled "Villages Dammed, Villages Repossessed: A Memorial Movement in Northwest China." His analysis illustrates how memories of defeat and suffering arising from dislocation, economic loss, and political persecution can be transformed into a collective force of recovery. The case of Yongjing shows how a life can be destroyed and how a grassroots movement to commemorate that destruction and its associated suffering can facilitate what she analyzes as "repossession." Repossession is about reclaiming history and identity. It is about setting the record straight. Jing uses the concept of repossession to evoke the activation of a silenced voice of resentment, of a damaged livelihood, of a ruined religious landscape in Yongjing in the context of emerging freedoms of expression in provincial China.

Since 1949 the development strategies of the People's Republic of China have promoted construction of large hydroelectric projects, resulting in the displacement of 10.2 million people (Human Rights Watch/Asia 1995:10 as quoted in Jing 1999:326). In the early period, the vast majority of these people were resettled involuntarily, with major economic losses that the government largely concealed by glorifying the benefits of large dams. The case of Yongching province in

Northwest China fit clearly into this pattern. A major government plan involved building forty-six dams on the Yellow River to control flooding, provide irrigation, and produce 110 billion kilowatt hours of electricity per year. Three of those dams were constructed in Yongching province, the last being completed in 1975. The dams affected 101 villages and displaced 43,829 people after 7,900 hectares of farmland were submerged.

The original plan for the region was to resettle people in remote areas, but the affected villages protested. Government officials realized that resettling people in distant regions would be too costly, so they consented to relocate people in the local area, but on lands of lesser quality and with less access to water. When villagers discovered that resettlement entailed serious declines in welfare, they protested again but were quickly silenced. The Communist Party ejected those who complained, sending one leader to a labor camp. All overt resistance was suppressed during the "big manhunt" of 1958 (mid August to mid September). The government equated resistance to resettlement with resistance to the Great Leap Forward and preemptively arrested 855 people, including landlords, leaders of dissent groups, and organizers of religious societies. Public executions of twenty-one people effectively ended overt resistance for decades.

The peasants lost their homes, ancestral tombs, religious monuments, lands, and spiritual and economic well-being. Even after post-Mao economic reforms began to improve the economic lives of people in rural China, the peasants of Yongching continued in poverty because they had been resettled on inferior land without compensation for their losses. After the dissolution of collective farming, as Yongching peasants experienced greater local autonomy and personal freedom, low levels of protest and resistance to the state began. People refused to pay taxes in groups or interest on loans they had received from state-run banks. Ironically, to voice their complaints with the Communist authorities, the peasants employed the Communist practice of the "recalling bitterness tradition" that was used to generate hostility toward the old pre-Communist system.

In 1981 a memorial movement began, commemorating the losses and persecution people suffered in the displacement and resettlement, to force the authorities to acknowledge their plight and to demand reparations. The movement employed three basic forms of collective action: the staging of public, frequently ritualized protests to evoke the grievances suppressed in the past, the circulation and submission of petitions insisting on adequate compensation for the loss of the means of agricultural production, and the documentation and reconstruction of lost temples and tombs of the families of the displaced. The kinship and lineage system normally provided the organizational basis for the development of resistance networks that carried out these strategies of collective action.

The staged protests often consisted of carefully orchestrated narratives of suffering that emphasized and compressed two separate events—the dismantling of homes and the flooding of villages—into one sudden, unexpected assault. These cataclysmic narratives were designed to rewrite the history of the resettlement period, obliging the authorities to recognize that the people had sacrificed a great deal in the name of national development. The protests also made clear that the state had not fulfilled its promises to the people. Through petitions to the government for economic reparations, the movement addressed the material losses. Even twenty years after the resettlement, villagers were still so poor that they depended on emergency food rations. The villagers organized sit-ins at government offices and submitted 322 petitions for financial restitution. Although the government refused to pay reparations, it did provide low-interest loans and free irrigation equipment in an effort to alleviate the poverty. The peasants further rejected the bureaucratic label *shuiku yimin* (reservoir relocatees) applied to them by the government, employing the local term *kumin* (reservoir people) to mean, through tonal change, "embittered" or "embittered people."

In the search for transcendental meaning in the trauma of political persecution and loss, people recovered their religious tradition and identity through two strategies: they created memorial texts and new genealogical records, and they reconstructed village temples. The displacement had destroyed one hundred village temples and forty-four thousand family tombs. Temple reconstruction and reconstructed temples became centers for unofficial, sometimes secret, networks of religious association. The rebuilding of mosques was equally impressive. In Yongjing, sixty-three mosques were rebuilt for a population of only twenty thousand Muslims. Plaques on reconstructed temples criticized Maoist policy on resettlement. Newly written texts memorialized the importance of deities' statues to community.

The Yongjing case indicates that the social reconstruction of memory and the assertion of that memory's relevance, through resistance, are crucial to recovery after displacement. In Yongjing, individual memories of suffering that had been suppressed by the government were transformed into a collective consciousness of rights that provided a moral justification for resistance and for protest of old and new grievances. Their main goal was to hold the government to its word. They argued that the government had reneged on its promise to compensate the losses they suffered in the name of national development. The movement combined invoking rights of public expression, the "recalling bitterness" tactics, and open but controlled confrontation with government authorities for recognition of Yongjing's losses.

The memorial movement publicly undermined the notion of people's indebtedness to the party. By commemorating the experiences of resettlement, hunger, and political persecution—in demonstrations, petition drives, temple reconstruction, and recording the destruction of family tombs—the villagers were able to reconstruct the official doctrine of popular indebtedness to the party; they demonstrated that the party was indebted to them. The path chosen by the villagers of Yongching is increasingly seen elsewhere in China. Village religious life and organization are emerging as an alternative base of power and authority precisely because this base is closely linked to the re-emergence of kinship organizations, temple associations, and village autonomy.

History and memory become the means by which community members oblige authorities to acknowledge their losses and injuries and to redress these through reparations and reconstruction. As their material losses are recognized and validated, people feel validated, which furthers social reconstitution. Not only are land and buildings repossessed, but also the history and identity of the community. Protest and resistance, even twenty-five years after the displacement and resettlement process, enable people to create a politics of identity and to undertake processes of recovery that are meaningful in terms of fidelity to local cultural tradition (based on Jing 1999:324–343).

POLITICAL VIOLENCE–INDUCED DISPLACEMENT:
THE REFUGEE CAMP OF TONGOGARA, ZIMBABWE

Displacement due to political upheaval can present significant challenges for the reconstitution of community, in part because resettlement takes a variety of forms. In some instances, refugees are resettled as individuals or families in totally new environments into which they must be assimilated, thus eradicating any possibility of community reconstitution. In other instances, refugees are resettled in camps that may exist for months or for decades. Although refugee camps frequently attempt to create forms of community organization based on the spatial density and nucleation of camp settlements, diversity can challenge the reconstitution of community. The need to cooperate often forces refugees in camps to form networks for mutual advantage, but ethnic, religious, and class barriers, or the temporary nature of the camp, may impede the establishment of community.

The Tongogara Refugee camp in Zimbabwe eventually became home to fifty-two thousand people displaced during the guerrilla war waged against the government by the National Resistance Movement (RENAMO) in Mozambique (Mabe 1994). After its independence in 1975, Mozambique participated in the struggle against white minority rule throughout southern Africa, giving shelter to the guerrillas of the Zimbabwean African National Union (ZANU). In response, Rhodesia created RENAMO, although it was primarily armed and financed by South Africa in the 1970s. After the fall of Rhodesia and the independence of the new nation of Zimbabwe, RENAMO, now fully under the South African Military Intelligence Directorate, turned its attention to Mozambique in order to inhibit any possibility of challenge that the emerging nation and its plentiful resource base might present to South African hegemony in southern Africa (Nordstrom 1992; Ball and Barnes 2000). RENAMO embarked on a guerrilla war in Mozambique that killed more than half a million people, destroyed the government, and drove millions to seek refuge in Malawi and Zimbabwe from the terror of village massacres, torture, and the destruction of homes, crops, and livestock (Mabe 1994:79). Because Mozambique had provided Zimbabwe's independence fighters sanctuary during their struggle, Zimbabwe felt a special sympathy and an obligation to assist the refugees.

The Tongogara Refugee Camp was run by a thirty-four-member staff of social workers, nurses, and administrators appointed by the government of Zimbabwe. The refugee population was divided into seventeen largely self-managed "base camps." Tongogara was relatively close to the border, so residents often returned to Mozambique to bring friends and relatives to safety. When refugees arrived, the camp administrator interviewed them to establish their cultural background and lineage identity. Four major languages were spoken in the camp: Shangani, Ndau, Chinyungwe, and Sena. All the cultures represented in the camp were related to Shangani, a cultural system drawn from Zulu and the MaShona culture of Zimbabwe. The camp administrator himself was a descendent of a prominent Zulu lineage, which provided him with a source of traditional authority. On the basis of this interview, the refugees were given a tent and assigned to a base camp whose population shared a similar regional and cultural background.

Tongogara base camps were organized around traditional patrilineages and administered through traditional law. Base camp leaders were village leaders charged with settling disputes, judging criminal offenses, and reporting problems and needs to the camp administrator. Shangani society is patrilineal and patrilocal, with clan and lineage elders holding authority based on the respect accorded their age. Leadership of the base camps emerged from the assignment of people of the same clan or patrilineage to the same camp. Because kin must always be accepted into the group that takes responsibility for them, ties of mutual obligation automatically linked new and established residents (Mabe 1994:83).

The organization of the base camp as a lineage-based settlement was not complete, however, without establishment of contact with the ancestors. Unless contact is established with the ancestors, the lineage (as community) will lack protectors and counselors. The ancestors also act as mediators between the creator and the people. Ancestors select their own spirit mediums, through whom they speak to the people. The process of choosing a spirit medium is lengthy and involves signs, often in the form of misfortunes that befall an individual. Traditional healers interpret these signs as the power of the ancestors at work. Once chosen, the spirit medium carries out the rituals that communicate with the ancestor who is essential for maintaining the continuity of the community (Mabe 1994:88).

The camp structure would be difficult to maintain without the validation of the ancestors who provide continuity through the customary law and ritual of the Shangani and related ethnic groups. Among the important symbols in ancestor rituals, snakes are seen as the messenger animals of the ancestors. The low-lying plain where the camp was located is also home to poisonous and nonpoisonous snakes. The python, in particular, is regarded as the emissary of the creator; its presence is a sign of great importance and power. That pythons actually visit the camp is also a sign that it is protected by the creator, as well as a reminder to the people of proper behavior during crisis (Mabe 1994:93).

In effect, the people view the occasional visits by pythons in the camps as completing the re-establishment of the lineage by bringing together all kinsmen, living and dead. The presence of pythons in the immediate environment, as well as in the camps, assures the stability and continuity of lineages and communities. When the pythons visit the camps, the Shangani refugees from Mozambique interpret this as a blessing and confirmation that they, as a community and as individuals, have a duty to continue. Thus, their survival acquires a purpose beyond the individual; life in the camp takes on meaning, and the continuity between the past and present, the living and the dead, and of the lineages forms the basis on which community is reconstituted.

Because of this social, political, and cultural foundation, as Mabe (1994:94) indicates, refugees in Tongogara lived in *villages*, not camps. The political sympathies of the host government and the cultural similarity of the host society in the surrounding villages also supported the establishment of viable, working communities instead of the disarticulated, violent refugee camps that have, unfortunately, become the standard elsewhere. When the war came to an end and peace was re-established in Mozambique, refugees were free to stay in the villages of Tongogara or return home. The vast majority returned home. The Tongogara Refugee Camp still exists today, although the population now totals fewer than two thousand from all over Africa. The camp is the site of a successful sustainable-farming project (ReliefWeb 2004), even though the cultural diversity of the refugee population initially impeded participation—an indication, perhaps, that the formation of village communities when the Mozambican refugees were in residence will not be forthcoming. Furthermore, there is some concern that increased pressure from urban refugees seeking relocation to Tongogara will put a significant strain on resources, services, and facilities (UNHCR 2004:5).

The value of culturally sustained restoration of social relationships as the basis for community among political refugees is supported by further evidence. When refugees are able to self-settle with culturally similar groups, the result is eventual integration, as in the case mentioned earlier of Angolan refugees in Zambia who resettled with co-ethnic Luvale villages or the case of the deterritorialized moral community of Hutu refugees (Hansen 1992; Malkki 1992). When refugees are repatriated, the cultural resources I have discussed become more relevant, particularly when the major sociocultural challenge is the reestablishment of trust. The violence and uncertainty of civil conflict undermine trust in the larger society as much as in the community itself. Research on rebuilding social capital in the post-conflict regions of highland Peru and Guatemala suggests that a prior process of reestablishing trust through specific social networks furthers the process of community reconstitution (Bebbington and Gomez 2000).

CONCLUSION

Over the past thirty years, the role of applied anthropologists in working with the uprooted peoples of the world has expanded significantly. Initially, anthropologists were primarily engaged in applied research on displacement and resettlement. The post-war concern for the welfare and fate of the enormous numbers of refugees in World War II inspired the research on displacement. The pioneer document is Alexander Leighton's (1945) *The Governing of Men: General Principles and Recommendations Based on Experiences at a Japanese Refugee Camp.* Although his research was based on a case of politically forced relocation, Leighton introduced many issues—particularly in the realms of stress, social organization, and resistance—that would become central to the concerns of anthropologists undertaking research with people variously displaced in the 1950s (for example, Colson 1971; Firth 1959; Scudder 1973; Wallace 1957).

Subsequently, anthropologists have become involved in an extremely wide array of activities and domains in their work with displaced peoples, activities as diverse yet related as applied research, policy formation, theory building, evaluation, planning, implementation, and resistance. Anthropologists were among the first to recognize and report on the impoverishment, social disorganization, and violation of human rights that occurred among uprooted populations. Applied anthropologists have worked in many dimensions of post-conflict social reconstruction, including troop demobilization, repatriation, refugee camp organization, and refugee resettlement. Among people uprooted by natural and technological disasters, anthropologists have worked on social reconstruction issues in the areas of hazard vulnerability analysis, urban planning, housing, post-disaster aid programs, and, very recently, policy formation.

Unquestionably, anthropologists have been most active and influential in the area of development-induced uprooting. Within multilateral institutions such as the World Bank, the Interamerican Development Bank, and the Asian Development Bank, applied anthropologists have played major roles in developing more appropriate policies for planning and implementing resettlement projects. They have authored the guidelines for best practices and procedures that require compliance by borrower nations. Often, as consultants to these and other institutions, anthropologists have carried out the applied research necessary for informed planning and implementation of humane and developmentally oriented resettlement projects. Throughout the lifetime of projects, anthropologists have also evaluated performance in restoring incomes and enhancing social re-articulation among the resettled for individual and community recovery.

Anthropologists have also been actively engaged in advocacy work with all kinds of uprooted peoples. Currently, anthropologists are in leadership roles in NGOs that work at many levels to assist communities facing resettlement in gaining better conditions in various reconstruction and resettlement projects. Working closely with groups and communities, anthropologists have also joined resistance efforts against development-induced resettlement. They are part of the larger community of activists and scholars who keep close watch on policy formulation in both national and international organizations dealing with the displaced, as well as those international lending institutions that fund development projects that uproot communities. The participation of applied anthropologists in all the activities associated with social reconstruction will take on increasing importance as the environmental vulnerability, social conflict, and large-scale infrastructural development that displaced so many people and communities in the twentieth century continue in the twenty-first.

The findings of researchers and practitioners alike over the past quarter century reveal that, even under the most harrowing of circumstances occasioned by natural, social, or (for lack of a better term) administrated violence, communities are not without significant cultural resources to regain and re-establish meaningful places in the world, even when they have been permanently torn from their homes. As other chapters in this volume reveal, the local resources, or assets, come in many forms: skills, voluntary organizations, institutions, natural and physical resources, and economic power. In this chapter, I have chosen to focus on local cultural resources and the power of cultural tradition to mobilize people facing the destruction of community. Rather than clump these varied traditions under some abstract construct of social capital, I prefer to explore the substance of the resources articulated and acted on by people themselves in the process of recovery and reconstitution of community life, as revealed in the cases discussed in Peru, China, and Zimbabwe.

This is not to say, however, that poorly informed reconstruction and other social policy cannot render vital resources useless. The wreckage from uprooted communities around the world is as much due to poor policy as it is to the violence to which they have been subjected. Nonetheless, as we enter the early years of the twenty-first century, we are undeniably the protean creatures that Lifton spoke of, but not to the degree that we can do without such elements of the self as place, kin, and community. The displaced around the world teach us that, when torn from these fundamental elements, we draw on the cultural constructs of space, time, and people to re-create them again and again in theme and variation. The displaced reveal to us the adaptive capacities of individuals and peoples and also the centrality of the grounding concept of community to the human sense of self and society.

4

The World as It Should Be

Faith-Based Community Development
in America

Robert V. Kemper and Julie Adkins

Generations of anthropologists have sought to comprehend the diversity of communities in America. Literally hundreds of ethnographic studies have been carried out—ranging from early efforts to salvage the spirit of Native American cultures to more recent projects designed to understand inner-city ethnic populations, middle-class suburbs, and even farming, fishing, and mining communities. Within the genre of American community studies, considerable effort has been made to analyze local religious practices. Yet, for all the ethnographic attention to beliefs and traditions, symbolism and syncretism, little has been written by anthropologists about a long-standing feature of American religious practices: the role of faith-based organizations in transforming communities.

The significance of faith-based organizations in American life has been affirmed by none other than the president of the United States: "Faith-based and other community organizations are indispensable in meeting the needs of poor Americans and distressed neighborhoods.... [By this Executive Order] there is established a White House Office of Faith-Based and Community Initiatives...that will have lead responsibility…to establish policies, priorities, and objectives for the Federal Government's comprehensive effort to enlist, equip, empower, and expand the work of faith-based and other community organizations to the extent permitted by law" (President George W. Bush, Executive Order, January 29, 2001).

The sheer size of the religious sector in America suggests its potential as a player in community development programs. Recent surveys by Independent Sector (2000:5) estimate that in 1997 there were more than 353,000 religious congregations, synagogues, mosques, temples, and other places of worship in the United States, with a collective annual budget of more than $80 billion. For example,

> since 1983, the Los Angeles United Methodist Urban Foundation (based at First United Methodist Church of Los Angeles) has given some 300 grants totaling $3.3 million to more than 200 different faith-based and social justice agencies in the metropolitan region. Recently, the Urban Foundation has become a faith-based intermediary, positioned to receive grants (more than $1.4 million to date) and to offer capacity building and technical assistance to other agencies. The Urban Foundation also supports the Mildred M. Hutchinson Chair of Urban Ministry at Claremont School of Theology, where Professor Michael Mata works in clergy education and community-oriented ministries training (information included with LAUMUF 1999 annual report).

Beyond local congregations, other faith-based enterprises include numerous higher-level denominational agencies, their social service agencies (for example, Catholic Charities and the Catholic Campaign for Human Development, Lutheran Social Services, the Presbyterian Health, Education and Welfare Association), and independent faith-based organizations with diverse missions (for example, Habitat for Humanity International, The Salvation Army, YMCA, and YWCA). The following two examples demonstrate the contributions of regional and cooperative community development ministries.

In the western part of Maine, nine Presbyterian churches in 1954 formed a cooperative parish ministry known as MATE (Mission at the

Eastward). Serving a mainly rural area, this cooperative is dedicated to community development broadly defined, including housing ministries, a nursing program, youth programs, and employment programs (Waldkoenig and Avery 1999:152–186).

In West Virginia, the Commission on Religion in Appalachia (CORA) was created in 1965 to bring churches and community groups together in partnership with the people of the region. Working with communities to confront the structural causes of injustice in Appalachia, CORA helps people become powerful enough to control their own lives. CORA supports numerous projects, including Project EAR (Economics in the Appalachian Region) and the Appalachian Development Projects Coalition (ADPC), and also encourages cooperative congregational development enterprises. The newest program, based in Jellico, Tennessee, is the Woodland Development Corporation's Individual Development Account program, which helps people to achieve their saving goals and to draw on matching funds for purchasing tangible assets (CORA web site).

In addition, a few national faith-based enterprises focus primarily on community development and organizing issues (for example, Industrial Areas Foundation, the Gamaliel Foundation, Direct Action and Research Training [DART], and Pacific Institute for Community Organization [PICO]). These community-organizing networks are discussed in greater detail later in this chapter.

In contemporary America, traditional institutions such as families, schools, the courts, and all levels of government seem to have fallen on hard times as bastions of moral values. Faith-based organizations, in contrast, find themselves distinctively positioned to provide leadership in our communities. Whether in distressed urban neighborhoods or in depressed rural towns, local religious groups often represent the best hope for community development and empowerment (Hinsdale, Lewis, and Waller 1995; Shirley 2002). Despite current concerns about sex abuse scandals in the Roman Catholic church and in other denominations, for many communities—rural, suburban, and center-city— "the church is one of the few remaining institutions of trust" (Carle 1997a:1). In new communities and among new immigrant populations, religious institutions provide places of confidence where people find relief from culture shock through the continuing practice of familiar rituals and ceremonies known from generation to generation.

Congregations, synagogues, mosques, and temples are repositories and stewards of significant resources—"time, talent, and treasure"—that often are undervalued in the public marketplace (Smidt, ed., 2003). Their philanthropy, which can be translated as "loving one's neighbor," extends far beyond the 15–20 billion dollars and millions of volunteer hours that they collectively contribute each year to community improvement (Castelli and McCarthy 1997, cited in Vidal 2001:6). Every community has one or more "power" churches where influential persons worship. When the mayor of San Francisco shows up at the Glide Memorial United Methodist Church to present a placard-size check to support one of the church's community development projects, the event makes the six o'clock news.

A FRAMEWORK FOR FAITH-BASED COMMUNITY DEVELOPMENT

It is not, of course, a foregone conclusion that congregations or other faith-based organizations will engage in community development, or even express an interest in the matter. Congregations particularly struggle with the question, what is our "community"? Is it defined on the basis of affinity? Is the community those people and families who are part of the congregation no matter where they live or work? Or is it a matter of geography? Is the church's neighborhood its community, regardless of where the members live? This is particularly an issue for congregations in neighborhoods that have changed. If, for example, a mainline Protestant church of aging Anglo members finds itself surrounded by young, Hispanic, Catholic immigrant families, that congregation's entire life and program will depend on which definition of "community" it has chosen (or had imposed upon it by higher church authorities).

Congregations and institutions that have decided to engage their local communities may move forward in a number of ways. Analyzing these trends historically and currently, we see two interacting dimensions, each representing a continuum of possibilities. The first examines the type of response an organization makes to its community's needs: Is its goal primarily to assist individuals and families in need, whether that help takes the form of rent assistance, food and clothing,

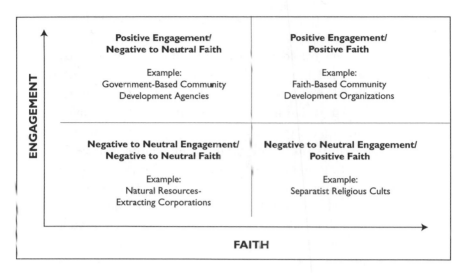

FIGURE 4.1

A framework for contextualizing faith-based community development.

job training, or legal aid (Poppendieck 1998)? Is its goal to transform the entire community by addressing problems with slumlords, redlining, and lack of access to medical care? This continuum—ranging from charitable assistance to community transformation—we have labeled the *engagement* dimension, represented by the vertical axis in figure 4.1.

A second dimension, which we refer to as the *faith* dimension, is shown on the horizontal axis in figure 4.1. Faith-based community organizations are far from monolithic in terms of the role that faith plays in their organization and their programming. While we can assume that any particular organization and its founders were and are motivated by some kind of faith commitment, beyond that point exist vast differences. Sherman (2002:61) has developed a helpful typology for examining organizations to ascertain where they fall on a continuum from "faith background," through "faith-related" and "faith-centered," all the way to "faith-saturated." An organization of the faith background typology probably does not require that its staff and board members share a particular faith background, nor does religious content play a part in its programming. At the other end of the spectrum, a faith-saturated organization may require that its staff belong to its particular faith group

75

and likely mandates participation in religious programming for all who benefit from its services.

In creating this typology for engagement and faith, we recognize that there is a broader context within which faith-based organizations carry out their missions. Clearly, possibilities for neutral and negative values exist along both the engagement and the faith dimensions. After all, some organizations may contribute greatly to the development of communities from an entirely faith-neutral stance—ideally, local governments would fall into this category. Other kinds of organizations may be detrimental to a community's life and health and even hostile to a faith perspective. For example, many multinational corporations engage in activities that demonstrate a negative commitment to the welfare of local communities and their citizens. Within this broader context, most faith-based community development falls into the upper-right quadrant of figure 4.1; that is, it is engagement-positive and faith-positive.

This useful two-dimensional diagram is incomplete without a third dimension—the locus of control. Most faith-based community development organizations are local—founded, staffed, governed, and funded entirely by local individuals and resources. Decisions affecting the community are made in and by the community. Others are chapters of national organizations, with some local control over decisions but with policies generally set at a higher level (for example, the US Department of Housing and Urban Development). A few are international in scope, far removed from the communities subject to their development programs.

The currently heightened awareness of faith-based community development is the culmination of a long history. Before we can deal with twenty-first-century issues, we must step back to see how *community* and *development* came to be combined into a single phrase to which *faith-based* only recently has been added.

HISTORICAL BACKGROUND

The eminent sociologist Robert Nisbet (1966:47) once observed that "the rediscovery of community is unquestionably the most distinctive development in nineteenth-century social thought." Nisbet's analysis of the sociological tradition demonstrates that, during the nineteenth century, "community" held the same pivotal importance that "social contract" had held in the Age of Reason. For a wide range of the nineteenth century's leading social thinkers—Jeremy Bentham, John Stuart Mill, Alexis de Tocqueville, Herbert Spencer, Auguste Comte, Frédéric LePlay, Ferdinand Tönnies, Max Weber, Emile Durkheim, Georg Simmel—an important task of social science was to explain the transformation of social relations accompanying urbanization and industrialization in European and other contemporary societies. In that context, the concept of community was understood by nineteenth-century theorists to encompass far more than neighborhood, the essence of propinquity (Alperson, ed., 2002; Amit 2002; Brown, ed., 2002; Poplin 1979).

Community was equated to the image of the good society, that is, the world as it should be. *Community* became a code word for "all forms of relationship which are characterized by a high degree of personal intimacy, emotional depth, moral commitment, social cohesion, and continuity in time....Community is a fusion of feeling and thought, of tradition and commitment, of membership and volition" (Nisbet 1966:47–48). This ideal type of community was most clearly explicated by Tönnies (1963) in his influential contrast between *Gemeinschaft* and *Gesellschaft*.

Benjamin Disraeli's (1845) famous essay "Sybil, or the Two Nations" also distinguishes between community and society: "It is a community of purpose that constitutes society…without that, [people] may be drawn into contiguity, but they still continue virtually isolated. Christianity teaches us to love our neighbour as ourself; modern society acknowledges no neighbour."

The Beginnings of Faith-Related Community Engagement

As is often the case with theory and practice, these theories about community generally came into existence independently of the ways in which US-based religious organizations were dealing with social problems related to housing, labor, education, health, and immigration, especially in the poorest urban neighborhoods.

In the United States, where individualism was at the heart of an expansionist entrepreneurial culture during most of the nineteenth century, popular views about progress and poverty focused on treating persons in light of what the astute French observer Alexis de Tocqueville called "self interest rightly understood" in his widely acclaimed *Democracy in America* (1835–1840). The challenge, for religious organizations and for other private charity organizations, was to reform particular persons rather than to transform the prevailing "powers and principalities." One well-known example, that of the YMCA, will serve.

> Founded by George Williams in England in 1844, in response to the unhealthy social conditions (in particular, gambling and drinking) arising in London and other large industrial cities, the Young Men's Christian Association (YMCA) sought to fight idleness among young men through Bible studies, prayer meetings, and (eventually) recreational activities. The YMCA movement spread to America in 1851. The first YMCA in the United States was established in Boston; dozens more were founded in other cities within the coming decades. The outbreak of the Civil War a decade later virtually paralyzed the movement, but the association soon developed a program of civilian volunteers dedicated to the welfare of war prisoners and other servicemen. Whether in peace or in war, the YMCA focused its programs on individuals in need, rather than transformation of the underlying social system. By the 1870s, leaders of the YMCA movement were focusing their attentions on working-class industrial and railroad workers. With the goal of reducing political radicalism and labor unrest, the YMCA developed programs to foster team spirit, moral conduct, and new standards of manhood that would avoid conflict and instead would encourage cooperation along the lines of a Christian, pious manliness (Winter 2002)

In the period before the Civil War, some religious groups (for example, Shakers, Oneida, and Mormons) elected to abandon the individualist emphasis in mainstream American culture, choosing instead to establish utopian communities where higher standards of behavior might be pursued. In a sense, these early communitarians took the concept of community development to its extreme—in different ways, they sought to develop holistic (and holy) communities from the ground up.

Slavery, the dominant issue of nineteenth-century American life, also played a significant role in the agendas of religious reformers. In shifting their position from encouraging the manumission (or escape) of individual slaves to urging the transformation of the entire slave-based social system of the South, several Protestant denominations suffered wrenching debates and eventual schism. A related effect was the post-war emergence of independent African-American churches and denominations, many of which would come to play significant roles in urban community development in the twentieth century.

After the depression of the 1870s, "scientific philanthropists" were urging that sentimental approaches to the "undeserving" urban poor be replaced by proper standards for deciding eligibility for assistance and that mentors (usually, well-educated middle- and upper-class women) be provided to instruct the poor on budgeting, child care, household maintenance, and other skills. To many Americans, contemporary urban social problems seemed insurmountable in the face of the growing waves of (mostly) European immigrants. Whereas individual religious organizations once had been content to provide limited charitable assistance to widows, orphans, and other unfortunates, now many private charity groups began to coordinate their efforts so as to reduce the growing rolls of paupers. In New York City, the Charity Organization Society (established in 1882) and other groups worked "to make New York less attractive to the needy by cutting back on outdoor relief and general giving" (Winston 1999:30)—a precursor to many subsequent attempts to reduce the welfare rolls, the most recent being the Personal Responsibility and Work Opportunity Reconciliation Act of 1996, which would give rise to "Charitable Choice options" and "faith-based" initiatives.

The Social Gospel Movement

The situation in the last two decades of the nineteenth century was ripe for new religious and social thinking. Many Protestants began to join the emerging Social Gospel movement, which was intended to respond to the worsening economic and social conditions associated with urban-industrial "progress." In 1885 Josiah Strong, a leading spokesman for the Social Gospel movement, organized an Inter-denominational Congress at his Central Congregationalist Church in Cincinnati. Additional congresses were held in 1887, 1889, and 1893—this last one, located at the Chicago World's Fair, being especially significant for its visibility to and impact on the public at large (Ahlstrom 1975:266).

Walter Rauschenbusch, a professor at Rochester Seminary and pastor for eleven years at the Second German Baptist Church, located just north of the notorious Hell's Kitchen area of New York City, summed up the Social Gospel movement in two highly influential works, *Christianity and the Social Crisis* (Rauschenbusch 1907) and *A Theology for the Social Gospel* (Rauschenbusch 1917). The crisis in contemporary American life, he argued, demanded that Christians answer the call to transform urban-industrial structures of power and inequality. Near the end of his 1907 bestseller, Rauschenbusch (1907:342) stated that "the conviction has always been embedded in the heart of the Church that 'the world'—society as it is—is evil and some time is to make way for a true human society in which the spirit of Jesus Christ shall rule." Then, in words that sound hauntingly contemporary, he proclaimed the following: "We are assured that the poor are poor through their own fault; that rent and profits are the just dues of foresight and ability; that the immigrants are the cause of corruption in our city politics; that we cannot compete with foreign countries unless our working class will descend to the wages paid abroad. These are all very plausible assertions, but they are lies dressed up in truth" (Rauschenbusch 1907:350).

In speaking about church-state relations, Rauschenbusch (1907:380) continues to sound like a prophet for our own times: "The machinery of Church and State must be kept separate, but the output of each must mingle with the other to make social life increasingly wholesome and normal. Church and State are alike but partial organizations of humanity for special ends. Together they serve what is greater than either: humanity. Their common aim is to transform humanity into the kingdom of God."

The power of the Social Gospel movement touched Protestant congregations and denominations across the nation. For instance, in 1887 "a group of New York Episcopalians founded the first Social

Gospel organization, the Church Association for the Advancement of the Interests of Labor" (Gough 1905:253). This expanding commitment of the Church to confront the "powers and principalities" was in line with broader political forces urging the breakup of corporate monopolies, eventually culminating in the Sherman Anti-Trust Act of 1890 and the work of Theodore Roosevelt and his Trust Busters.

Organizations that we would now label "parachurch" also prospered in the environment of the Social Gospel movement, although they tended to concentrate on providing charitable assistance for the poor rather than transforming unjust social structures. For example, in 1880 The Salvation Army arrived from England and initiated its street ministries in New York City. Beginning with its pursuit of lost souls, then moving on to humanitarian aid among the urban poor, The Salvation Army developed a significant social services network—including soup kitchens, rescue shelters, employment bureaus, thrift shops, and clinics—in the city's poorest neighborhoods. In her excellent history of the organization, Diane Winston (1999:3) argues that "while other religious traditions survived, even thrived, in New York, they were not urban religions. In the city but not of the city, they served discrete memberships by offering a respite from the outside world. Sunday (or Saturday) was a spiritual time distinct from the rest of the week just as the sanctuary was a place apart, designated for private worship. Catholics might get out for the annual *festa*, Jews for *tashlich*, but only The Salvation Army pounded the pavements each day of the week."

Urban missions were another significant development (Carle 1997b). The Water Street Mission in New York City and the Pacific Garden Mission in Chicago were the best known of these so-called "rescue missions." By the 1880s every city boasted one or more rescue missions. Eventually, city mission societies throughout the country were launching a wide range of programs for the poor, including homes for working mothers and children's hospitals. They were especially important because of the absence of Protestant congregations in the poorest and most blighted urban neighborhoods. The rescue missions were designed to minister to the "dregs of society—vagrants, alcoholics, former convicts, jobless men, and fallen women" (Hudson 1965:297).

The rapidly expanding city of Chicago gave birth to the Settlement House movement when Jane Addams and her friend Ellen Starr established Hull House in 1889. Addams (who was awarded the Nobel Prize for Peace in 1931) was an active Quaker; the Quakers also supported the Friends Neighborhood Guild in Philadelphia. Settlement houses, many of which had religious connections, focused on improving living conditions, especially among the growing ethnic immigrant populations flooding into the poorest urban areas.

The late nineteenth century also saw the short-lived approach to the problems of urban community life known as the "institutional church"—a late nineteenth-century precursor of today's megachurches. The institutional church was defined by its leading apologist, Edward Judson (1907:436), as "an organized body of Christian believers, who, finding themselves in a hard and uncongenial social environment, supplement the ordinary methods of the gospel—such as preaching, prayer meetings, Sunday school, and pastoral visitation—by a system of organized kindness, a congeries of institutions, which, by touching people on physical, social, and intellectual sides, will conciliate them and draw them within reach of the gospel."

By the end of the nineteenth century, there were more than 170 such institutional churches in the nation's major cities, most of them affiliated with the principal Protestant denominations (Baptist, Congregational, Episcopalian, Methodist, and Presbyterian). The Open or Institutional Church League was formed in 1894 to promote "educational, reformatory, and philanthropic" activities (Hudson 1965:300–302). This initial success tended to absorb more and more of the congregations' energy in the provision of humanitarian services, rather than in evangelization. Hudson (1965:302) reports that "as a result the congregations dwindled almost as rapidly as they had increased. In the end, far from being a means of building up a congregation to support a ministry in areas of deterioration, many of the institutional churches became social agencies which other churches had to find money and leadership to maintain and support."

The Early Twentieth Century

In the first half of the twentieth century, the United States became a (reluctant) global power driven by an ever-growing industrial output generated largely by a workforce of immigrant and ethnic-minority laborers. The so-called "Great Migration" of African-Americans from the South to northern cities was accompanied by the "urbanization of black Christianity" (Franklin 1996:78). This "ministry of resettlement" was structurally similar to efforts by Roman Catholics, Jews, and Protestants to assist newly arriving Europeans. For example, in 1907 the Presbyterian Church created an Office of Immigrant and Industrial Work, and in 1914 the Presbyterian Mission Board built the Labor Temple in New York City to provide office and meeting space for newly organizing unions (Todd 1996:152).

The experience of Jewish immigrants to America transformed their participation in community life. Once restricted to self-contained enclaves (ghettos) in European towns and cities, Jews in the United States found themselves embedded in a broader, more diverse society, with full rights and responsibilities as citizens. Here, the synagogue became the primary institution of Jewish life, often with several in a metropolitan area. Rather than being limited by ghetto walls, American Jews were able to participate in community life through a synagogue (Hudson 1965:329). The estimated two hundred fifty thousand Jews in the United States in 1880 expanded to nearly three million by the beginning of World War I.

In similar fashion, the Roman Catholic Church grew dramatically in the years from 1880 to 1914. In those days, Catholics often suffered discrimination at the hands of the Protestants, who outnumbered them in the urban areas of the northeast and midwest. According to Frederick J. Perella (1996:180):

> The parish was and remains the primary center for pastoral care and development of people in the Catholic urban experience.... Parishes were geographically defined, which meant that the clergy had pastoral responsibility for the care of all souls in their neighborhood. Therefore, Catholic parishes and their institutions, while ethnocentric and creed-centered, often extended their services to others in their area. In this immigrant-community stream could be found Catholic churches, elementary and secondary schools, and some local parish credit unions or small consumer cooperatives.... In addition, the immigrant-community church created volunteer, self-help social services, such

as emergency aid funds and volunteer mutual assistance groups like the St. Vincent de Paul Society.

World War II to the 1960s

World War II represents a watershed in the history of religious involvement in community development and social services programs. First, the five years of global conflict from 1941 to 1945 shifted resources away from the problems of rural and urban communities that had accumulated during the Great Depression of the 1930s. Then, after the war, the baby boom resulted in the dramatic growth of suburban America, accompanied by a continuing impoverishment of many old city centers, where African-Americans and other ethnic minorities would soon become demographic majorities. These trends were exacerbated by the "white flight" response of many Anglos to the 1954 Supreme Court decision (*Brown v. Board of Education of Topeka*) that declared school segregation unconstitutional.

During the 1950s and the 1960s, religious groups were faced with building thousands of new congregations in the expanding suburbs. At the same time, center-city churches were declining in membership and lacked the resources to meet their community's needs. For the new suburban churches, *community development* ceased to refer to social ministry in a congregation's surrounding community and, instead, came to mean the development of a sense of community within a congregation's own membership—not unlike the escapist utopian communities of the nineteenth century. During the period from 1940 to 1960, church membership rose from about 50 percent of the population to nearly 70 percent. By the late 1960s, at a time when the Vietnam conflict was just beginning to affect American society, a reversal of membership trends had become evident. Green (1996:17) reports that "in 1968 the ten largest Protestant denominations reported fewer members than in the previous year. Church membership was not keeping up with the growth rate of the population."

The civil rights struggles of the 1960s engaged the energies and passions of many religious groups—especially African-American congregations and Hispanic Catholic parish churches. In life and in death, charismatic leaders such as Martin Luther King Jr. and César Chávez challenged the national conscience. The involvement of churches in national human rights issues often created a tension with their ongoing participation in local-level community issues.

The urban riots in the summer of 1967 brought this tension home to congregations, synagogues, and parish churches throughout America. During that terrible time, Andrew White (then an assistant professor at Lutheran Seminary in Philadelphia) wrote a prescient article titled "The Churches and Community Development." He saw churches as potentially powerful forces for solving the problems billowing from the nation's cities:

> As strategies for constructive social change are being developed, the strategists are choosing between approaches which simply control the scope and consequences of ills resulting from individual dysfunction and those resulting from whole system dysfunction....The community development process, recognizing the deep-rooted source of system dysfunction, is one that, in its multi-variety of forms, views the community as a whole and is a search for the problem-solving activity which will attack root causes rather than offer merely symptomatic treatment (White 1967:372).

Although White's analysis focused on Lutherans, he and others (for example, Schaller 1965) also saw the need for a broader approach if urban neighborhoods were to be saved. As an example of this community development approach, White presented the case of the First English Lutheran Church, located in a poverty area of Columbus, Ohio. This congregation "had the courage to help the people of its community structure themselves to help themselves, rather than be continued recipients of hand-out aid" (White 1967:373). Thus, the people created the East Central Citizens Organization (ECCO), which offered its members "a new self-image for the individual, a new sense of identity in community, the dignity of freedom and self-determination, the power to make decisions and judgments, the respect of the whole community and its official agencies, and the right to choose its leadership, to control the actions of its officials and to reject manipulation by friend or foe" (White 1967:373–374).

Community-oriented projects often took place in the context of ecumenical efforts. Following the creation of the National Council of Churches in 1950 (after the founding of the World Council of Churches in 1948), the Second Vatican Council (1962–1965) not only opened the Roman Catholic Church to the world but also brought to the attention of the world's religious community a heightened concern for social justice ministries and liberation theology (originally elaborated in Latin America, Africa, and Asia). These new teachings "reinforced and enlivened an already strong Catholic commitment to improving urban life and encouraged Catholics to work together with other Christians in addressing problems of the city" (Green 1996:19).

The 1960s saw the beginning of church-based training institutes for urban community ministry efforts. According to Green (1996:19–20), twenty-seven centers were set up in twenty-two cities, with the Urban Training Center in Chicago and the Metropolitan Urban Service Training program in New York being among the best known. These centers were supported by fifteen national church agencies, including white and black Protestant, Roman Catholic, and smaller groups. Although most of these centers were short-lived, they collectively trained thousands of workers to do community ministry throughout the nation.

The 1960s to the New Millennium

A major emphasis in the 1960s was the community-organizing strategy inspired by the earlier work of Saul Alinsky and his colleagues. In the late 1930s Alinksy and others brought together Roman Catholic parish leaders and other local neighborhood leaders to organize the Back of the Yards Neighborhood Council in Chicago. Their experiences resulted in the establishment of the Industrial Areas Foundation (IAF) in 1940. In his 1946 bestseller *Reveille for Radicals*, Alinsky (who earlier had studied archaeology and urban sociology at the University of Chicago) elaborated his hard-won philosophy that community organizing demanded detailed ethnographic understanding of a community, required an outside organizer to serve as a catalyst for change, and depended on understanding power in terms of relationships.

After spending two decades traveling throughout the nation's cities developing his bottom-up, people-first methodology for community organizing, Alinsky was ready for another major community project. In 1959 he was approached by leaders of local churches in the Woodlawn area of Chicago to combat the University of Chicago's plans to expand its campus into this "depressed" neighborhood. At Alinsky's suggestion, the local association of Protestant pastors was expanded so that Catholic clergy could join, and, with this broader base of support, the IAF began to organize the residents of Woodlawn. With funding from the Archdiocese of Chicago, the Presbyterian Board of National Missions, and private foundations, The Woodlawn Organization not only dealt with the university but also organized campaigns for fair business practices by the area's merchants, led a series of tenant strikes, and—led by Alinsky's brilliant protégé, Nicholas von Hoffman (who later went on to become a well-known author and television commentator)—took on the Board of Education over the issues of segregated and unequal public education.

As P. David Finks (1984:167) has observed, "the close working arrangement between Alinsky and the Christian churches in ecumenical coalition became the model for the IAF's approach to organizing communities in the 1960s and 1970s and continues to operate today." According to Monsignor John J. Egan, then director of the Archdiocesan Office of Urban Affairs in Chicago, "the early 1960s were the 'Golden Age' of Church-community cooperation in Chicago because in a time of civic crisis Alinsky brought to the frustrated people in the churches and to the troubled people in the neighborhoods the tools they needed to create democratic power, pride in themselves, and the political skills to take control of their lives and communities. Nobody could have done it alone; it took the churches and the neighborhood people—and it required Alinsky and his organizers as the catalyst" (quoted in Finks 1984:169).

As a consequence of the Woodlawn project's success in Chicago and that of similar projects in New York and California, community organizing became the single most important strategy for church urban mission. Presbyterian leader George Todd (1996:164) has observed that "community organizing was recognized as a new form of ministry that carried forward the long line of the church's service in urban communities. Whereas in the nineteenth and early twentieth century the church had pioneered in establishing schools, hospitals, community centers, and other forms of social service, community organizing represented a transformation of church thinking from service to *empowerment.*"

In the wake of Vatican II, with its acceptance of new ideas about liberation theology, church-based community organizing was a logical extension of the historical role of Roman Catholic parish churches. As Perella (1996:209–210) has pointed out:

> Under the concept of congregation or parish-based organizing, networks such as the Industrial Areas Foundation and the Campaign for Human Development began to stress training and funding that make the parishes and the churches in a community the constituency for an organization. Rather than merely sponsor or physically host a neighborhood organizing project in which some parishioners and the pastor get involved, organizing strategies call for the entire parish to be interviewed and for an intensive program of leadership development to take place in each member parish....The agendas for these congregational organizing projects were developed in a process of consultations and prayer, which included theological and biblical reflection, about basic goals and values of the churches.

FAITH-BASED COMMUNITY ORGANIZING TODAY: NATIONAL STRATEGIES, LOCAL ACTIONS

Perhaps the greatest legacy of the faith-based efforts in the golden age of the 1960s is to be found in the continuing work of four national-level community-organizing enterprises. These enterprises—the Industrial Areas Foundation, the Gamaliel Foundation, PICO, and DART—collectively provide community organizers and offer training to hundreds of local-level community organizations throughout the country. Operating through local-level networks and mainly in metropolitan areas, IAF, Gamaliel, PICO, and DART collectively have operations in thirty-three states and the District of Columbia. They sponsor a wide range of "actions" and celebrate many "victories" each year as they work to expand their influence to new communities and new social issues (Jacobsen 2001).[1]

Just as Alinsky's earlier work in community organizing has continued to attract attention and has served as a model for current work, so, too, the effort of present-day organizers is being taken seriously by national-level governmental and private-sector enterprises. For instance, Ernesto J. Cortés, regional director of the IAF's Southwest Network for almost three decades, has received the Heinz Award in Public Policy and a MacArthur Foundation "genius" grant (Cortés 1993, 1996; Rogers 1990; Warren 2001).

Through Cortés's leadership, IAF has established a strong presence in Texas and throughout the Southwest with coalitions of congregations (mostly Roman Catholic, Protestant, and Jewish), along with labor unions, public schools, and other interest groups. Beginning with the establishment in 1974 of the COPS (Communities Organized for Public Service) organization in his hometown of San Antonio, Cortés has helped to build local networks based on relational power that have generated more than $1 billion worth of improvements in neighborhood infrastructure in San Antonio alone, with another $1 billion of improvements in the Rio Grande Valley area along the border. In 1999, when COPS celebrated its twenty-fifth anniversary, more than five thousand leaders from the IAF Southwest Network assembled in San Antonio to celebrate their thousands of victories. These include statewide educational reform through Alliance Schools, metropolitan living-wage policies for working families, organizing for the provision of water and wastewater services along the Texas border, the creation of affordable housing for low- to moderate-income families, and adult job training programs (Shirley 2002).

The work of faith-based community-organizing networks is surveyed in a recent report about the state of the field (Warren and Wood 2001). Of the 133 local organizations identified for inclusion in the survey, 100 responded. The responding organizations are active in thirty-three states and the District of Columbia—not the same thirty-three states served by the four national organizations, though there is significant overlap. Yet fully half of those one hundred organizations are clustered in six states (California, Texas, New York, Florida, Illinois, and Ohio). Warren and Wood (2001:6) found that the faith-based community-organizing field

> includes about 4,000 member institutions, of which 87% are religious congregations, and 13% are non-congregational institutions like unions, public schools, and a diverse array of other community organizations.... [T]he leaders...include

nearly 2,700 people serving on governing boards and roughly 24,000 core leaders actively engaged at any one time through the work of 460 professional organizers. Their combined efforts drew an estimated 100,000 people to at least one large public action over the 18 months leading up to the survey, which should be understood as a minimum figure for active support for the field's organizations.

Faith-based community-organizing groups involve a wide range of religious congregations. Catholics make up about one-third of the congregations; Baptists (mostly black) represent about one-sixth. United Methodists, Lutherans, Episcopalians, Presbyterians, and Congregationalists (UCC), together, represent another one-third of the participating congregations. The balance is composed of small percentages of Jewish, Unitarian Universalist, and black evangelical (mostly Church of God in Christ) congregations. Warren and Wood (2001:7) discovered in their survey that "white evangelicals and fundamentalists are noticeably absent, considering their prominence in American society."

In addition to being faith-based, these organizations are intentionally inclusive and broad-based within their communities, are locally constituted and locally focused, are driven to confront multiple issues in nonpartisan ways, and are usually directed by professional community organizers responsible for recruiting and training local leadership.

COMMUNITY DEVELOPMENT CORPORATIONS: A COMPETING APPROACH

Even though the community-organizing paradigm has proven itself to be an effective mechanism for transforming power relationships in local communities, it is not the only approach used by faith-based enterprises. The major competing paradigm is that of community development, principally manifested through local-level Community Development Corporations (CDCs). Among African-American congregations, it is common practice to spin off one or more separate nonprofit 501-c(3) organizations in which local pastors also may play key roles.

Not all faith-based organizations are involved in community development, much less in their communities. A key finding of a recent report (prepared by Avis C. Vidal [2001:i–ii] of The Urban Institute for the US Department of Housing and Community Development [HUD]) states that "relatively few faith-based organizations participate in community development activities," although "faith-based organizations are uniquely positioned to have a significant impact beyond simply sponsoring community development projects."

This same report suggests that community development activities are not distributed evenly among religious groups. Size is an important variable because larger congregations are more likely to have more financial resources, more paid staff, and more members willing to serve as unpaid volunteers. While income per se does not appear to be a significant variable in determining whether congregations will be involved in community activities, theological orientation does make a difference. Theologically liberal congregations are more than twice as likely as conservative congregations to engage in social services and to carry out community-oriented activities. Congregations located in areas where more than 30 percent of the residents earn incomes below the federal poverty line also are more likely to be involved in work in their communities. Finally, the presence of charismatic leadership in a congregation is a significant factor in the congregation's commitment to community work.

Given these tendencies, it is no surprise that congregations with a predominantly African-American membership are more likely than Anglo-dominated congregations to participate in community development activities (McDougall 1993; McRoberts 2001). Usually, African-American churches establish CDCs to operate their community projects (Orr 2000; Owens 2000). In this way, African-American churches "have traditionally worked…to preserve ownership of projects that are 'in, of, and for' the African-American community" (Day 2001:193). Moreover, "through investment of new resources from government, academia, denominations, and the philanthropic communities, [African-American] churches are more strongly equipped to carry out large-scale economic development projects. As a result, entrepreneurial churches are able to tackle whole neighborhoods and a plethora of issues within them—education, business development, housing, commercial development, job training, crime and safety, and so on" (Day 2001:194).

CDCs have proven to be a viable mechanism for dealing with community issues for more than thirty years. Indeed, they have reached such venerable status that an oral history project has been conducted among the founders, leaders, and supporters of nineteen of the pioneering CDCs across the country. Supported by major funding from the Ford Foundation, the Pratt Institute Center for Community and Environmental Development (PICCED) of Brooklyn carried out this project. To inform the broader public about the mission, history, struggles, and accomplishments of the community development movement, PICCED and Charles Hobson of Vanguard Films drew upon the CDC Oral History Project interviews to produce *Building Hope,* a one-hour video documentary that was aired nationwide on PBS in April 1994.[2]

According to the recent National Congregations Study (Chaves et al. 1999), nearly 57 percent of congregations engage in social services or community-oriented activities. Only 18 percent participate in housing programs, even though this is the most common community development activity. Recently, HUD has been reinventing itself "to serve communities." HUD now sees its mission as including work with faith-based organizations to enhance community development programs. A crucial piece of HUD's reinvention is the new Center for Faith-Based and Community Initiatives, established in response to President Bush's Executive Order of January 29, 2001, to replace HUD's Center for Community and Interfaith Partnerships. This new center does not make grants. Rather, it assists faith-based organizations by making it easier for such organizations to participate in HUD programs, thereby helping HUD to achieve its mission. HUD is committed to working with faith-based organizations not simply because of a presidential mandate; the significant involvement of diverse faith-based agencies makes it impossible for HUD to avoid such involvement.[3]

ASSET-BASED COMMUNITY DEVELOPMENT: TURNING THREATS INTO OPPORTUNITIES

Writing three decades ago about the trajectory of community development and cultural change in Latin America, anthropologist Norman B. Schwartz (1978:237) suggested that "the core of the community development movement and method was to help people help themselves improve the material and nonmaterial conditions of their lives because the assumption is that 'there, in the long run, lies the salvation of the community'" (quoting Dunham 1963). Schwartz (1978:237) continued his analysis of the Latin American situation by observing that community development "aims to help a community realize its own aspirations and needs by using its own human resources, although the community, usually poor and deprived, may require private or public support at various stages on the path to self-realization. Within this context, change agents regard the 'felt needs' of their clients as primary. Further, the felt needs of the entire community are important; no segment of the community may be neglected."

More recently, John M. Perkins, co-founder of the Christian Community Development Association (CCDA), established in 1989, proclaimed that Christian community development is dedicated to meeting three universal felt needs: (1) the need to belong, (2) the need to be significant and important, and (3) the need for a reasonable amount of security (Perkins 1995:20–21). The CCDA brings together a wide range of faith-based organizations concerned with meeting the felt needs of urban and rural communities. Through its quarterly newsletter "Faith in the Community" and its annual national conferences, the CCDA spreads its message, especially among African-American clergy and laypersons.

One of Perkins's colleagues, Phil Reed (senior pastor, Voice of Calvary Fellowship, Jackson, Mississippi), has defined what he calls the "3 Rs" of community development: reconciliation, redistribution, and relocation. First, people must overcome divisions of all kinds. Second, people must have access to opportunities to obtain the skills and economic resources necessary to work their way out of poverty, whatever the cause of their situation. Third, the people must bring God's resources into the community of need in a personal way. For Reed (1995:36; Perkins 1993), "relocation is the method by which we accomplish reconciliation and redistribution. Neither reconciliation nor redistribution can be done effectively long distance.... Relocation is personal. It involves putting ourselves in threatening situations, coming into areas that others have long since abandoned, or merely planting our feet in neighborhoods that 'smart' people are leaving."

In their call for the restoration of at-risk communities, Perkins, Reed, and their CCDA collaborators actually demonstrate the importance of relationships—what we can label the "fourth R." For instance, in discussing the local church and community development, Glen Kehrein (1995:179; Ferguson and Dickens, eds., 1999), executive director of Circle Urban Ministries in Chicago, points out that "relationships are key. Partnership takes intentional effort; it won't happen just because we want it to happen. Staff and leaders must commit time and energy to relationship building. To have integrity and longevity, ministry must grow from our fellowship."

These 4 Rs have been taken to another level by John P. Kretzmann and John L. McKnight, the directors of the Asset-Based Community Development (ABCD) Institute, located at the Institute for Policy Research at Northwestern University. The ABCD approach involves six steps: releasing individual capacities, releasing the power of local associations and organizations, capturing local institutions for community building, rebuilding the community economy, mobilizing the assets of the entire community, and providing policies and guidelines to support ongoing asset-based development.[4]

The ABCD approach focuses on developing a Community Assets Map of local institutions (businesses, community colleges, hospitals, parks, schools), citizens' associations (block clubs, churches, cultural groups), and gifts of individuals (including artists, the elderly, youth, and "labeled" [differently gifted] people). The detailed gathering of information about a community, household by household, building by building, block by block, is intended to reveal its unique inventory of assets. Assembling and analyzing the assets map and developing the inventory are necessary steps before these assets can be mobilized for development purposes (see also Hyland and Owens, chapter 5 of this volume).

According to Kretzmann and McKnight (1993:9), the ABCD approach to community development starts with what is present in the community, the capacities of its residents and workers, the associational and institutional base of the area—not with what is absent, what is problematic, or what the community needs. This community development process is internally focused to stress the primacy of local definition, investment, creativity, hope, and control. Finally, this community development process is designed to be relationship-driven. Therefore, one of the central challenges for asset-based community developers is to sustain the relationships between and among local residents, local associations, and local institutions.

The asset-based approaches of the CCDA and the ABCD Institute are precursors of a social capital approach to community organizing and development (Foley, McCarthy, and Chaves 2001). Made popular by Robert Putnam's (2000) bestseller *Bowling Alone: The Collapse and Revival of American Community*, social capital can be understood as the stocks of social trust, norms, and networks that people can call upon to solve shared problems. Neighborhood associations, cooperatives, sports clubs, and religious congregations represent separate elements in a community's portfolio of social capital. The more these associational networks overlap, the more likely that a community can be mobilized into effective action. Social capital tends to be below the radar screen of formal assessment methods. The associational networks and the individual "funds of knowledge" (Vélez-Ibáñez and Greenberg 1992) that compose the networks are hard to measure through sample survey techniques. On the other hand, careful community analysis through ethnographic procedures, especially spatial mapping (Cromley 1999) and social network analysis (Trotter 1999), is more likely to reveal the richness of local communities.

Faith-based community development may be characterized as social capital development to the extent that it builds on relationships within the community of interest and then expands these relationships to include external individuals, associations, and institutions. When religious institutions join with labor unions, schools, banks, and other enterprises, the chances for transforming the community increase dramatically beyond what typically occurs when top-down planning approaches are imposed by external agencies. And when faith-based organizations are able to join metropolitan, regional, and even national networks composed of like-minded individuals, there is no need to reinvent the wheel or suffer through situations that other communities have already resolved. Instead, there is a significant multiplier effect for faith-based community development in such contexts.

IMPLICATIONS FOR ANTHROPOLOGICAL THEORIES AND PRACTICES

Faith-based organizations offer excellent opportunities for putting anthropological theories and practices to the test. At a time when the need for studying the diversity of American communities is obvious to all, congregations and other faith-based groups provide an entry into places where ethnographers might otherwise *not* be able to conduct field research. Congregations cross all the lines of contemporary America—rich and poor, ethnic minorities and majorities, urban, suburban, and rural. Churches and parachurch organizations are found everywhere, from east to west, from north to south.

Thus, it is possible to construct large-scale comparative projects (Woolever and Bruce 2002), as well as to carry out small-scale, indepth analysis of faith-based community development enterprises (Ammerman et al. 1998). Most of these studies are being conducted *not* by anthropologists, but by scholars in other disciplines (for example, sociology, social work, demography, and theology) who have come to appreciate the value of ethnographic inquiry (Cnaan with Wineburg and Boddie 1999; Cnaan et al. 2002; Goldsmith 2002; Rubin 2000). Even though few anthropologists have been involved directly in research projects focused on faith-based community development, anthropological perspectives are very much in vogue (Bartkowski and Regis 2003).

Persons with skills in community assessment, evaluation, strategic planning, and grant writing are in great demand among faith-based organizations involved in community development projects. There is no end to the opportunities for doing consulting assignments, whether for local congregations, for regional judicatories, or even with national denominational offices. Many anthropologists' experiences with ethnic and immigrant populations can be very useful to religious organizations committed to working with these groups.

But it is both awareness of and commitment to "culture" that continue to be the most important components in contemporary analysis of faith-based community development projects. Attention to "cultural models of local religious life" (Becker 1999) can be an important step toward framing "cultural" approaches to understanding the internal workings of faith-based organizations involved in community development.

Throughout America, in inner-city neighborhoods and small rural communities, historic churches are in decline or even face being closed. The generational transition inside these churches reflects the broader changes in the surrounding neighborhoods. At the other extreme, the rise of new, affluent suburbs on the edge of metropolitan areas brings with it the building of new congregations, representing not only mainline denominations but also independent and nontraditional churches.

In a sense, faith-based organizations are institutions with their own life cycles, played out across several generations and sometimes spread across the landscape—as congregations move from one place to another or expand from an original site to a wider range of localities. In such contexts, anthropologists interested in longitudinal and historical studies will find congregations and their members very receptive to studies of their impact on the broader community.

CONCLUSION

Wayne G. Bragg (1984) has suggested that, for community development to achieve community transformation, it must have the following elements: life sustenance, equity, justice, dignity and self-worth, freedom, participation, reciprocity, cultural fit, ecological soundness, hope, and spiritual transformation. Unfortunately, this commendable list of qualities is rarely made explicit in the goals and objectives laid out in Requests for Proposals for community development projects.

A recent president of the Community Development Society, Ronald J. Hustedde, has decried the absence of soul in community development. He believes that integrating "soulful practices" into community development projects would help us to "respect the diversity of the peoples we serve" (Hustedde 1998:155). He goes on to say that "soul can make sense out of paradox. It thrives on it. The many paradoxes within community development cause its practitioners to draw upon their intuition and their discerning spirits in deciding what is right when dealing with them" (Hustedde 1998:160). Hustedde is enough of a realist to know that, despite our best efforts, sometimes nothing is accomplished, at least in the short time frame of a funded project. As he states, "in the end, all one may have left to show for their efforts is the saving power of relationships to sustain us. Community is not abstract. It is about real people with real names. The community developer's relationship with people is unique....We seek to strengthen the skills of the communities so [that] they no longer need us.... When practitioners nourish these relationships, they are engaged in a soulful act" (Hustedde 1998:161–162).

Finally, Hustedde (1998:163) reminds us that community development involves giving and receiving a blessing: "The most subtle blessing we give is the blessing of being there to truly listen and walk with people in their pain, joy, and questioning....Additionally, there are the blessings of affirmation in which we tell community people in words and touch the importance of the journey they are on. We affirm their accomplishments, the difficult questions they raise, and the lessons they learn along the way."

What Hustedde claims for specialists in the community development profession applies just as well to anthropologists. Our theories, methods, and practices are valuable for understanding and implementing faith-based community development projects, whether carried out by anthropologists or used by non-anthropologists. But beyond this obvious connection, we believe that involvement in faith-based community development also offers to anthropologists the possibility of self-transformation and, perhaps, even disciplinary development. Contrast the difference between consulting for a corporation driven to extract profits from consumers and working in partnership with congregations determined to be prophetic social critics to their communities.

Speaking about the soul of community development brings to mind the biblical sense of community welfare and partnership, represented in the Old Testament by the Hebrew term *shalom* (peace, welfare) and in the New Testament by the Greek term *koinonia* (community, partnership). Following Roy H. May Jr. (1985:2, emphasis added), we suggest that "development does not mean *having* more, but fundamentally *being* more in terms of the quality and relationships of life that emerge from a community's own cultural tradition....It is the creation of new cultural, political, and economic patterns and conditions that enhance dignity, critical consciousness, and interpersonal communication and cooperation based on the principles of participation and community self-determination."

In this ancient tradition, turning around begets repentance begets transformation. Change is not merely material; it also is spiritual. The Greek term *metanoia*, which can be translated as "transformation of the mind," captures the power of the spirit that thrives in faith-based community organizing and development. Establishing relationships and building a base for political and economic power are worthless without spiritual engagement. In this sense, transformation is more than a human endeavor; it is God's will made visible through human actions in community (Linthicum 2003; Livezey, ed., 2000). Change comes about *not* because of solitary individuals who act through their "self interest rightly understood"—*pace* Alexis de Tocqueville—but because people form lasting partnerships and voluntary associations based on common interests rightly understood. Ultimately, effective community development—and the role of anthropologists as students and agents of change—depends on being in communion, being together with others who see the world as it is and share a vision of and commitment to the world as it should be.

Notes

1. Because these national organizations devote most of their energies to local-level community organizing, rather than to national-level publications and conferences, they can be contacted most easily through their respective websites:

- The Industrial Areas Foundation: http://www.tresser.com/IAF.htm
- Gamaliel Foundation: http://www.gamaliel.org
- Pacific Institute for Community Organization: http://www.piconetwork.org
- Direct Action and Research Training: http://www.thedartcenter. org

2. Their website (http://www.picced.org/) provides profiles of fifteen CDCs across the nation.

3. For more information on HUD and other governmental partnerships with faith-based community organizations, consult the http://www.knowledge plex.org website powered by the Fannie Mae Foundation. Also useful is a Fannie Mae–funded publication titled *Faith-Based Affordable Housing Development and Finance Resource Guide*, prepared by the College of Biblical Studies, Houston, Texas.

4. These steps are described in detail in the excellent manual *Building Communities from the Inside Out: A Path toward Finding and Mobilizing a Community's Assets* (Kretzmann and McKnight 1993) and are taught through annual three-day learning events and five-day learning retreats. In addition to these training programs, the ABCD Institute began (in 1997) a Religious Network for faith-based community builders that has received significant financial support from the Presbyterian Church (USA). In 1999 ABCD established an ABCD Neighborhood Circle network for bringing together local community project

leaders investigating ABCD approaches to mobilizing whole neighborhoods in community training. Regional ABCD networks have developed in recent years in California, Oregon, Connecticut, South Carolina, and Wisconsin.

5

Revitalizing Urban Communities through a New Approach to Computer Mapping

Stanley E. Hyland and Michelle Owens

Much like the transformation of rural villages after World War II and the reconstruction of settlements after catastrophes (Oliver-Smith, chapter 3 of this volume), the processes of globalization have dramatically changed the community life of urban neighborhoods. Assumed to be relatively stable by virtue of ethnicity, income, religion, kinship, or other social bonds, urban neighborhoods have undergone assault by the ecological processes engendering decentralization of American cities, global industrial restructuring, public and private policies favoring suburban development, and disinvestment associated with racism and classism (Macionis and Parrillo 2003). The resources needed for viable urban neighborhoods have systematically diminished with the growth of suburbs and urban fringe settlements through hidden subsidies and job relocation. The literature on the restructuring of urban space has become synonymous with ethnographies of marginalization and displacement, homelessness, social injustice, and the hopelessness of inner-city residents (Sanjek 1990; Low 1996). Only descriptions of downtown revitalization via gentrification and gated residencies seem to offer counter-images of urban space (Low 1999).

Outside responses to inner-city development via government, private sector, and nonprofit initiatives have been largely top-down, driven by definition of needs and administered through powerful intermediate agencies and institutions. Whether in health, housing, job training, or social service programs, top-down responses parallel those described in catastrophic relocation projects (Oliver-Smith, chapter 3 of this volume). Their ineffectiveness to produce viable neighborhoods has been documented by social scientists and residents in terms of lack of citizen participation and grassroots empowerment (Gans 1962b; Greer 1965; Edelman 2001; Greenbaum 2002). Components of this growing literature include discussions of community-based assets, civic/community infrastructure, healthy neighborhoods, and the social capital of the inner-city residents attempting to rebuild their neighborhoods (Kretzmann and McKnight 1993; Putnam 2000; Saegert, Thompson, and Warren, eds., 2001). This literature, including Kemper and Adkins' chapter 4 and Schensul's chapter 8 of this book, has challenged the more top-down development approaches.

Interestingly, anthropologists' ethnographic descriptions of social networks and community-based adaptations in their studies of both rural villages and urban neighborhoods share similarities with this literature. Writing in the 1970s about the future survival of local communities, Gallaher and Padfield (1980) stated that all associational forms share what we believe to be the most basic of all purposes—group survival, through the development of collective solutions to problems. This common purpose defines a community. Gallaher and Padfield (1980) raise several critical issues for anthropological research today. The first is an understanding of the internal processes associated with community disintegration, the individual and group values and behaviors that are detrimental to community-building efforts. The second is an understanding of the intervention (change) approaches to both the internal and external processes that contribute to the dissolution of local communities.

These issues are as germane today as they were thirty years ago. Researchers in inner-city neighborhoods, particularly US public-housing developments, have produced an overwhelming literature on crime, substance abuse, gang activity, and violence (Popkin et al. 2000; Venkatesh 2000). Popkin and others (2000:6) note that the kind of violence occurring in Chicago Housing Authority's (CHA) high-rise developments is incomprehensible to most Americans. They list a few of the stories that made the news during an especially violent four-month period, between January 1 and April 30 of 1997:

- A nine-year-old girl (labeled "Girl X" by the media) was kidnapped, sexually assaulted, poisoned, and left for dead in Cabrini-Green (*Chicago Tribune*, January 10, 1997).

- CHA police and drug dealers in Cabrini-Green engaged in a shoot-out ending with the police firing into an occupied building (*Chicago Tribune*, March 5, 1997).

- The head of the Chicago public schools announced a plan to transport children from an elementary school in Cabrini-Green to another location to escape constant gunfire (*Chicago Tribune*, April 12, 1997).

- A thirty-one-year-old man was killed in the Henry Horner Homes in a gang-related shooting (*Chicago Tribune*, April 14, 1997).

- A five-year-old boy was sexually assaulted by six ten-year-olds in a community center in the Robert Taylor Homes (*Chicago Tribune*, April 21 and April 23, 1997).

The neighborhoods around CHA's developments have few services or stores and even fewer jobs. Popkin (2000:1) notes, "Most residents are unemployed; they depend on public assistance or the underground economy. Only a few older, stable individuals are capable of enforcing standards of acceptable behavior. Without this underlying social structure, there is little mutual trust and cohesion that can encourage or even allow residents to unite to fight their common problems." Chicago's public housing is not unlike troubled housing developments throughout urban America, in Memphis, New Orleans, or Baltimore.

Of relevance in today's urban neighborhoods are the polemics surrounding community and community building. To reclaim community, many housing authorities have proclaimed war on the street gangs that live in public housing developments and prey upon residents, but gang members and their networks often claim to *be* the community.

Disputes over who belongs to the community further divide it, pitting tenants with gang ties against those without. Community building cannot be achieved with efforts totally controlled by residents, or through war. Today, community-building approaches do not have remedies that are simply either top-down or bottom-up. The current literature suggests agendas that may contribute to a reconceptualization of community building. This process, actively facilitated by scholars, involves the collaborative efforts of multiple stakeholders to make comprehensive changes through computer community-assets mapping (Kubisch et al. 2002).

THE COMMUNITY-BUILDING APPROACH IN URBAN NEIGHBORHOODS

At the turn of this century, community activists and scholars (Briggs and Mueller 1997; Kingsley, McNeely, and Gibson 1997; Kubisch et al. 2002; Mattessich and Monsey 1997) converged on a definition of community building as a continuous, self-renewing, collaborative effort by community residents and professionals to engage in problem solving and enrichment. The effort would result in improved lives; greater equity; strengthened relationships, networks, institutions, and assets; and new standards and expectations for life in the neighborhood. Key components in this conceptualization of community building include the development of residents' capacities and skills, the power of community-based voluntary associations in defining a vision of action, and the ways these resources, institutions, residences, and agencies are connected. The conceptualization also values the resources of local institutions—their natural and built physical resources and their economic power.

Community building can be viewed as one critical dimension of community development. It is as much about the *process* of action through relationship building as the outcome. Community development, on the other hand, focuses on the achievement of a common goal and improvements within the community associated with material products, without necessarily working on relationship building and social capacity (Mattessich and Monsey 1997). Using the example of US public housing, a community development approach may result in the re-creation of a safe, mixed-income population that enjoys new quality-of-life amenities. The revitalized neighborhood, however, does not necessarily include all the relevant stakeholders in the design, planning, and implementation of the redevelopment, much less the former residents of public housing. When anthropologists, scholars, policy makers, and practitioners do not perceive this distinction, they unwittingly contribute to the undermining of community-based initiatives.

THE ROLE OF INFORMATION IN COMMUNITY BUILDING

In an age of information, one critical question is how information contributes to community building and neighborhood revitalization. Sassen (1991), among other scholars, has argued that global cities are being restructured in terms of their relationship within the information loops of global market systems. New York, Hong Kong, and Paris are key corporate locations for access to the ever-expanding information networks and industries. As large corporations strategically relocate in cities, using information technology and community building to enhance their competitive edge, many traditional residential neighborhoods find themselves being displaced. Baba's chapter 6 clearly illustrates how multinational corporations are harnessing computer technology and information to expand their domination of various markets. Similarly, computer technology and information on physical, economic, and social resources are critical to the short- and long-term planning efforts of community-based organizations (CBOs) to maintain their neighborhoods.

A growing body of literature has revealed the disparity resulting from poor access to information. In a very real sense, information has become as essential to the creation and maintenance of wealth as the control of capital, land, and natural resources. Historically, factors such as high automobile and highway use and policies such as urban renewal have accelerated the deconstruction of communities. Today, community deconstruction continues to intensify when the power elite charts patterns of disinvestment and redevelopment through the monopolization of information. Similarly, one could argue that the inaccessibility of information to community-based groups further alienates neighborhood stakeholders, leading to increased violence and crime. Community-based activists must respect the imperative that people at all levels of society have an equal chance to obtain information and use it to construct their communities and determine their quality of life.

In today's knowledge-based economy, the accumulation, management, and analysis of relevant information require tremendous and expensive infrastructure. Many moderate- to low-income homes and communities seldom have access to such infrastructure. The disparity in Internet access levels between the rich and poor, white and non-white, well educated and undereducated, has been dubbed the "digital divide." The digital divide takes the pre-Internet term *information gap* to a whole new level.

A report from the US Commerce Department (1999), "Falling Through the Net," states that the digital divide widened between 1998 and 1999. Black and Hispanic households are approximately one-third as likely to have home Internet access as households of Asian/Pacific Islander descent and roughly two-fifths as likely as white households, according to the report. The disparity does not follow only racial lines. Even at the lowest income levels, those in urban areas are more than twice as likely to have Internet access than those in rural areas.

The British Broadcasting Corporation (Black 1999a, 1999b), quoting a recent UN Human Development Report, stated that industrialized countries, with only 15 percent of the world's population, are home to 88 percent of all Internet users. Less than 1 percent of people in South Asia are online even though it is home to one-fifth of the world's population. The situation is even worse in Africa. With 739 million people, there are only 14 million phone lines. That is fewer than in Manhattan or Tokyo. Eighty percent of those lines are in only six countries. There are only 1 million Internet users on the entire continent, compared with 10.5 million in the United Kingdom. Even if telecommunications systems were in place, most of the world's poor would still be excluded from the information revolution because of illiteracy and lack of basic computer skills. In Benin, for example, more than 60 percent of the population is illiterate. The other 40 percent is similarly out of luck because four-fifths of all websites are in English, a language understood by only one in ten people on the planet.

While revealing the digital divide's negative impact on individual households, the available literature also poses many questions for researchers: How does lack of access to technology and information by individual households affect the community-based agencies and organizations that serve them? For instance, does the information and technology disparity of individual households discourage local agencies from investing in and sustaining technology as part of their work in and with the community? How can we integrate the value and knowledge of technology into the culture and processes of individual households and community agencies and organizations so that technology becomes a customary part of their community-building activities?

Within the past decade, the digital divide has been monitored on international and national platforms. For example, Yahoo provides computer links to a variety of agencies working to understand and remedy the digital divide (http://dir.yahoo.com). Web pages provide numerous links to international and national efforts aimed at bridging the digital divide. In addition, the US Department of Commerce has released a series of four "Falling Through the Net" reports that examine the digital divide from multiple perspectives. World Resources Institute, an environmental think tank, is searching for sustainable ways to bridge the global digital divide.

COMPUTER MAPPING APPROACHES TO BRIDGING THE DIGITAL DIVIDE

Within the context of community building, this chapter examines one type of computer access: computer asset mapping. This tool holds real promise for community-based organizations trying to acquire information rapidly in a concise and visual form. In addition, computer mapping can be used to layer resource information including physical, economic, and social variables. Neighborhood maps, for example, can show the physical condition of housing and commercial units, their assessed value, and their proximity to health care or transportation facilities.

In this chapter, we review three approaches to bridging the digital divide with computer asset mapping: intermediary data providers, participatory mapping, and computer community-assets mapping. All of these have evolved since 1986. We also examine major challenges incumbent in the use of computer mapping as it relates to community building. Next, we describe and evaluate the Memphis experience with community building through computer community-asset mapping. Finally, we suggest how the expertise of anthropologists, sociologists, and practitioners involved in engaged scholarship can be used to create new approaches for meeting the challenges of community building.

The past fifteen years have seen initiatives from the private, government, foundation, and nonprofit sectors. During this period, the private and university sectors have developed many software applications to graphically display information sets. These developments, geographic information systems (GIS), evolved into easy-to-use, efficient applications that run effortlessly on personal computers, thereby enabling GIS use by a greater public.

Within the same time frame, the Clinton administration pushed to make federal information available to the public by requiring each federal department to develop a plan for increasing accessibility to its data. Towards our interest in information access and more user-friendly software, especially in computer mapping, President Clinton signed an Executive Order in April 1994 that created the National Spatial Data Infrastructure. This order declared that "within one year of this order, each (federal) agency shall adopt a plan...establishing procedures to make geospatial data available to the public" (Sawicki and Craig 1996:512).

By July 1997 the Department of Housing and Urban Development introduced its Community 2020 GIS software to aid citizen groups, universities, colleges, state and local government offices, and citizens with their community projects. The idea behind Community 2020 is that it is easier to master than other GIS products used by mapping professionals (Kingsley et al. 1997). For instance, Community 2020 contains a large amount of data, such as census data and HUD program data, that enable users to quickly and easily produce maps showing public housing or Section 8 unit locations in a defined census tract.

Intermediate Data Providers

Despite these federal government initiatives and state and local data sets, linkage to computer mapping remains outside the grasp of most community-based organizations. In light of this divide, Sawicki and Craig (1996:516) document the rise of "sophisticated information providers—those acting as intermediaries between the agencies producing the data and the community groups that need it. Although these intermediate agencies take many forms, they essentially are housed in larger institutions that control how the data will be analyzed, manipulated and displayed. The institutions range from public libraries and universities to nonprofit groups and private foundations."

In St. Louis, the public library acts as an intermediary between organizations that generate various types of numerical data and the general public. Anyone can go to the library and use a "foolproof" GIS application to map his or her own data. With the library's electronic atlas, the general public also can access thirty-five standard map views of city and county census data. Similarly, in Minnesota, the Minneapolis GIS Cookbook offers standardized mapping information that anyone can access for a fee. It falls under the auspices of the city's Public Works Department.

At Georgia Tech in Atlanta, the Atlanta Project (TAP) offers a broad range of support to neighborhood leaders via its Data and Policy Analysis Office, which uses databases of land records, tax records, and building conditions. TAP has digitized about 150,000 land parcels in the poorest area of Atlanta. This parcel-level GIS database came in handy not long after its creation, when the city and county sold a large group of tax-delinquent properties in a poor area to a private financial institution. Because neighborhood leaders had access to the GIS database and maps, they were able to strike a deal placing certain properties on a "hold-harmless" list.

Milwaukee Associates in Urban Development (MAUD) operates the Neighborhood Data Center in Milwaukee, a cooperative resource center for approximately 240 nonprofit member groups. It houses public data such as master property files and also trains the nonprofits to analyze and map the public data or their own data.

The Urban Institute's National Neighborhood Indicators Project is the umbrella for a variety of local initiatives aimed at placing the power of electronic data into the hands of local groups. Among these groups are TAP and the Piton Foundation in Denver, Colorado. Piton collects, analyzes, and distributes data to individual organizations on request.

Challenges to Intermediary Efforts

Intermediaries in data collection and use are helpful in many instances. Yet for all its merits, this approach remains a top-down, agency-driven venture that excludes neighborhood leaders from deciding which data will be collected and how data will be processed for the community's benefit. Like agencies that give raw data to the intermediaries, the intermediate agencies require highly skilled professionals to manage the data for their clients. Unless intermediaries offer training to their clients, client access to the data remains limited.

In addition, many intermediaries must charge for their services. Those that do not are quickly overwhelmed with requests and must pick and choose which requests to meet. Those organizations that are too cash-strapped to pay remain alienated from the data. For example, the Milwaukee GIS Cookbook project charges twenty-five dollars for a color parcel map and fifteen dollars for each additional identical map. Such costs can quickly accumulate. With the software, hardware, and know-how, a neighborhood group can manipulate the same public information to produce as many maps as it needs.

Global and Local Participatory Mapping

A second approach to bridging the digital divide is participatory mapping. Writing in the journal *Human Organization*, Herlihy and Knapp (2003) define participatory mapping (PM) as a new way to produce geographic information about people and places for research and applied work. Similar to the participatory action research (PAR) methodology advocated by Jean J. Schensul in chapter 8 of this volume, PM calls for the effective engagement of community-based organizations and individuals in the construction of maps. PM is particularly appropriate for eliciting spatial understanding from informants (both rural and urban) without literary traditions.

Schensul has defined PAR as a method of bringing about social change. Similarly, Herlihy and Knapp note that PM often links research with action to meet society's needs. In both methods, the people most concerned about a problem help identify that problem, participate in the research, and use the results to bring about change. PM efforts are predicated on the belief that individuals at the community level have important knowledge that can be layered upon baseline maps of the neighborhood.

Applications of PM are rapidly increasing in geographic locations and social issues. Some examples of the PM approach developed by social scientists and planners can be found in agricultural resource planning in the rural Philippines (Rambaldi and Callosa-Tarr 2000), documentation of subsistence and community lands, land and natural resource management issues in indigenous Latin America (Herlihy and Knapp 2003; Smith 2003), urban centers in South Asia (Pelto 2002), HIV risk behavior in New York City and Puerto Rico (Oliver-Velez et al. 2002), urban heritage park planning in Philadelphia (Taplin, Scheld, and Low 2002), and city planning in inner-city Chicago (Al-Kodmany 2001).

Part of the PM work has been linked to computer applications to address the digital divide issue. Rhoda M. Gonzalez, a GIS expert at the University of the Philippines, used GIS mapping to help Ifugaos farmers manage their resources and protect their rapidly degenerating, two-thousand-year-old terraced agriculture methods. She noticed that even though the old Ifugaos farmers did not understand GIS, they did use spatial information concepts in carrying out basic activities such as delineating their territory, determining the highest water source on which the highest possible terraces depend, and choosing irrigation canal routes (Gonzalez 2000).

Even though the farmers were not adept at computer mapping, their participation in the mapping was crucial in saving their terraced agriculture system. To include them, Gonzalez used a model of participatory mapping that met the farmers on their own level: she had them interpret aerial photographs of the area. GIS software experts then used the farmers' information to make digital maps.

Eventually, the results were relayed to the Community-Based Natural Resource Management Council of the Barangay and became the basis of action plans. From her research, Gonzalez concluded that "limitations in computer know-how are not a deterrent to engage in GIS-assisted joint learning for channeling efforts towards new platforms to debate about environmental futures." She found that local participation "is precisely the key in systematically taking stock of the resource base, monitoring and understanding local conditions by sharing perspectives, and debating collective action for sustainable natural resource management" (Gonzalez 2000).

Similarly, the University of Illinois at Chicago and a nearby low-income neighborhood employed a web-based, participatory planning technique to discover what residents liked and disliked about their community. Using a web-based interactive map of the community, the university surveyed participants about their feelings on topics such as commercial and industrial sites. From the survey data, the university made several maps. One map used dots to indicate the intensity of like-ability and dislikeability of an area. The two-way method of communication employed by the university and neighborhood produced information that was used to improve the neighborhood's appearance (Al-Kodmany 2001).

Challenges to Participatory Mapping

Taken together, these examples show that the global applications of PM are creating valuable knowledge bases and, in so doing, are engaging participants to change the conditions around them. Stocks (2003:345), in his PM research in Nicaragua, however, states the challenge for community building: "Geographic Information Systems (GIS) and Global Positioning System (GPS) technology enable many people to produce maps cheaply and quickly in support of indigenous land or resource claims, but often without much thought about the next step, or indeed any orderly process dealing with the more difficult aspects of indigenous land and resource rights."

The participatory methods of data collection and analysis—with their emphasis on the inclusion of local knowledge—are not enough to ingrain computer mapping into the recurrent operations of many community-based organizations in rural and urban areas. In fact, many CBOs fail to see how mapping can push forth their agendas.

A recent survey of community and economic development professionals by the National Consortium for Community/University Partnerships (2000) supports this point.

The survey asked participants to rank a list of twenty-nine core competencies needed to carry out community and economic activities. GIS ranked dead last, after such choices as grant writing, advocacy, community organizing, community planning, housing, and data gathering and analysis (NCCUP 2000).

The national survey parallels a local effort by the Center for Urban Research and Extension (CURE) at the University of Memphis. In 1999 CURE sponsored a HUD Community 2020 training session for the twenty most active community-development corporations in Memphis. Upon successful completion of the two-day training, each CDC was given the $250 software package and free technical assistance. After one year, only four CDCs were still using the software, primarily for grant writing to show housing-related needs in their neighborhoods. When asked about the importance of GIS to their planning efforts, most CDCs saw computer mapping competing for limited staff time and resources. We infer from these results that community groups are slow to understand how computer mapping can enhance bottom-up community-building efforts.

Computer Community-Assets Mapping and Community Building

Given the limitations of the existing efforts to bridge the digital divide, we discovered through the Atlanta Project "that neighborhood leaders react very negatively to receiving data dumps of measures of pathology (for example, teenage pregnancy rates); indeed, that is a good way for a provider to lose their trust forever" (Sawicki and Craig 1996:518). The Atlanta Project conclusion suggests that the question must be reframed to emphasize the community's interest at the front end; that is, how can computer mapping enhance grassroots redevelopment efforts?

To address this question, we can follow three seminal cases of community organizing and community-based mobilization in Boston and New York: *Streets of Hope* (Medoff and Sklar 1994), *Organizing the South Bronx* (Rooney 1995), and *Upon This Rock* (Freedman 1993). Three themes appear central to these efforts: (1) the mobilization of multiple stakeholders around critical issues that threaten the community, (2) the power to make decisions that affect the control of community infrastructure such as land and housing, and (3) the ability to generate wealth and social capital through local exchange within the community.

In Boston's Dudley Street neighborhood, the neighborhood leaders and community organizers mobilized residents and seized power with the rallying cry "Don't dump on us!" They carefully built consensus for a neighborhood vision among diverse populations of African-Americans, Latinos, Caucasians, and Cape Verdeans living in the neighborhood. They were then able to change public policy on code enforcement, build affordable housing, and entice commercial development to the area.

The South Bronx of the 1980s was the universal symbol for urban decay—often compared to the rubble-strewn cities of postwar Europe. Seeking to ameliorate the wrecked landscape, a coalition of forty minority congregations formed to battle the City of New York for vacant land in order to build owner-occupied, affordable row houses. In Rooney's account, *Organizing the South Bronx*, the ministers taught citizens of low-income neighborhoods that, when banded together, they had a powerful voice that could evoke change.

In another account, *Upon This Rock: The Miracles of a Black Church*, by Samuel G. Freedman, the Rev. Johnny Youngblood mobilizes his fractured congregation at St. Paul Community Baptist Church to build community, within the walls of the church and outside in its decaying South Bronx neighborhood. Like the residents of Dudley Street and other South Bronx areas, they overcame personal and institutional obstacles to build a better community.

The leaders in these case studies were successful because they were following the "Iron Rule" of community organizing purveyed by Saul Alinski and, more recently, Kretzmann and McKnight. That rule is, "Never do for others what they can do for themselves" (Rooney 1995:75). Kretzmann and McKnight further advocate the use of assets mapping for successful community organizing and mobilization. Communities inventory the gifts and skills of individuals first and then organizations in and around the targeted areas, arranging them on a cognitive map. The inventory provides the social capital and wealth necessary to negotiate with larger, more formal interests (Kretzmann and McKnight 1993).

With the improved accessibility and user friendliness of GIS applications, the logical progression of the Kretzmann and McKnight cognitive maps is towards spatially arranged assets maps in community building. Computer mapping helps, not hinders, CBOs seeking to mobilize, gain power, and create social capital and wealth (such as those in the National Congress for Community Economic Development (NCCED) survey and in the case study). Computer community-assets mapping enhances community building through its role in communication processes that identify and protect the interests of all stakeholders and lead to collaborative decision making (Pearce 2001). How does computer community-assets mapping actually accomplish this?

COMPUTER COMMUNITY-ASSETS MAPPING IN MEMPHIS

Memphis is a trade city of stark class and ethnic contrasts that sits on the Mississippi River and serves a 200-square-mile agriculture hinterland based on cotton, soybeans, and catfish farming. The city and the region have struggled against the image of a backwater city in a poverty region, sometimes described by national politicians as Third World (Farney 1989). Per capita income in Memphis is among the lowest in the nation; the city school system is characterized by low academic achievement. Public housing was among the worst in the country. Nonetheless, Memphis has incubated some of the nation's greatest entrepreneurial businesses (Holiday Inn, FedEx, AutoZone) and birthed eminent music traditions.

The complex character of this region and city has exerted a powerful influence on the applied anthropology program at the University of Memphis. Begun in 1977, the M.A. program was established with the stated purpose of applied research and training "that examines the nature of poverty and the impact of industrial restructuring and national policy on the distribution of resources and on quality of life in the Lower Mississippi Delta region. We proposed to train a new type of employee for the regional labor market" (Hyland and Collins 1991:7). Over the past three decades, faculty, students, and practicing anthropologists have engaged in a series of applied initiatives related to neighborhood revitalization, housing, health care, refugee settlement, and community building. From this venue, two case studies provide insight into the question of how neighborhood residents, especially youth and community organizations, obtain the desire and ability to use asset mapping for community building.

The Ghostwriters Project

The first case study, the Ghostwriters project, was initiated in 1995 by the University of Memphis anthropology department and the Boys Club. The neighborhood was low-income, almost entirely African-American, and the site of the worst public-housing development in Memphis. The City of Memphis had received federal funding in the form of a Hope VI grant to demolish the public housing development and rebuild the neighborhood. Given this context, the Boys Club needed to evaluate its effectiveness in the neighborhood, and the university sought to fulfill its mission of urban outreach (Key and Barlow 1998).

The aim of their collaborative effort was to create a neighborhood directory relevant to the boys in the LeMoyne Garden area. Committed to the community-building approach of assets mapping rather than information dumping, the project began as a service learning course in urban anthropology. Because it would take time for the anthropology students to establish trusting relationships in the community, the project was continued through directed research courses over the next year.

Trust first developed as participants built a visual picture of what the neighborhood was really like and who was most important to everyday life. Eventually, the boys created an identity (the Ghostwriters) and decided to tell the neighborhood's story through maps, pictures, music, and art. Their enthusiasm for the project soared as they "mapped" their territory with a camera. When the pictorial directory was published, it received local and national media attention. The book not only empowered the boys but also raised the level of pride among neighborhood residents. In that respect, the project fulfilled its community-building mission.

From the larger perspective of the multimillion-dollar HOPE VI, the Ghostwriters project had no direct effect. HOPE VI did not involve any youth, much less the Ghostwriters, in the planning, design, or implementation of its massive neighborhood-revitalization effort. This case illustrates that community building has no relation to community development and, conversely, that the community development of a revitalized neighborhood does not necessarily involve community building.

Although the Ghostwriters project appears to be insignificant, four important results relate to present community-building efforts and computer community-assets mapping in Memphis. First, one of the anthropology students leading the Ghostwriters project became director of development for the emerging community-development corporation in the area and has, for the past five years, actively worked a community-building agenda into the significant accomplishments of neighborhood revitalization in the area. Computer community-assets mapping has been one of the tools used in planning and marketing (Hyland et al. 2004). Accomplishments include the building of the Stax Music Museum, which provides an avenue for youth from the neighborhood to develop their musical talents and perform. Second, the efforts of the community development corporation have been linked to the local, historically black college in the neighborhood;

these two institutions have continued in joint efforts to involve multiple stakeholders, including students. Third, the documentation of the Ghostwriters story became a significant reference point for leaders in the nonprofit sector to rethink their outreach strategies (LeMoyne Owen College Community Development Corporation website). Fourth, the Ghostwriters project received media attention from a variety of sources, including a sponsored book signing by the youth and coverage by the national news.

Maps to Success

Seeking to build on the insights gained from the Ghostwriters project, the university's Department of Anthropology began a partnership with a neighborhood-driven collaborative in the historic African-American neighborhood of Orange Mound. Over the course of a four-year partnership, faculty, students, and practicing anthropologists worked with the Orange Mound Collaborative to create a neighborhood newsletter, a community development corporation, neighborhood oral histories, and educational modules for the two elementary schools.

Within this context and through a federal program of the Clinton administration for inner-city revitalization, the City of Memphis chose Orange Mound as one of its three Enterprise Communities. Simultaneously, the University of Memphis received a federal Community Outreach Partnership Center Grant from the US Department of Housing and Urban Renewal to support the city's Enterprise Communities efforts. The university involved anthropologists who had been working with the Orange Mound Collaborative.

In a series of community meetings, Orange Mound residents determined five major needs: neighborhood maps, market gap analysis, technical assistance to the local community development corporation and neighborhood Family Resource Center, and the identification of recreation opportunities (Hyland 2000). The first of these needs called for computer mapping of parks and recreation areas, housing code violations, street maintenance, public transportation routes, crime statistics, housing values, morbidity, and community assets.

To achieve this, the anthropologists explored various options within the university. One option was to have university experts produce the maps and to sell them to the community. Another was to train community residents and/or high school students to produce the same maps. The second option was far more complicated in that it involved new resources, computer equipment and software, personnel training, student stipends, space, and approval and commitment from the relevant public school officials and parents. The advantage, however, was that it clearly linked the community assets approach to community building with computer mapping.

The Orange Mound Collaborative overwhelmingly supported the computer map training approach and offered some financial support. The remaining financial support came from the City of Memphis Division of Housing and Community Development, the Memphis City School System and the local high school, the Community Foundation of Greater Memphis, the Community Services Agency, a local bank, and the University of Memphis. The initiative was called "Maps to Success" and was overseen by a community advisory board that would answer to the city's Enterprise Committee.

The university team, including anthropology faculty and students, as well as practicing anthropologists, in collaboration with Orange Mound community groups, recruited a teacher with GIS experience from the local high school. With university assistance, the teacher further developed his GIS skills and recruited two high school teachers and a group of high school students for training. This team began a survey of the neighborhood's assets and liabilities from the neighborhood students' perspective.

Descriptions of the summer program were announced to the general student population at the local high school. To appeal to a broad base of students, academic performance and conduct were deprioritized in the selection process. Eight students whose interests matched the program activities were given the opportunity to participate. Varying in age, academic background, skills, and interests, the selected participants included students with a history of criminal delinquency and one honors student. Stipends were offered as an incentive to greater participation.

The students took part in a six-week, all-day summer program that offered computer mapping (GIS) training in theory and practice. The curriculum was designed to meet four learning-development objectives

as defined by the superintendent of the Memphis Public Schools: communication, productivity, reasoning, and civic and cultural knowledge.
Integrating community-assets mapping and computer technology, the
curriculum's youth activities included collecting neighborhood geographical data and photographs of neighborhood assets, GIS database
construction, data input and management techniques, field trips to
agencies presently utilizing GIS technology, and a presentation of other
associate occupations. Unlike the Ghostwriters project, Maps to Success
linked community assets mapping to computer technology via GIS.

Maps to Success resulted in student portfolios illustrating their
accomplishments. A major part of each student's portfolio comprised
a series of computerized neighborhood maps of sociodemographic
information (US census data and local agency data) and neighborhood assets as defined by the student. The maps depicted landmarks,
restaurants, zoning, services, retail businesses, youth facilities, schools,
recreation facilities, and points of interest in the Orange Mound
neighborhood. At a graduate ceremony, the students presented the
portfolios to the Community Advisory Board, parents, and other neighborhood stakeholders. In addition, before one hundred students and
guests at their high school, the students performed a play that drama-
tized what they had discovered in their mapping of neighborhood assets.

Maps to Success generated discussion and enthusiasm about the
students' computer community-assets maps. It effectively engaged a
diverse group of stakeholders, including the Enterprise Communities
Board, in the future of the Orange Mound neighborhood. In fact, one
of the high school participants became a member of the Enterprise
Communities Board.

As in the Ghostwriters project, involved anthropology students
gained critical skills in community building. One went on to become
the executive director of the Orange Mound Community Development
Corporation and continues to use computer assets mapping in her
development work. Another became the program director for a nonprofit intermediary that supports capacity building for community
development corporations.

The following year, Maps to Success expanded to two other inner-
city neighborhoods and recruited high school students from their
respective neighborhoods. This six-week summer GIS training program

was called "Memphis Maps" to connote its broader focus (Hyland, Cox, and Martin 1998). The high school teacher who coordinated this effort eventually created his own minority GIS business.

Continuing its collaboration with agencies and nonprofits, the City of Memphis subsequently conducted a transportation planning effort that used the students' maps. The University of Memphis extended its involvement outside the Department of Anthropology. The City and Regional Planning Department did a marketing study, the College of Education became involved in a participatory evaluation study, and the Department of Sociology conducted an extensive problem-property survey. Beyond the university, more nonprofit and government agencies expanded their engagement in Orange Mound. The Police Department established a substation.

The Maps to Success program proved that useful community-assets maps could be produced by neighborhood youth. For its best practices, Maps to Success received a national award from the US Department of Housing and Urban Development. The various community-building activities and recognition contributed to a new perception of Orange Mound as a vibrant neighborhood.

Despite the attainments of Maps to Success, the project and the federal Enterprise program made no noticeable, overall impact on the Orange Mound neighborhood in terms of creating businesses and neighborhood jobs, reducing crime, building new housing, or even producing a new, comprehensive neighborhood plan. In addition, the computer-mapping lab that had been established in the local high school was not sustained. From an outsider's perspective, neither program yielded outcomes to any significant degree indicative of a revitalized neighborhood, that is, community development. From an insider's perspective, however, both programs enhanced community building within the respective neighborhoods by engaging a number of stakeholders though assets mapping.

The Ghostwriters and Maps to Success projects promoted participation, networking, story telling, linking to the larger community, and the production of multilayered computer maps by community development corporations. In short, fundamental community-building processes did take place. But sustained computer community-assets mapping by the residents, which was part of the desired outcome, was only partially achieved. Possible reasons include the lack of a major ongoing crisis threatening the local community, the lack of a stable physical presence in the neighborhood, the lack of sustained presence of university personnel in the neighborhood, the lack of sufficient resources for the computer community-assets intervention, the lack of comprehensive databases directly relevant to the neighborhood's problems, and the lack of committed, collaborative efforts by agencies and nonprofits.

UPTOWN: A Public Housing Crisis

Presently, a wide range of crises is brewing in US inner cities—environmental Superfund sites, wholesale abandonment by upper and middle classes, a dearth of affordable housing, concentration of poverty, decaying public housing, and public health epidemics such as asthma, diabetes, and obesity. Of these, the decay of public housing is one of the most pressing problems. Once a temporary, affordable living situation, public housing has now become a long-term alternative of last resort, often ignored, isolated, and neglected. Many neighborhoods containing public housing have also been abandoned. In 1993 the US Congress created HOPE VI, a program to replace high-density, decaying public housing with a less dense, mixed-income alternative. The policy guarantees that neighborhoods will change. But in what ways?

The situation presents a critical opportunity to examine community response to the pending transformations and to discover whether computer community-assets mapping can affect the outcomes. The Urban Institute's National Neighborhood Indicators project has implemented a few studies, and several universities are beginning to research this area as well (Popkin et al. 2004). Although these case studies and others are trickling in from across the country, the issue largely remains unexplored.

In light of the ongoing inner-city crises mentioned earlier, a third Memphis effort, UPTOWN, was initiated in another Memphis inner-city neighborhood in 1999. The design of the initiative took into account the best practices of the Ghostwriters and Maps to Success projects and addressed their deficiencies. The University of Memphis anthropology faculty and students, and practicing anthropologists in collaboration with related academic departments at the university, decided to focus on public housing conditions—a serious issue in Memphis (Cox et al. 2004). With the city's receipt of a new HOPE VI grant in the low-income Greenlaw-Manassas neighborhood, the University of Memphis took the opportunity to engage its anthropologists in designing a program that made long-term sustainability of computer mapping a primary goal.

The neighborhood met six aforementioned criteria for successful sustainable mapping. First, it faced a major crisis: public housing demolition and possible neighborhood gentrification. The historic but decaying neighborhood sits between a multimillion-dollar downtown redevelopment project, a billion-dollar hospital expansion by St. Jude Children's Research Hospital, and the upscale Harbor Town riverfront neighborhood. The thirty-five-million-dollar HOPE VI grant enabled the city to raze the troubled Hurt Village housing project. With its neglected Victorian homes, canopy of sycamore trees, and views of the downtown skyline, the neighborhood stood a good chance of gentrification unless the residents intervened.

Second, the University of Memphis had a stable presence in the neighborhood. Mindful of lessons learned in Boston, New York, and Memphis, the University of Memphis collaborated with the City of Memphis Division of Housing and Community Development in securing a building in the Greenlaw-Manassas area. St. Jude Children's Research Hospital donated an historic building on the edge of the neighborhood to house a resource center. The city and the developers renamed the area "UPTOWN" as part of the HOPE VI renewal effort. As a result, the house was named the "UPTOWN Neighborhood Resource Center" (URC) and opened in February 2002.

Third, as part of its effort, the university provided a full-time, on-site staff person and a graduate assistant to manage the operations and link with both the surrounding community and the university. Specifically, the university staff actively sought to engage faculty and students from a variety of disciplines to address the community-driven needs. The URC continues to serve as an optimum point of university engagement, especially for internships and service learning.

Fourth, the University of Memphis secured resources in the form of a major grant from the US Department of Housing and Urban Development to create and maintain a computer lab in the URC. The lab consisted of fourteen workstations and a server that linked it to the university. Also, the university committed to maintaining the lab and providing software that would support GIS mapping, as well as offering basic and advanced computer training programs.

Fifth, the university effort included the creation of a comprehensive data system that would track the plans of developers and the city, as well as changes in the neighborhood. The databases ranged from the United States 2000 census to crime data, property ownership and tax records, land use data, and health data. In addition, the university collected primary data on problem properties from windshield surveys conducted by students. An inventory of community assets was also incorporated in the effort. All of this data was compiled in a GIS format that enabled spatial display and analysis.

Sixth, there was extensive collaboration. In discussions of design, planning, and implementation, the URC engaged many stakeholders—displaced public-housing residents, homeowners, the neighborhood community-development corporation and nonprofits, the City of Memphis, St. Jude Children's Research Hospital, private developers, the HOPE VI management team, and the University of Memphis. The UPTOWN initiative was predicated on a willingness to follow the lead of the community residents, rather than on simple provision of services deemed appropriate by the city or the university. To achieve this goal, the university held a series of focus group sessions with neighborhood residents, conducted personal interviews and surveys, and attended community meetings to determine preferences. In addition, the UPTOWN effort emphasized university student involvement in the planning process. Students in anthropology and city and regional planning drafted proposals for community-centered programs. Designed to meet needs identified by community residents, the programs fostered partnering with established service agencies and utilizing existing resources in innovative ways. Some focused on collecting and analyzing voter registration data and school performance data for the UPTOWN area schools; one program developed an initial proposal for the creation of a volunteer bank.

The UPTOWN Neighborhood Resource Center continues to be a work in progress. Through computer assets mapping, several accomplishments have helped bridge the digital divide. The URC computers are interconnected and have high-speed Internet access. In addition, university faculty and students have provided continuous technical support that includes hardware, software, Internet access, and on-site system maintenance, as well as computer training for community residents. The lab has had a variety of uses. Currently, the local YWCA is using it to train economically disadvantaged individuals in basic computer repair and maintenance. Similarly, the university has coordinated computer self-help workshops such as the volunteer income-tax assistance program. Approximately 20 volunteers assisted 108 residents in filing their returns, resulting in more than $207,000 in taxpayer refunds. The UPTOWN site was the most successful first-year program in the Memphis area.

In the first year, the center primarily focused on technology infrastructure maintenance, software management, and training. Simultaneously, considerable efforts have led to the layering of critical information about neighborhood change and assets critical to stakeholders. In addition to the baseline data on crime, property values, housing, transportation, businesses, and services, students have been working on an inventory of community assets in various ways. For example, one innovative approach to assets mapping was the creation of memory maps. Students from the applied anthropology graduate seminar developed a plan to collect neighborhood student maps and art for use in the URC and UPTOWN website. Six junior and senior high school students from two community public schools were selected for the program and were paired with undergraduate anthropology students from the university to collect data. In addition to its aesthetic contributions, the Community Arts Project (CAP) provided youth with an opportunity for active community participation, served as a link among youth from various segments of the community, and offered tangible community-building and engagement results. Partners in CAP include the University of Memphis Department of Art, Memphis College of Art, Urban Arts Commission, The Art Center, Hutchinson School, and Clear Channel Media. Future plans include a Spring Folk Art Fair at the URC featuring the work of community artisans.

Another accomplishment was the development of the UPTOWN Neighborhood Resource Directory. Paid student interns compiled lists of faith-based organizations, nonprofit organizations, neighborhood and civic associations, community development corporations, businesses, child care facilities, schools and other educational institutions, and elected officials from the UPTOWN neighborhood, along with a brief description of their services and their contact information. The information was geocoded and published in electronic and hard copy. Plans to convene the nonprofits and educational institutions for a planning summit are underway.

Neighborhood-level data sets, maps, and community assets and resource directories are available on an UPTOWN website maintained by the university (http://www.people.memphis.edu). Plans are to link this website to nonprofits and educational institutions in the neighborhood to encourage use by residents, faculty, students, developers, and civic and community organizations. There is also a community newsletter that keeps residents, university students and faculty, and other community stakeholders current on activities in the neighborhood.

The staff continues to work toward integrating technology with community building to ensure that residents not only have access to information but also can improve their individual capacities and those of the greater community. For example, staff developed a plan to increase residents' ability to participate in collecting, accessing, and analyzing information. This plan also provides training for students and residents in survey research, community assets mapping (including the GIS), and windshield survey methods to assemble information about community preferences and assets.

Lessons Learned

Like the Ghostwriters and Maps to Success projects, the UPTOWN Neighborhood Resource Center has witnessed community building but has experienced failures in getting neighborhood residents into the lab. Even with training in using the technology and information, most residents found it too difficult to navigate the website and access information on their own. Low literacy rates and educational levels posed major obstacles. Residents did not recognize how the information could directly benefit their participation in the revitalization process. The Memphis experience with assets mapping has shown that computer mapping, in and of itself, in any of its forms, is not enough to help residents bridge the digital divide. Melissa Checker (2004) described similar experiences in her anthropological research in urban areas.

Certainly, some of the problems stemmed from a failure to meet the residents' needs; engaging them at their levels of ability constituted one challenge. An equal challenge, however, was the integration of the computers and mapping data into their life as a community and as individuals. Similarly, information and computer mapping were not comprehensively shared with the other key stakeholders in the neighborhood.

Therefore, the task ahead is to institutionalize computer mapping systematically into community-building activities that are part of residents' daily life. Technology and information must encounter residents in their schools, churches, and meeting places and in those critical issues directly related to their quality of life. At the same time, because technology and urban revitalization are so complex, requiring the collaboration of participants and resources and many simultaneous efforts, computer mapping must be more broadly contextualized, not just situated in singular groups and outcomes.

The URC continues to train residents about access to computers and information related to individual achievement and future neighborhood revitalization efforts. It is also shifting focus to better serve the residents, for they, collectively, are a primary partner in the revitalization process. Future programs will concentrate on literacy, which will also help residents access and use the information in the neighborhood asset database, on the website, and in the newsletter. Tutorial programs and computer training, among other programs, will be offered in the schools and nonprofits, as well as at the URC, strengthening the connection between the residents and the schools.

The URC also has plans to expand the database to include information that motivates residents individually and collectively. A volunteer bank for residents is already in development. This database will contain a list and description of residents' talents and skills so that these can be matched with other residents' needs. This will also help residents understand why and how information is a fundamental part of their neighborhood revitalization. In addition, the university is pursuing the design and implementation of a kiosk in the URC so that individuals can access information through comfortable and inviting icons, images, and vocabulary.

Another approach is to link case management (a HOPE VI requirement of former public-housing residents wanting to return to the new, mixed-income UPTOWN neighborhood) to computer training and community building. Case management is potentially the most comprehensive, practical approach to developing an individual's capacity, which is fundamental to both the private life of the individual and the civic infrastructure of the community. Case management supports and gives voice to residents' needs. The URC plans to give incentives (such as a free laptop computer and home installation of Internet access) for residents to complete the case management program successfully.

RECOMMENDED COMMUNITY-BUILDING METHODS

Returning to the chapter's initial thesis, access to information via computer technology is critical not only to multinational corporations and the global city (Baba, chapter 6 of this volume; Sassen 1991), but also to inner-city residents in terms of their future success and quality of life. We have explored various efforts to bridge the digital divide through a linkage with community-building initiatives. Based on the US case studies, the lessons from Kretzmann and McKnight, and the Memphis experiences, it is appropriate to conclude that bridging the digital divide through community building is complex and requires multiple, simultaneous strategies. Simply giving inner-city residents computers or access to computers, providing training, linking training to mapping, collaborating with other agencies, or even dealing with life and death issues still are not enough.

From the Memphis community-building experience with computer community-assets mapping initiatives, we have learned that the following methods have been effective in diminishing the digital divide and revitalizing community.

Tackle High-Risk Issues. High-risk issues demand much effort; however, the rewards are greater, and outcomes have a broader policy impact on issues of systemic inequality. The high-risk issues in neighborhood revitalization could include problem-riddled public housing, residential displacement, gentrification, environmental brownfields, and neighborhood decline in a specific geographic area. Equally important are internal community issues such as gangs, violence, illiteracy, and disease. High-risk issues draw more community stakeholders to the table.

Engage Top and Bottom. When possible, all relevant stakeholders should be identified and should engage in the process, not only residents but also local government, educational institutions, developers, bankers, nonprofits, faith-based organizations, community-based organizations, and university administration, faculty, and students. Engagement includes active discussions, planning, activities, and sharing of information. Each stakeholder brings a distinct viewpoint that must be acknowledged and respected.

Create Products and Processes. Larger institutional stakeholders such as government and developers favor initiatives with visible, tangible, or otherwise quantifiable outcomes. These include maps and comprehensive information. Equally important are the community-building processes often associated with community assets, social capital development, capacity building, and community-based mapping.

Be Present in the Neighborhood. The predictable and ongoing presence of staff on-site in the area significantly contributes to a program's effectiveness. Physical presence enhances participant observation, participatory action research, participatory mapping, and coordination of related outreach activities necessary to the community-building process.

Find the Necessary Resources. Very little community development can be sustained without major financial and human resources. To close the digital divide, labs, computers, software, wiring, connections, and (most important) trained and dedicated personnel are needed. The pursuit of resources must be conceived as an ongoing effort.

Collaborate with Other Stakeholders. In the current economy, institutions and individuals face fiscal constraints. Further, comprehensive community development involves multifaceted, sometimes complex solutions and multiple points of attack. Addressing community issues demands interagency collaboration and pooling of resources. To bridge the digital divide, neighborhood stakeholders must work together to produce a plan that is viable and meaningful for diverse groups of individuals in the neighborhood.

Understand Contexts and Trends. A comprehensive knowledge of the legal, educational, and funding aspects of social action related to computer technology and access to information is an important prerequisite to community development. Local and federal policy, national and international technical assistance agencies and networks, and funding foundations contribute in critical ways to sustaining community building and community development issues related to the digital divide. In addition, awareness of the best practices employed by other initiatives is imperative.

Make a Long-Term Commitment. Community residents must be assured that the higher education institution and other institutional stakeholders are invested in the project for the long term, not just through the project period. Long-term relationships with the community have inspired significantly more resident buy-in and support.

Integrate Individual, Family, and Institutional Concerns. The most challenging method is to design computer technology and information initiatives that appeal to residents' mentality and relate to their lives, such as user friendly, interactive, touch-screen kiosks. Methods that link to case management requirements also ensure more meaningful use. Institutions such as universities and nonprofits must continually prioritize these initiatives as part of their ongoing mission.

Form a Vision. Following the *Streets of Hope* lesson, collaborative efforts must work to create future initiatives that actively involve residents. Specifically concerning computer technology and information initiatives, collaboration should produce ongoing, interactive changes.

CONCLUSION

These methods are neither linear nor exclusive. They are like the spokes of a wheel; each spoke contributes to the wheel's overall stability and optimum function. Just as a wheel revolves continuously, a community is always changing. To be effective in community building, one must have a command of each method. One must discern when to employ a particular method and how to keep all the methods balanced according to their appropriateness to the opportunities available. The other chapters in this book illustrate how these methods can be adapted to the varying characteristics and circumstances that distinguish one community from the next. For example, visioning in Baba's virtual work community differs from the visioning of Kemper and Adkins's faith-based community. Likewise, Oliver-Smith's discussion of collaboration in working with displaced communities takes on different dimensions than Schensul's use of research collaboratives, or the collaboratives in Chrisman's discussion of community building for health. Anthropologists are assembling an important array of methods to effect community building in various locations and political-economic contexts.

In chapter 8, Schensul highlights the challenge facing engaged scholarship, applied anthropology, and community building for the future. She notes that "It makes sense, therefore, to ask how research conducted by anthropologists and other social scientists can not only describe local community capacity to promote and sustain community, but also strengthen it. How can our research improve the survival of families and individuals, the growth of their communities and quality of life, their social, cultural, and economic well-being?" We ask, what challenges do anthropologists face in future community-building initiatives concerning the digital divide?

From the Memphis experiences, we recognize that training future engaged scholars and practitioners who are capable of making a difference is one such challenge. We must educate students about comprehensive computerized data systems, collaborative approaches, engaged scholarship, and policy-oriented publications.

Another major challenge is the construction of comprehensive computerized information systems that include data sets from stakeholders such as nonprofits, government, business, community-based groups, and individuals. How do we prepare the next generation of students to negotiate data-sharing agreements that ensure both privacy and access? How do we take part in the storage and management of these data systems? How do we design software that enhances public access?

Learning how collaborative community-building processes relate to the way we educate students is another challenge. How do we train students in community problem-solving approaches predicated on working with multiple community stakeholders with different values, goals, and languages? Anthropology as a discipline needs to evaluate the kinds and quality of service learning courses, internships, and practica in its curriculum that prepare students to enter into these complex negotiations.

The documentation and dissemination of efforts involving the various stakeholders with whom we collaborate constitute the final challenge. Traditional academic journals are not written for the public. How are we training students to write for new audiences? How much importance do we place on producing and publishing policy papers? What proportion of our courses deals with participatory action research and participatory evaluation studies? If anthropology is to continue growing as a discipline, it must address these challenges and instruct students in community *building*—not just community development—in the twenty-first century.

6

Virtual Community

An Oxymoron at Work? Creating Community in a Globally Distributed Work Group

Marietta L. Baba

Work in America and elsewhere across the globe is being reorganized to enable collaboration among individuals in different geographical locations. In companies large and small, employees commonly work in groups or teams whose membership crosses nations, cultures, and languages. Ideally, such globally distributed work groups can achieve a perspective spanning multiple marketplaces around the world, closely integrate globally distributed information, and still act locally (O'Hara-Devereaux and Johansen 1994; Baba 2001). The paradox inherent in this global-local vision raises a question: how can people from different cultures around the globe work together closely enough to integrate disparate sets of localized information and coordinate local action while still maintaining their diverse points of view?

Not surprisingly, the answer in our American technological utopia almost invariably is information technology. The rapid advance of computing and telecommunications technologies has produced a suite of new work tools that support distributed communication and collaboration. Known collectively as "computer-supported collaborative work" (CSCW) tools, these devices enable distributed groups separated by time and space to work together (Monplaisir 1999). Corporate decision makers believe that the evolution of these tools eventually will permit people to accomplish everything they need to do together without ever being co-present in the same location. Yet, while it is true that globally distributed work depends on information technology as a medium for communication and coordination, technology has proven to be insufficient for effective work performance. As demonstrated in this chapter, working together from different locations around the globe can create challenges that surpass the capabilities of CSCW tools, regardless of their sophistication.

In the meantime, corporations have not waited for a better answer before plunging headlong into a massive process of trial-and-error learning, with theory lagging behind. The emergence of global distribution as an organizing principle is radically altering the context of work, yet our knowledge of these new organizational forms trails corporate practice. Much of what we know about work comes from the study of collocated work groups with relatively homogenous membership. Certain classes of workers have long functioned on a distributed basis (salespersons, airline flight personnel, academics), but our theories of work generally have not been founded upon an assumption of significant spatial distribution, let alone multicultural membership. Rather, in studies of work, we often take for granted the opposite case—people of a single nation working together in the same place at the same time. This assumption is becoming obsolete.

The importance of world markets and global competition to economic systems worldwide suggests that globally distributed work groups will emerge as a fundamental form of organizing during the twenty-first century (Gibson and Cohen, eds., 2003). We need to know more about the impact of global distribution on human work experience, particularly its effect on the development, performance, and sustainability of work communities. For our purposes, a work community is defined as a group of people who consider themselves to be engaged in the same type of productive work activity, whose identities are shaped by their work, and who share a set of work-related practices, norms and values, and meanings that influence not only their work but their social lives as well (Van Maanen and Barley 1984). Work communities are important both economically and socially. They play a vital role in training new workers, solving production problems, and integrating new tools and processes (Baba 1990). They also contribute substantially to the quality of work life and the moral fabric of organizations (Roethlisberger and Dickson 1939; Kunda 1992). The ability to create and sustain work communities is therefore of vital importance to a nation's welfare. Yet, whether work communities can come into being and thrive in a global virtual workplace is an open question. Many companies are betting that they can, but the evidence thus far is mixed, with some success stories and many reports of failure (Gluesing 1995, 1998; Jarvenpaa, Knoll, and Leidner 1998; Jarvenpaa and Leidner 1999; Maznevski and Chudoba 2000; Gibson and Cohen, eds , 2003).

In this chapter, I explore the consequences of global distribution for the development and performance of a work community over time, guided by an ecological model of human development (Bronfenbrenner and Morris 1998). Ecological analysis of ethnographic data drawn from the study of a globally distributed work group in a major American corporation reveals the unique interplay of factors and forces that influence the emergence of community in the globally distributed workplace. This analysis also suggests conditions that organizations need to establish to ensure greater success in building virtual work communities in the future.

WORK COMMUNITIES AND VIRTUAL WORK

The Latin root of *community* is *communis*, which means "common," and the notion that people at work form communities is founded on an observation that commonality of work establishes the grounds for common life. As Durkheim (1951:578; see also Van Maanen and Barley 1984:293) noted, "Besides societies of faith, of family, and of politics, there is one other...that of all workers of the same sort, in association, all who cooperate in the same function; that is, the occupational group or corporation. Identity of origin, culture, and occupation makes occupational activity the richest sort of material for a common life."

Van Maanen and Barley's (1984) classic work on occupational communities identifies several characteristics common to all of them:

1. Boundaries of the community are set by the members themselves, rather than on the basis of ascribed characteristics.

2. Identities and self-images of members derive from work roles.

3. Members define other members as their primary reference group, leading to the sharing of values, beliefs, and norms.

4. Distinctions between work and leisure activities are blurred.

To this set of classic features must be added the collaborative learning and sharing of behavioral practices and innovations, a critical quality of work communities more recently defined as "communities of practice" (Lave 1991; Brown and Duguid 1991). I will return to this idea shortly.

Note that the features of work community as defined above do not require physical collocation, even though some formal definitions of community assume proximity as a fundamental defining feature (Watson 1997). The possibility of separating community from proximity is readily apparent in professional communities such as those formed by members of academic disciplines. One does not need to be in close quarters with other anthropologists to consider oneself a member of that community.

Nevertheless, collocation or physical proximity does provide a critical source of stimulation and support to the formation of community identity and social bonds. People who are physically proximate communicate more with one another than those who are more distant (Allen 1977). Further, people in contact with one another on a regular basis are more likely to report friendly feelings toward one another (Festinger, Schacter, and Back 1950). Through face-to-face communication, people discover similarities in attitudes (Newscomb 1956). Additionally, people who must see one another regularly tend to like one another (Darley and Berscheid 1967). In physical proximity, people are more likely to share the same social context and experiences and engage in mutual sense making with respect to those experiences. As a result, collocated individuals are more apt to share overlapping cognitive schemas that contribute to a shared understanding (that is, intersubjectivity; Rogoff 1990), which, in turn, provides a foundation for community.

Work communities have been an object of intense interest among organizational scholars and practitioners ever since Western Electric's Hawthorne Project revealed that groups of workers create miniature social systems that operate outside the control of management (Roethlisberger and Dickson 1939). At Hawthorne, these communities exerted power over the production process because it was they who controlled the actual process of work "on the ground," not only the speed of production but also the quality of products and processes and the flow of improvements to production systems (see for discussion Baba 1990). These considerable powers, combined with the community dimension of work group activity operating outside management control, make work communities significant from the standpoint of industrial productivity and economic value.

More recently, we have discovered that the economic value produced by work communities is even greater than originally conceived. Besides influencing production, work communities share practices that embed highly specialized bodies of knowledge. This knowledge has its own economic value in modern terms. Anthropologist Julian Orr's (1990) research on repair technicians at Xerox Corporation provides an illustration. The technicians swap war stories of difficult machine repairs, and these stories contain diagnostic clues and technical solutions that the technicians develop as part of their practice. Sharing the stories transfers the knowledge embedded in technicians' practice to other members of the work community. This knowledge then becomes a key asset for Xerox, an asset that is partially responsible for the success of its technical repair services. Many other examples of knowledge creation and sharing have emerged in the literature, documenting the intellectual assets created by communities of practice (Brown and Duguid 1991; Nonaka 1994; Davenport and Prusak 1998).

In the 1990s, major corporations (with the help of the consulting industry) introduced a new set of managerial goals and activities known as "knowledge management" to encourage the formation of communities of practice and the transfer or appropriation of knowledge produced by these work groups for other corporate purposes (see Baba 1998a, 1998b). Such efforts contain inherent contradictions. The knowledge value added by communities of practice is based only in part on the resources and conditions of work provided by management acting as agents of the corporation (formal training, technology, work projects, physical setting). To these material factors, work communities add their own social and psychological resources, including informal relationships and networks that facilitate work flow, know-how that compensates for flaws in formal processes, ideas that lead to improvements in work practices, and a sense of common identity and moral support that enables the group to keep production going even when the equipment or some of its own members are not performing optimally (for example, Roethlisberger and Dickson 1939; Kusterer 1978; see for discussion Baba 1990). Such resources, contributed voluntarily, reflect the interests, needs, and volition of community members but often are unacknowledged in formal job descriptions and employment contracts (Baba 1998a). At the same time, it is fair to say that these social and psychological resources would not come into being without the prior existence of the corporate organization and its rational agenda.

This discussion points to a distinction between modern work communities and communities that come into being more spontaneously, without the visible hand of management. Work communities experience a tension between the instrumental demands of management, on the one hand, and the natural call of community life, on the other. Management wants its due in exchange for providing the conditions for work and wages—it wants access to all the value embodied in the fruits of the community's labors. A substantial component of that value, however, is generated directly from a zone of discretion and autonomy in which workers produce something of value, of, by, and for themselves. Its offering cannot be forced, and its true ownership can be contested. The tension or struggle between the managerial demand for an ever-increasing return on a corporation's investment in its human resources and the work community's fundamental requirement for autonomy and discretion in the creation of economic value form a basic paradox at the heart of modern work organizations. Geographical distribution intensifies the tension inside this paradox. Now corporations are requiring work group members to produce new kinds of value while working at a distance from one another. In other words, they are making production of economic value more difficult but simultaneously demanding more of it. Whether work communities can even form under these conditions, let alone deliver on expectations, remains to be seen.

To get a sense of the economic value that geographically distributed work communities can generate in the *absence* of managerial demands, we can turn to the community of hackers who produced the Linux operating system (Moody 2001). These software developers collaborate intensely and over extended periods of time to create new and improved software capabilities that are freely available for use, that is, open-source code. (Open-source code is not copyrighted by any authority but, instead, uses an ingenious invention known as a "copyleft" to guarantee free access to software.) During its early years, the open-source code movement was populated entirely by volunteers who earned no income from their labors and received no direction or resources from a corporate hierarchy. These extraordinary individuals were passionately committed to creating high-quality software that was controlled by them, not by a corporate authority. They gained international reputations for their technical prowess through electronic communication with a worldwide network of colleagues, most of whom they never saw. The well known technical powers of Linux, which is capable of competing successfully against traditionally copyrighted and proprietary systems, attest to the efficacy of the hackers' collaborative work processes and to the strength of their community.

Significantly, the hackers were never collocated and were seldom in physical proximity—the exception being attendance at professional conferences by some (Moody 2001). This suggests that strong communities of practice do not require physical co-presence when other factors provide the basis for a common identity—in this case, a devotion to technical excellence, the chance to gain an international reputation among peers, and an anticorporate theory of economic value. This community was expert in the use of electronic media as an alternative to face-to-face communication. Further, the Linux hackers were not required to cope with the managerial demands for enhanced production that can be counterproductive. When a globally distributed work community is free to design its own incentives, processes, and expectations for productivity, the results can be highly competitive.

In comparison with the success of the hackers' virtual community and its robust work products, however, the experience of corporations in creating effective distributed work groups is not impressive. Distributed groups in a corporate setting might not be highly motivated to cooperate. Certainly, they confront numerous handicaps when compared with their collocated counterparts. For example, research on computer-supported collaborative work tools shows that technology-mediated communication filters out social cues critical to smooth interpersonal interaction (facial expressions, gestures, tone of voice; Sproull and Kiesler 1986). Because typing takes longer than speaking, distributed groups in a corporate setting need more time to accomplish a work task at the same level of quality as an equivalent collocated group (especially during the early period following group formation). Distributed group members also tend to exchange less socially relevant information and to focus more on task-related communication (because of the extra effort required to convey social information via technology; Siegel et al. 1986). With thinner social information, bonds of friendship and trust do not form at all or form very slowly. In addition, distributed work groups are more prone to miscommunication due to a reliance on email communication (wrong addresses, misinterpreted silence, lack of sufficient attention to all parts of a message). These errors can create barriers to trust (Cramton 2001), which inhibits open sharing of information (Baba 1999).[1] When distributed groups also are multicultural, the potential for misunderstanding and distrust increases because individuals must translate words and concepts across cultural and linguistic boundaries, as well as cope with differences in work-related motivation, values, and behavioral practices (Gluesing 1995, 1998).

Unlike the hackers, whose work practices resemble those of a medieval guild (Coleman 2000), corporation employees do not own the means of production and do not work for themselves. Rather, they are doing a job assigned to them by the management hierarchy. The overall corporate context, as well as employees' individual characteristics, strongly influences their motivation and work processes. In many cases, the resources, support, and motivational inducements provided by the corporate environment may be insufficient to overcome the handicaps associated with distributed work. As a result, the group fails to achieve its goals and is subsequently disbanded. In human terms, such failures can signify a low quality of work life associated with distributed work (intragroup conflict, increased job stress, reduced job satisfaction) and potentially negative consequences to employees' jobs or career prospects. The important point is that, for whatever reason, when the people involved cannot find enough in common to serve as the foundation for a work community, the potential benefits to the employees, the corporation, and society do not materialize.

THE ECOLOGY OF DEVELOPMENT IN WORK COMMUNITIES

Every work community begins as a collection of individuals who, by virtue of what they hold in common, develop social bonds that support their productive activity and shape their social lives at work and beyond. Research on work groups suggests that this developmental process is influenced by the environmental context in which the group is situated (Tuckman 1965; Gersick 1998; McCollom 1990; Chidambaram and Bostorm 1996). People who interact with a common environment are more likely to share overlapping patterns of thought, feeling, and behavior that can facilitate community formation. Those who are distributed across several environments, however, likely will find it more difficult to converge on a common perspective regarding their work—what it is and how to do it.

To gain a better understanding of the process by which individuals may converge to form a work community (or may not), we adopt an ecological framework specifically designed for research on human development (Bronfenbrenner 1986, 1989; Bronfenbrenner and Morris 1998). Bronfenbrenner's ecological theory provides a richly detailed conception of the environment. Originally designed for the study of individual development, this model has been adapted to the study of globally distributed groups (Baba and Ratner 2003). The adapted ecological model identifies four environmental spheres of influence: the microsystem, mesosystem, exosystem, and macrosystem. These nested systems may be represented visually as a set of concentric circles surrounding the group. The innermost circle, the *microsystem*, represents the immediate context of the global work group itself. This includes the local work groups in which each member of the global group is based and their immediate work settings.[2] The *mesosystem*, next in the series, represents interrelationships among the various contexts of the microsystem, for example, the interactions among the distributed members of the GDT or among local work groups that influence the activity of global team members. The *exosystem* is composed of those social, economic, political, and religious forces in which an individual may play no direct role but which influence the microsystem, therefore affecting the global team and its members. An example would be a corporate merger and downsizing that threatens to reduce the membership of the global work group. Finally, the *macrosystem* represents larger historical and cultural forces that affect all the other systems. The macrosystem could include the culture(s) of the nation-state in which a local work group is embedded. This framework is particularly well suited to the study of globally distributed groups because it highlights the significance of larger settings for group development, that is, settings beyond the local environment. Each member of a globally distributed group is situated locally but must interact with members who are not part of the local context (co-workers around the globe). The ecological model enables us to investigate this unique arrangement by providing a framework that incorporates both micro- and macro-level settings and influences.

According to Bronfenbrenner, the primary causal mechanism for human development is the process of interaction between persons (or groups) and their environments over time. What this means for a work community is that the effects of the developmental process are moderated by characteristics of the individual actors and by time. In the remainder of this chapter, I draw on concepts and relationships expressed within this ecological systems framework to explore the processes that enable and that impede the convergence of globally distributed individuals toward the formation of a work community.

CASE STUDY DATA AND METHODS

Data in this chapter is drawn from a fourteen-month study of a globally distributed team based in a Fortune 100 corporation with headquarters in the United States. A *team* is a special type of work group comprising diverse individuals who are interdependent with respect to achievement of a common goal. The team was studied between summer 1999 and fall 2000. The corporation manufactures and sells goods for consumer markets and has globally distributed manufacturing and sales operations. The purpose of the team under investigation was the creation and execution of a global marketing strategy for corporate interactions with a major European customer.

Traditionally, the focal work communities studied by ethnographers primarily have represented face-to-face, collocated groups. In this case, it was necessary to modify ethnographic practice for the study of a distributed work group (see for discussion Baba 2001). Observing the activities of a global team under distributed conditions was challenging, to say the least. Multiple methods of data gathering were utilized. These included direct observation of face-to-face meetings and videoconferences of the full global team or its subgroups, listening in (with permission) on teleconferences, interviewing individual team members (both face-to-face and virtually, using video and audio technology), collecting team documents (charters, presentations, surveys, reports), and collecting email communication (sent through email distribution lists). Interviews concentrated on the ethnohistory of the team, its purpose, leadership, structure, communication and interaction patterns, use of technology, and the changes in any of these dimensions that had taken place since the team's inception.

Case study analysis focused on the team as a whole and its development over time. Drawing on multiple sources of data, a narrative ethnohistorical case study was constructed. The backbone of the case is a time line running from the period surrounding the team's formation through the present (see Baba 1988). The case study data are configured around this backbone in a way that recounts the story of the global team's development, as reflected in team members' accounts and supplemented by the researcher's observations. The goal was to understand objective changes over time (what happened each month in terms of team membership changes, technology deployment or implementation, primary tasks, critical incidents such as conflicts or crises) and changes in subjective states (the emotional climate at various times, perceptions of team members' interactions, attitudes toward technology).

Below is the condensed version of this case study analysis. Interested readers may want to consult a more extended discussion of the case material, including excerpts from interviews with study participants (see Baba et al. 2004). All proper names associated with the case are fictitious.[3]

CASE STUDY: THE CELESTIAL CORPORATION'S FRENCH CUSTOMER TEAM

The Celestial Corporation is an American-based manufacturing and sales organization with several major global retail customers. One key customer—Group Voila—is a French retail company with head-quarters in Paris. Because the two firms' corporate policies were based on zero sum negotiations related to prices and profit margins (that is, on sales of Celestial goods to Voila), relations at the top were often strained. Fortunately, the same could not be said about the French people in the two organizations who had worked together on a daily basis for many years. Celestial had a long-standing French Customer Team in Paris (mainly French nationals) that maintained a very good working relationship with Voila's top and middle management. The Voila managers also were French, conducted business in French, and shared with their Celestial colleagues similar ideas about how business should be conducted. For example, they all agreed that relations between the two firms should be organized hierarchically through Celestial's French team leader, Henri Couture. Couture was a member of the French elite and had long-term relationships with the leadership of Voila. His close relations with Voila's management gave his team members confidence that business would continue to be good even though the two corporations (in a corporate policy sense) often dis-agreed over business terms. Because business results in France were excellent for both companies, the French people at both firms felt sat-isfied with their work and saw no reason for a major change.

In the late 1990s the formal relationship between Celestial and Voila became so strained that Celestial's top management called in a senior American manager, James Morris, to lead a study team to assess the situation. At the same time, Celestial was undergoing a major orga-nizational restructuring to globalize its operations. The intent was to break down long-standing regional divisions in its organizational struc-ture that prevented effective and efficient coordination of resources located around the world. Like many other corporations at the time, Celestial wanted to use its globally distributed resources to "think glob-ally, act locally," that is, create an integrated network of resources to understand and respond better to global opportunities and threats, wherever these happened).

As a result of Morris's assessment and Celestial's new global strate-gy, it was decided that the French Customer Team in Paris would be reconstituted with additional talent and given a new charter to create and execute a worldwide strategy for strengthening business relationships with Voila. Morris was put in charge of the new Global Customer Team for Voila, and he invited two other Americans to work with his team—Gerry Hanover and Cathleen Drummond. Morris had worked closely with these individuals previously, and he respected their capabilities and trusted them as colleagues.

Hanover was an organizational development facilitator with many years' experience helping diverse teams to perform more effectively. Drummond was an expert in a new management method, Product Family Management (PFM). PFM was a means of improving sales volumes and profits through the creation of joint manufacturer-retailer strategies focused on targeted categories of products.[4] PFM required close collaboration between the goods manufacturer and the retailer, as well as cooperation across various functions in both companies.[5] Morris believed that PFM could improve relations between Celestial and Voila by expanding volumes and profits for both companies. In addition to Hanover and Drummond, regional managers responsible for Celestial's interaction with Voila around the globe, including managers based in Asia, Latin America, and Europe, would join the new Global Customer Team. Most of these managers were Europeans, mainly French.

For various personal reasons, Morris, Hanover, and Drummond decided not to relocate to Paris, even though the newly constituted global team charter called for their relocation near Voila's headquarters. Instead, Morris and Hanover (both based at the US headquarters) commuted to Paris on a periodic basis. Drummond (based in Tokyo) also commuted while continuing to cover other responsibilities in Asia. The new globally distributed team would operate through regular video- and teleconferences and quarterly face-to-face meetings. The official operating language was English.

None of the Americans who joined the team spoke French fluently, so they could not work directly with Voila, whose managers preferred to conduct business in French. Morris had to go through Henri Couture to make appointments with Voila's management, a dependency that inverted the formal superior-subordinate relationship. Further accentuating the differences between French and American members of the Celestial team, the Americans did not agree with the French style of hierarchical organization and interaction with Voila, in which all interactions were channeled through Couture. This precluded the broad-based, multifunctional cooperation necessary for PFM to succeed. Morris, Hanover, and Drummond also shared a very American belief that good business results today are no reason not to introduce dramatic changes that could make business even better in the future.

The situation became more complex almost immediately after Celestial's new Global Customer Team was launched. Abruptly, Voila announced its plan to merge with a major French rival, Jardin. This had a serious impact on Celestial, which had Global Customer Teams in operation for both Voila and Jardin. Their merger also meant the merger of Celestial's Global Customer Teams. Celestial decided to merge these two teams immediately, which proved to be premature. Regulatory review within the European Union delayed the Voila and Jardin merger for some months, throwing Celestial's newly combined Global Customer Team into a "merger limbo." Before taking any further action with its customers, the new team had to wait to see whether the merger would be approved.[6] To make matters worse, the premature team merger had doubled the number of Global Customer Team members at a time when there was not enough work to go around.

During this merger limbo, conflict erupted among team members. The conflict was complex, with two major dimensions. First, French members were anxious about their future, given the "double heads" situation created by the merger, and wanted to know whether they would have a job on the team in the future. The tension around this question was heightened because everyone knew that Celestial planned to downsize as part of its globalization strategy. Some French members were upset that Americans had joined the team when the future of the original European members was unclear. Morris had no patience for such worries. He directed the team members to get together with their functional counterparts (for example, Celestial marketing people from both the Voila and Jardin teams) and determine who would stay on the merged team and who would go. This directive triggered even greater anxiety; people in certain functions were unsure how to make such a decision and wanted Morris to make it for them.

Second, as previously implied, there was criticism of Morris because neither he nor the other two Americans (Hanover and

Drummond) had relocated to Paris. Fulfilling his role through travel and virtual meetings meant that Morris had not developed close relationships with French team members. He did not realize the extent of their anxiety, in part, because he was seldom in Paris. As a result, Morris's leadership role was delegitimized. Henri Couture, who was daily on site in Paris, continued to be viewed as the legitimate head of the team. Couture felt that the arrival of the high-ranking Americans had undermined his leadership role, and he experienced a loss of face as a result. Couture did little to discourage the French team members who looked to him for leadership, especially because he was present in Paris and still held the keys to contact with Voila.

Given these tensions, the resistance to Morris's idea of implementing PFM in Paris is not surprising. The French members of the Global Customer Team believed that Voila was not interested in working as closely with the Celestial Corporation as PFM would require. They preferred a more arms-length way of dealing with suppliers, as in the past. Indeed, some in the Voila management believed that too cozy a relationship with any supplier was an invitation to unethical conduct, and they certainly did not want such a relationship with an American firm.[7]

Morris, realizing that he could not implement PFM in Paris under these conditions, made contact with another American executive, David Hyde. Hyde had recently joined Voila as head of merchandising, a position perfectly situated to support the implementation of PFM. Morris and Hyde had worked together previously in the United States and had high regard for each other. These two men worked out an arrangement for the PFM concept to be piloted at a Voila store in Asia. The economic recession in Asia made Voila store managers based in Asia eager to try new approaches. Through a pilot project, Morris believed that he could prove the value of PFM (by improving business results) and convince Voila's top managers to adopt the new approach more widely. David Hyde was concerned about resistance to the pilot from his own subordinate managers in Paris but felt that he could keep a PFM pilot "off the radar screen" of these resistant managers by trying it out in Asia first.

This latter analysis proved to be inaccurate. Voila's managers in Paris were in close communication with French members of the Celestial Global Customer Team, who received regular updates on the pilot project in Asia. In addition, Celestial's regional manager for Asia (also a French national) fed bits of information about the pilot to his French colleagues in Paris. All of this meant that the Francophone information network foiled Hyde's plan to keep the pilot project "off the radar screen," even though information was not flowing in the "proper" way (that is, top-down from formal sources). Tensions mounted as Voila's middle managers in Paris and the French members of the Global Customer Team worried about what was happening in Asia, a worry made more intense by their job insecurity. No one wanted to be left out of an important project that might represent the future for Celestial and Voila.

Partly in response to tensions that were building around the PFM pilot, Henri Couture entered into an agreement with Voila managers in Paris to launch a special project, Nourriture Excellente. Like PFM, this project used research and data analysis to improve corporate buyers' decisions about products to be sold in retail stores. Unlike PFM, Nourriture Excellente did not require close, multifunctional collaboration between the manufacturer and retailer. Voila middle managers found this aspect of PFM especially threatening because it challenged their traditional power base, which rested in a hierarchical structure. Nourriture Excellente soon was touted as a "French approach" to PFM that would be better than the American-inspired version in Asia. Arguments broke out between the French and American members of the Celestial Global Customer Team regarding what is "real" Product Family Management and which of the two projects had the greater potential for improving business and being accepted by the customer. Through their contacts within the customer organization, French and American factions on the team tried to kill the other side's project.

Although the team polarized around which project was best, no one knew for certain. The PFM concept had not yet been fully developed or documented for use outside the United States. Each application of PFM at a customer firm depended, in part, on the particular structures and processes of the customer organization. Voila was quite different from the American organizations that had implemented PFM. Significant aspects of the method still had to be adapted within the French context. The team was on a knowledge frontier—no one had an exact blueprint for the project. New knowledge about implementing PFM in a French organization needed to be created, but the team was going about it in an inefficient way—by creating two competing projects based on separate premises and then seeing how each survived an all-out attack. The PFM pilot suffered a serious setback when Voila's top managers reviewed its results, which were quite successful in business terms, but rejected it for reasons that were not entirely clear to the Americans.

In light of these circumstances, Morris ordered the French and American factions on his team to figure out how to link their competing projects, giving them a short deadline. A series of meetings ensued toward that objective. At one face-to-face meeting in Paris, Celestial team members successfully developed a plan to change the name of the Asian pilot project to "Nourriture Excellente" to convince Voila managers in Paris that Nourriture Excellente should be more like PFM. Celestial dispatched one group of team members to Asia; another group remained in Paris. Each group tried to implement the next steps on which they had agreed. Cathleen Drummond led the group that went to Asia, which included a Belgian and an American marketer who usually worked in Paris. These latter individuals were "non-aligned" in the sense that neither played an active role in either warring faction. The Celestial regional manager for Asia (who was part of the Francophone information network) also joined this group. The team members who remained in Paris were French "partisans" (aligned with the French point of view regarding PFM).

Unfortunately, when the French group met with Voila middle managers in Paris to fulfill their part of the linkage plan, it became clear that Voila was dead set against this plan. The French Celestial team members realized that the plan would never work. Significantly, the team members who went to Asia were not informed of this.

A follow-up videoconference connecting Paris, Asia, and the United States was planned to enable further coordination of the linkage plan (which, unbeknownst to the people in Asia, was now dead). The team members in Asia chose the Belgian marketer to lead the call for their side because she was perceived to be non-aligned, which would make for smoother communication. Meanwhile, in Paris, the French group determined that a relative newcomer who was being groomed for higher leadership would lead their side of the call.

Technological limitations prevented either side from seeing every-one present. The videoconference facility in Asia was located in a room about the size of a closet, with a stationery camera and only one person visible on the monitor. Likewise, the people in Asia could not see who else was in the room in Paris besides the one person visible on their monitor (Hanover also was plugged in to the videoconference, but no one could see her). As the video call began, the people in Asia did not know that Henri Couture, the former French team leader, was in the room in Paris. Those in Paris could not see that Drummond (also not visible) was becoming increasingly upset as the proceedings unfolded.

When the French team members in Paris informed their team-mates in Asia that the Voila managers had scuttled the linkage plan, they were greeted by surprise and anger. Even though two members of this "Asian" group had been non-aligned initially and a third one was connected to the French faction, working together on the linkage plan in close proximity to the pilot project had changed their point of view.[8] Now they all saw how the PFM pilot could improve retail sales, and they were excited about the possibility of convincing Voila to try this approach in Paris. The Belgian marketer demanded, "Why did you tell Voila about our plan? You knew they wouldn't be receptive." Drummond came in angry, her face suddenly appearing on the screen in Paris. She asked, "How could you have held these meetings with the customer and not involve me? I am the global director for this work!" This was met by a contemptuous denial on the part of the young French call leader in Paris, who interpreted Drummond's remark as "pulling rank": "You can't even speak French, so how can you expect to work with the customer? The customer doesn't want to do PFM with you, so we don't have a choice." Aggressive dispute ensued as each side blamed the other for the problem. The so-called "videoconference from hell" drew to a close as Drummond left the videoconference room visibly distraught and on the verge of tears, determined to resign from the Celestial Corporation.

People remaining in the videoconference realized that something had gone terribly wrong, something that could damage the company and their careers. Everyone, by virtue of long tenure at Celestial, understood how reputations are built and destroyed and that they were dangerously close to the latter situation. Suddenly, everyone became interested in cooperation. Hanover (who could not be seen but could be heard) quickly made arrangements to talk with each individual privately and then to get the group back together to resolve their differences. Over the next several days, Hanover implemented a form of "shuttle diplomacy" to learn each participant's point of view, which she then shared with the others, one-on-one. All the anxieties and tensions building below the surface during the preceding several months were brought out in the open. Team members became aware of the pressures facing their colleagues and recognized and accepted their viewpoints. Chastened by the crisis and now sensitive to issues others were facing, the two groups began to work in earnest on a plan to connect their two competing projects. One symbol of their shared understanding was the invention of a new term to designate both projects— *Produits Exemplaires*, a French phrase that joins key aspects of the two original projects. They decided to focus their future PFM activity on food-related categories, a product category already selected by Voila in the Nourriture Excellente project and also a passion of the Americans (who love to eat, it was said jokingly).

Significantly, the action plan for Produits Exemplaires was founded explicitly on a recognition by the Americans that they had been "going too fast" in introducing PFM to Voila. The customer obviously was not ready, and further efforts to force PFM on Voila could only be counterproductive. This insight emerged out of their experience in the videoconference from hell, as well as knowledge gained through shuttle diplomacy. Of course, French members of the global team had known this all along but had been careful not to push their views too strongly against those of the powerful American executive, Morris.

During this period, ironically, business results for Voila and the Celestial global team were strong. After the EU approved the Voila-Jardin merger, however, business began to deteriorate, largely as a result of problems experienced during implementation of the corporate merger. Voila lost interest in any new project with Celestial until sales volume and profits improved. The Celestial Global Customer Team turned its attention fully to the problem of boosting business results for Voila. Selling and marketing was a traditional area of work for everyone on the team, all of whom had been selected because of their excellent track records. Their shared knowledge in this domain inspired high emotional energy—lower sales meant fewer rewards for them. Shared knowledge had been shaped by many years of interaction with the larger corporate context of Celestial, which was heavily results-oriented all over the world, not only in the United States. As a result, the team members began to collaborate intensely, engaging in detailed discussions of core business issues and, through tele- and videoconferences, identifying problems and creating solutions that required team cooperation.

From this point on, the content and style of the team's virtual meetings changed from largely passive information sharing on a wide range of topics to an intense, exclusive focus on business results. Interaction dynamics reflected collaborative give-and-take, a higher content of problem-solving dialogue, and a new technology appropriation move related to the web-based team collaboration tool (which had not been used previously). For the first time, someone on the team suggested that they use the team web site as a means to share ideas and coordinate their activity. The web site had been in place from the beginning but had not been utilized as a team resource, primarily because the team as a whole had not been collaborative.

Not only did the team collaborate on solving the problem of declining business, but it also displayed other forms of behavioral convergence. For example, after reading a book on business practices across cultures, the facilitator realized that Celestial often tried to force-fit processes and methods from its American headquarters on to organizations and people in Europe, perhaps not the best way to achieve performance gains. The team discussed this issue at a face-to-face meeting, the first time such a topic ever surfaced on a team agenda, and considered organizational approaches that would feel more natural to European team members. Hanover began to resist the urge to reach automatically for a standard Celestial approach to every issue and consciously encouraged approaches that evolved more naturally from the team. Another form of convergence was the team's decision to send subgroups of people from different locations to important meetings with the customer, specifically to promote a shared understanding of situations and problems across sites. Probably the most significant form of convergence was the decision to relocate Drummond and her family to Paris and to identify a new team facilitator who also would relocate to Paris. The latter objective was accomplished, and the new facilitator, an American based in China, came to Paris to meet team members during a quarterly face-to-face meeting before his move.

As our research team prepared to depart the field, we said farewell to a global team whose members were working together actively across time and space to develop plans for boosting business with their French customer. Collaboration was a hard-earned achievement based on team members' shared experiences.

DISCUSSION: THE ECOLOGY OF COMMUNITY DEVELOPMENT

The case study documents the development of a would-be virtual community, revealing some of the reasons globally distributed teams fail but also suggesting that distributed individuals can converge around common work goals and collaborate. At the end of the case, the people involved began to display signs of community. They started to define themselves as a group with common interests, they oriented their behavior around shared norms and values, they began to pool their knowledge and ideas, and they even created parts of a new vocabulary. While the team was not yet a classic work community as defined by Van Maanen and Barley (1984), it had the potential to become one, especially if collaboration succeeded in the members' own terms and they continued to build on what they had learned. Certainly, the convergence of individuals toward the end of the case was a surprising contrast to the near civil war conditions that prevailed over most of the story, indicating that something significant happened to these people. They somehow gained a sense of *commonality* from the ruins of their competitive struggle for dominance, and that sense of commonality is the most fundamental basis for community in the long run.

To gain a better understanding of the dynamics at play in the development of commonality in a globally distributed work setting, I will draw upon ecological systems theory, which argues that changes in patterns of group behavior (that is, development) arise from the *process of interaction among persons and environments over time*. I will explore each key dimension of the ecological model and attempt a theoretical reframing of the question, how does commonality develop in a globally distributed work group?

The Interaction of Environmental Contexts in a Global Setting

Strong interaction dynamics among the various contexts, from macrosystem to microsystem, explain the internecine conflict observed in this case.[9] Globalization is a macrosystem phenomenon being implemented within Celestial (exosystem; see also note 9) as a means to enhance competitiveness in world markets. Celestial's globalization strategy was intended to break down organizational barriers between regions (for example, North America and Europe) so that corporate resources could flow more effectively and efficiently from anywhere they were located to anywhere they were needed. This is the ideal vision of globalization: a coordinated, worldwide network of resource flows unhampered by barriers of culture, nation, or organization. This image of globalization forms the backdrop for the case study.

In the globalization process, local microsystems (the business scene in Paris, Celestial headquarters, the Asian retail market) suddenly were thrown into juxtaposition. Localized sets of practices and meanings, grounded in each microsystem, were thrust together, with little understanding or even recognition of their differences. Morris's formula for achieving commonality across the diverse microsystems was PFM. The new Global Customer Team would adopt PFM to improve business relationships with Voila and would introduce this methodology to its customer. PFM was to be the language of commonality, both for team members and for the customer, even as their actual languages remained mutually unintelligible.

PFM was an American-born business method, and embedded within it were numerous American concepts and practices. In addition to the culturally alien demand for close relations between customer and supplier, foreign elements included the American expectation of continual improvements in business results and the need for dramatic organizational changes to make that happen, the individualistic choices of Americans with respect to (not) relocating to Paris, the Americans' desire for a flatter, multifunctional organizational structure, and a nonchalance about downsizing.

In effect, Morris was attempting to hijack the corporate globalization project to transplant an American business ideology and methodology in France. In this scenario, commonality does not mean a shared understanding as much as it does American domination. The French, for their part, experienced a nationalistic distaste for the American "takeover" of their previously autonomous operation in Paris, a sentiment echoed at the macrosystem level in French resistance to

American business dominance. Such differences formed the foundation for conflict in the case study.

These differences might have been ameliorated or even transcended if PFM had been implemented effectively. Given its American roots, PFM needed to be modified to incorporate knowledge from the French context. To extend the linguistic metaphor, if PFM was to become a common language, it had to evolve to incorporate elements from its new environment. Yet such evolution was stymied when the PFM pilot project was established in Asia rather than Paris, out of the French global team's reach.

Morris's effort to force American business practices on colleagues or partners in another nation is nothing new. American managers have a long history of introducing their business methods without modification to other nations and of adopting unmodified methods from elsewhere (for example, TQM from Japan), often with disastrous results (see Gluesing 1995; Brannen, Liker, and Fruin 1999). Yet certain aspects of the present case do appear to be novel and result from globalization (the increasing interconnections among nations and peoples and the blurring of boundaries at the global level).

First, in this case we observed not a direct transplant from the United States to France, but a "back door" strategy that utilized a third nation as a leverage point for overcoming French resistance. When Voila balked at adopting PFM in Paris, Morris and Hyde took the method to Asia, where they found a more willing Voila partner. This approach was made possible by Celestial's globalization strategy, which opened to Morris a pathway to Voila stores in many countries and regions. Previously, under the older "international business" regime, Morris might have had little recourse if the French had resisted PFM, for introducing this method to France via Asia would have been unlikely under an organizational structure based on regional control.[10]

Second, Morris was able to establish the pilot in Asia while ignoring Voila in Paris because of his own organizational power. Global projects such as the one described in the case have very high stakes because they affect a large piece of the company's business and, consequently, attract high-level attention and intervention. Morris was a high-ranking executive with a broad scope of authority. All he had to do was deliver business results—how he did it was up to him. Morris's greater organizational power relative to Couture and everyone else in the case was a result of globalization, which brings higher-level corporate powers to bear on local activities previously managed at the regional level.

Third, globalization also provided a rational cover for managerial actions that otherwise might have appeared ill conceived or self-serving. Morris was able to explain himself through the rationale of "global thinking, local acting"—to achieve his global objectives with Voila, he needed to circumvent Paris and work through Asia. This logic eliminated the need to further scrutinize what was going on in Paris or even to worry about it. The clever global game plan looked good on the surface.

Unfortunately, Morris's strategy for building commonality was based on the very American assumption that strong business results in the pilot would convince the French to adopt PFM. It did not occur to Morris that the French might reject PFM even if it had strong business results. The Voila managers were not persuaded by Morris's logic of globalization primarily because they were operating on the basis of a different logic, which Morris had rejected out of hand. As a result, Morris's formula for commonality (convince everyone to do it the American way) did not just fail—it failed spectacularly.

Couture and his Parisian colleagues, though not as powerful as Morris, still had global reach. The effort to hide PFM in Asia was picked up by the globally operative Francophone information network as a signal of exclusion (which it was), increasing French anxiety and resistance. The Americans' exclusion of the French crystallized the formation of two factions, intensified the debate around PFM, and ultimately led to the videoconference from hell, during which the team nearly was destroyed. Rather than achieve commonality, Morris's global strategy created two factions obsessed with their differences, each trying to undo the other. Clearly, the American pathway to commonality did not work in this case.

The Interaction of Persons and Contexts

Environmental contexts do not simply interact in an impersonal and autonomous fashion. Their interaction is shaped by the characteristics and behaviors of individual people within the local microsystems. It is postulated that the behavior of specific individuals is a key mechanism that mediates the effects of one level of context upon another. In the case study, two key individuals were the factional leaders (Jim Morris and Henri Couture). These men were motivated in large measure by a personal power struggle to establish or regain independence and autonomy. Couture had autonomy before Morris's arrival, but he lost some of it when placed under a new American boss. Morris was accustomed to operating at the executive level in Celestial, where he more or less decided for himself what he would do. When he agreed to lead Celestial's customer relations effort with a Francophone company, he lost this independence. Both men were uneasy about being caught in this mutual web of interdependency and struggled to break free. Morris took the PFM pilot to Asia. Couture took on a competing project (Nourriture Excellente) with the customer, but without Morris's knowledge or blessing. These competitive actions led to the videoconference from hell.

Morris, having superior power in Celestial, was able to travel from context to context almost at will. He easily maneuvered among the local microsystems (US headquarters, Paris, and Asia) whenever he wanted. Just as importantly, he was able to travel up and down the ecological scale, sometimes drawing on globalization logic (for example, claiming that he could create a global marketing strategy for improving relations with Celestial), sometimes focusing on the interaction of the microsystems (directing the two factions to link their projects), and sometimes being firmly implanted in his local microsystem (pushing the American-born PFM all the way). He had a great facility for moving across and among contexts. Couture was more constrained. He did not command a corporate executive's budget and authority and could not claim to be an agent of globalization. But he could draw upon the interaction of microsystems (the Francophone information network in Asia) and certainly his own local microsystem (long-standing relations with Voila) to enhance his individual power.

In their multifaceted maneuvers, these two individuals actualized their personal agendas by manipulating resources rooted in disparate contexts. In so doing, they connected these contexts and deepened the intensity of the conflict in unanticipated ways. Both men sought personal power, as well as organizational autonomy. Other characteristics, motives, and preferences also played a role. For example, Morris's inability to speak French, his alliances from the past (Drummond and Hyde), and his personal reasons for not relocating to Paris were significant factors in shaping the interaction of contexts. Likewise, Couture's membership in the French elite bonded him more strongly to Voila than to the American headquarters of his own firm, a generative factor with respect to factional competition.

The culture of the Celestial Corporation (exosystem) certainly must be implicated here, for that culture appears to have produced two leaders on opposite sides of the Atlantic with traditional hierarchical characteristics. Had the leaders differed in personality, experience, and/or ability, they likely would have maneuvered among the ecological contexts and utilized the resources found there quite differently, and the story would not have been the same.

The Shift in Individual Self-Interest from Local to Global

A turning point in the story was reached in the videoconference from hell. Before this critical incident, each faction treated the other as an external entity with little held in common. Afterwards, however, the boundaries between the microsystems became porous, and a shared understanding began to align the factions around a common set of interests. This process of incipient community formation involved several key events or developments.

First, members of each faction had a shared or convergent experience that brought them closer to one another. The videoconference from hell convinced members of both factions, simultaneously, that they were on the wrong track. That videoconference—a logical consequence of the deadly power games being played on the team—did not end with one faction as the winner, as hoped. Instead, both were losers. This sobering realization transformed willing combatants into fearful penitents and made everyone receptive to alternative pathways.

Second, after the videoconference, the team members co-constructed a shared understanding of what had happened during the entire period preceding the crisis. Through the facilitator's shuttle diplomacy, each member gained an appreciation for the others' points of view and came to understand why the French so distrusted the Americans. The Americans also learned that they had been "going too fast"—forcing PFM on Voila would not be acceptable no matter how excellent the business results. Much more time, and a different approach, would be necessary for a successful introduction of new business methods. Of course, the French understood this all along but had not been consulted. Here, the French team members could provide some guidance, thereby equalizing the power balance on the team. All of this produced a rough consensus on what needed to be done next.

A third factor that supported community formation was a shift in team member self-interest—from factional self-interest to individual self-interest. Ironically, the shift to individual self-interest actually drew the team members closer together. The only way they could control the damage and save their careers was to cooperate and salvage what they could of the situation. Anyone who did not cooperate would quickly be labeled unfit for global duty, something that nobody wanted in a globalizing (and downsizing) corporation. The motivational calculus changed, from seeking factional gain to avoiding personal loss, perhaps a more compelling form of motivation. Only when individual interests were freed from their factional focus were team members able to concentrate on a common interest—saving the team from dissolution and their careers from ruin.

When the team members realized that they needed one another to achieve their individual goals, they were able to negotiate a "third way"— a new approach to PFM that combined French and American knowledge of the customer and the methodology (Produits Exemplaires). A commitment to this negotiated solution was realized through a series of concrete projects and action steps that the team designed together as a means to move forward with Voila. After this successful effort to forge agreement, several other types of behavioral convergence were observed on the team, including one with most dramatic personal consequences—the relocation of two Americans in Paris (an ironic form of success for a "global team"). Having finally found the commonality of mutual understanding and shared goals, the team members were able to create an ongoing spiral of open communication, collaboration, and trust that permitted them to draw ever closer to one another. Their platform of commonality became the heart of an incipient community.

It is significant that the behavior of an individual also played a central role in the turn to commonality. The shift from global to local probably would not have happened without a facilitator—in this case, Hanover. Trained to build teams across various industry functions (and not a traditional leader herself), Hanover was able to transfer this skill to an analogous situation involving national cultures. The facilitator was the pivotal individual whose expert knowledge and skill shifted the articulation of the entire team from individual-local to individual-global. At the point of communication breakdown, the facilitator understood what was happening, based on her training and prior experience in the corporation, and immediately switched from acting as an agent of the factional American interests to acting as an agent of the global corporation. Importantly, and unlike Morris, Hanover did not claim to have a preconceived formula for commonality. Rather, she engaged the others for mutual *discovery* of shared understanding and common interests. This was exactly the approach needed—in a complex global reality, the basis for commonality is likely to vary in each case. The people involved must co-construct an emergent foundation of shared understanding and common interests. Significantly, the facilitator role is a recent development at Celestial (and many other corporations), in contrast to the more traditional leader role, and it may draw upon a separate framework of concepts and practices. Persons who can adapt their behavior to the facilitator role may become the new leaders of twenty-first century work organizations.

CONCLUSION

Through our project—the School of American Research/Society for Applied Anthropology's seminar on community building in the twenty-first century—a group of anthropologists approached their diverse fields of inquiry with a common aim: to stretch our understanding of the phenomenon of community and community building, and especially to challenge traditional conceptualizations based on social and physical features of community. Our emphasis was to be on the processes of building human relationships through which people work and live together.

The case study presented in this chapter challenged the orthodoxy of traditional community studies by suggesting that physical propinquity is not necessary for members of a group—even a group with a history of sharply divisive conflict—to discover the grounds for commonality. The bases for community in this case grew out of shared experience in a common environment, but *not* necessarily a common physical environment. The members of the global team described here, and especially the two factions, were seldom collocated.[11] The shared experience that triggered their convergence happened in cyberspace, and the co-construction of a shared understanding among them was supported by telephony while the individuals were distributed across three continents. Humans construct their environments, and these environments do not need to be embodied in a physical surround.

Perhaps even more startling is the notion that if these distributed individuals shared any environment, it was that of a global corporation—the Celestial Corporation and its incentive structure. Individuals' responses to crises were conditioned by shared knowledge from the corporate setting that pointed to the likely negative consequences of their actions with respect to their self-interests. Celestial provided a globally relevant framework of meaning that ultimately trumped the local meanings held by each faction, despite the influence of powerful leaders whose personal agendas depended on factional loyalty. The realization that a continuing orientation to the local would threaten their self-interests diverted their attention away from the local and toward the global, which demanded that team members cooperate with one another. Thus, we see the critical role of individual behavior and choice as a mechanism that mediates among and connects the various contexts in a global setting. But the framework of meaning in which these choices were made was shaped by a global company, one based in the heart of our advanced capitalist society, the United States.

The dynamics in the case reveal a kind of tug-of-war between local and global interests, with several forms of environmental context struggling to recruit or retain their members and, as events unfold, individuals shifting allegiances. The struggle gave birth to a new kind of virtual community—one that did *not* grow naturally or spontaneously from physically grounded commonalities, but one that needed a skilled midwife (facilitator) to pull the would-be community out into the light of day. The outcomes of the case study point to the potential power of global corporations in transcending local interests and give weight to the argument that corporate or organizational culture is beginning to rival national or ethnic culture in its capacity to influence human behavior. If there is any merit to this observation, then perhaps anthropologists should begin to take corporations and all organizations more seriously as legitimate and even urgent loci of investigation in the twenty-first century. If we do not, we could lose focus on the generative forces that will shape the cultures of the postmodern world.

We are perhaps accustomed in anthropology to casting the corporation in the role of a destructive force on the global scene, bringing devastation to local communities in ways that have negative consequences for people's lives. This case study does not deny such dynamics or their profound consequences, but it presents an alternative point of view from which to gaze upon the twenty-first century. Here we see the corporation as a potential constructor of a new global work community, bringing together otherwise divided people around a common goal, providing resources through which they can discover their commonality. The global corporation became the birthplace of a "third-way work culture," a genuinely new thing. Is this something that anthropologists should care about in the twenty-first century? I would argue that it is. The global corporation represents the workplace of the future, one that might produce a continuous stream of such emergent microcultures or nanocultures, whose influence on the larger world we do not yet understand. The global corporation is a complex phenomenon, both a risk and a resource for the peoples of the world. If we perceive only the risk and cannot or will not see the potential resource, then we will be half blind and will miss seeing what everyone else envisions.

Finally, we should consider the role of twenty-first-century technology in global community building. The case made clear that currently available technology for communication across globally distributed work sites does not necessarily provide a platform for commonality. Ironically, videoconferencing did provide a platform for a shared experience that would not have been possible otherwise, and ultimately its use precipitated a crisis that culminated in shared understanding. This incident, however, was chaotic (out of local control) and could have destroyed the team. Certainly, we would not advocate such risky incidents, or their technological supports, as a means to commonality if we had other options. Indeed, the team discontinued use of videoconferencing after the crisis, on the grounds that it was "getting in the way." Only after the team established common ground was it able to incorporate new technology (the website) in a way that supported collaborative work. While technology can support community, it cannot be relied on at this stage in its development to construct community without the help of many other human resources.

In conclusion, we find that humans are building new forms of community in the twenty-first century and utilizing new kinds of resources to build them. These new communities respond to the economic and political pressures that are gradually shaping our lives in ever more globally distributed patterns, whether or not we like it. Yet, at the heart of community, we still find the ties of common experience and interest that bind individual people and the choices people make to allow these bonds to embrace them, regardless of where they may be located in place or space. This is a human constant that is not likely to change as we go forward into the future.

Notes

The author expresses gratitude to Julia Gluesing, whose superior ability in French and knowledge of global teaming practices enhanced data collection and analysis, and to Hilary Ratner, who provided an introduction to Bronfenbrenner's ecological model. The author takes responsibility for what has been done with the resources they provided. Acknowledgment also goes to Wayne State University and the Institute for Information Technology and Culture for graciously contributing matching funds to this NSF-supported project. And thank you especially to the people of the Celestial Corporation for welcoming me into their homes away from home. I am in their debt for all that I have learned.

1. Distrust emerges when one expects another to do her harm (see Baba 1999).

2. Typically, members of a globally distributed work group are based within local work groups and have both local and global work assignments.

3. In addition, the gender of one participant was disguised, at the request of that participant.

4. Product Family Management (PFM) is an innovative system of management practices that creates a strategic business plan around specific families of

products (for example, food products). The PFM approach is grounded in detailed research about shoppers' purchases, practices, and preferences. A joint multifunctional team of experts from both the manufacturer and the retailer leads the research and planning effort. Using research data as a guide, the team designs and implements a store-level plan to offer product groups in ways that increase the overall volume of shoppers' purchases at that store (and the profits that derive from them).

5. People from marketing, logistics, information technology, finance, production, and other functions would need to coordinate and collaborate effectively to plan and execute the product-oriented strategies successfully.

6. A significant legal/regulatory problem could arise if members of Celestial's Global Customer Team inadvertently provided one of the two customer firms with inappropriate information about the other firm before the merger.

7. Celestial, for its part, had strict standards of ethical conduct and also was concerned about some questionable supplier-retailer practices it had observed in Europe and elsewhere. Celestial believed that formal customer contracts open to scrutiny by other levels of management could solve such difficulties.

8. Hanover referred to them as "Asian" in an interview, even though there were no ethnic or cultural Asians in the group.

9. *Exosystems* are the larger contexts of the corporation in which the group plays no direct role, but these also influence the group. *Macrosystems* are the broader social, cultural, and historical contexts in which the corporation is embedded. The *microsystem* is the environment immediately surrounding the group, and the *mesosystem* comprises the interactions among elements of the microsystem.

10. Prior to the era of globalization was the period of "international business," in which corporations invested resources in selected geographical regions, based on their proximity to markets or access to resources. Once invested, those resources were considered to be more or less fixed within the region, rather than elements of a flexible global network. The earlier period was marked by the rise of geographically bounded organizational structures that developed their own power hierarchies and priorities and carefully guarded their turf against encroachment from headquarters or elsewhere.

11. At one point in the case, people from different microenvironments were temporarily collocated, and this did affect their point of view significantly. The instance in question was when Drummond, the two marketers from Paris (neither one French), and the French regional manager for Asia worked together on the

PFM pilot project for several days. This brief period of co-orientation to the same physical environment was sufficient to produce a "gelled" microcommunity of the four teammates, as demonstrated by their solidarity during the videoconference from hell and Hanover's reference to them as Asians. This observation confirms the power of shared experience in a common microenvironment to produce a shared understanding.

7

Community Building for Health

Noel J. Chrisman

Applied anthropology in the 1950s and 1960s engaged in many discussions of health in community settings. In part, these reflected anthropology's central concern with the notion of community as a significant social unit in which culture can be expressed holistically (Arensberg and Kimball 1965; Redfield 1955). Benjamin Paul's volume *Health, Culture, and Community* (1955) was the classic in which basic principles were stated and clarified. Anthropologists learned that it was essential to discover community beliefs about illnesses or health problems, that community sensibilities and approaches were to be respected and used. Scotch's chapter on medical anthropology in 1963 reported similar studies in international health. Books on applied anthropology by Ward Goodenough (1963) and George Foster (1962) included health-related advice. Some of applied anthropology's success in health matters was due to similarities in the goals of anthropologists and public health practitioners.

What emerges from this fundamental work in applied anthropology is a set of principles that not only tell us where we have been but also, and more importantly, are completely congruent with what applied anthropologists do now and will continue to do in the twenty-first century. These long-standing principles underlie the participatory action research (PAR) and community-based participatory research (CBPR) that are so significant in anthropology's contributions to community and public health:

- Our proposals and procedures must be consistent with the community's values and beliefs.

- We must, therefore, analyze culture.

- We must discover and work with community wants and needs.

- Community members must participate in planning, delivering, and evaluating the project.

- We must work with and through existing organizations and their leaders.

- We must design and carry out projects that make sense to community members.

- We must respect the people with whom we work (beware of ethnocentrism).

- We must act as a catalyst, a change agent, by working with the people and not on them. (Little 1998; Chrisman 2000)

In the 1970s and 1980s these principles continued to underpin applied anthropology, but medical anthropology and public health began to diverge in their goals. Mainstream medical anthropology slowly shifted its focus away from community settings to medical systems and beliefs. Public health, with its long tradition of community health programs, began to emphasize prevention and control of diseases in population aggregates without the community context. It has seemed to me, however, that clinically applied anthropologists (for example, Chrisman and Maretzki, eds., 1982) interested in public health profited from advances in medical anthropology without becoming distracted by the heavy theory. We also continued to be involved with public health, even though it had become increasingly medicalized.

As we enter the twenty-first century, applied anthropology traditions of culture, community, and ethnography have served us well but must be strengthened to include capabilities to create partnerships at the macro level. While we engage in community building, our challenge will be to develop and maintain relationships with political and economic institutions whose money and influence can promote (or inhibit) community growth.

These trends form part of the continuity among the disparate chapters in this book. Participation in the SAR/SfAA symposium allowed the authors to see and discuss the similarities across our topics and approaches. You will see in this chapter that crucial changes in public health and in anthropology have synergistically promoted a stronger anthropology that will continue to have a powerful effect on public health in the twenty-first century. With new theoretical perspectives, methods, and many more studies, and with the commonalities of culture and community, of holistic ethnographic methods, and of a focus on grassroots participation in both research and practice, applied anthropology provides a strong foundation for our work over the next fifty years. This vision for the future will be further strengthened to the extent that we encourage more cross-fertilization, such as this volume represents.

This chapter explores current and future roles for anthropologists in public and community health.[1] I suggest that the views of population health and conceptions of public health practice formed in the past few decades offer important opportunities for applied anthropologists to engage in community building in multiethnic settings. Drawing on my own work in two community health projects, I illustrate the kinds of contributions applied anthropologists can make. Finally, I raise a few of the fascinating theoretical and methodological issues that we must work to resolve.

CHANGES IN PUBLIC HEALTH

In the 1980s, public health interest returned to the community because chronic diseases proved to be more complex to prevent and control than infectious diseases. Chronic diseases are much more embedded in lifestyle and community context. They are impervious to the "magic bullets" that medicine has offered to the nation. Large-scale community studies such as the Stanford Five-City Project (Fortmann and Varady 2000) and the Minnesota Heart Health Program (Luepker et al. 1996) modeled working with cities and used organizations and public media to get disease-prevention messages across. In addition, the Institute of Medicine (1988) report, "The Future of Public Health," exposed the disarray of public health across the country and recommended complementing its concern with diseases with an equal consideration of working more broadly on health and community. These changes have opened new doors for applied anthropology to ply its trade.

In Washington State, for example, there have been changes to the public health infrastructure in all the counties. A small group of visionaries began to write legislation in the late 1980s that was approved in 1993 and became the Public Health Improvement Plan in 1995 (Washington State Department of Health 1994). Although variously adopted throughout the state, this mandate for public health required setting and meeting goals for the health of populations and mobilizing communities to accomplish these goals. The basic ideas of the Public Health Improvement Plan are now being disseminated throughout the United States through the Turning Point project funded by the Robert Wood Johnson and Kellogg Foundations (National Association of County and City Health Officials 2001). Many of the skills necessary to work with communities are those of applied anthropology, particularly for assessment, community mobilization, and evaluation. For example, colleagues and I gave workshops throughout the state on community organization theory and qualitative data-gathering techniques for assessment.

At the national level, the Centers for Disease Control and Prevention (CDC) developed numerous community-based projects aimed at the AIDS epidemic. The experience gained in these projects seems to have provided tools and inspiration to continue such efforts. Two more recent national programs are the Urban Research Centers in Seattle, Detroit, and New York and the Racial and Ethnic Approaches to Community Health projects in more than forty locations across the country. These community-based public health activities are multiethnic, lodged in communities, and explicitly based on coalitions or community governing groups.

The new endeavors have been a stretch for public health. Public health programs for the past twenty-five to thirty years have tended to be what Rothman (1995) calls "social planning." That is, in these top-down projects, experts such as epidemiologists and health planners have determined the health needs of populations, constructed plans to solve those health problems, and implemented them with little regard for the people's desires or felt needs. Even the early projects in the 1980s, such as Minnesota Heart Health (Luepker et al. 1996) and the Commit Smoking Cessation trial (COMMIT Research Group 1995a, 1995b), included but did not stress community mobilization. Instead, they focused more on bringing their programs to the community through communication channels, but with relatively low levels of involvement. A continuing problem with these and many other projects is that not enough organization is left in place after the project's funding ceases (Sullivan et al. 2001). Consequently, hard-won advances in health have declined over time.

More important, communities, particularly ethnic communities, have recognized a pattern in their histories with researchers. White expert researchers full of promises have entered their communities like a whirlwind and have departed leaving few, if any, visible results for community members. Researchers' promises of jobs and sustained health programs have proved to be empty. Moreover, researchers have demonstrated little ability to work with the cultures of ethnic groups, consistently acting as if they were the only knowledgeable people in the project (McKnight 1995; Sullivan et al. 2001; Kone et al. 2000; Israel et al. 1998; O'Fallon, Tyson, and Dearry, eds., 2000). More and more, communities across the country have refused to allow medical researchers entry without agreeing on explicit benefits to community members (Norton and Manson 1996). Only now are current solutions to these problems emerging. Public and private funding agencies are calling for participation, power sharing, and attention to culture. These are prime areas for anthropological contribution.

The recent and slowly growing trend toward CBPR, community-based participatory research (Israel et al. 1998), is a response to past difficulties. In an excellent review article, Barbara Israel and her colleagues (1998:174) lay out the issues that CBPR is designed to address:

> Recognition of the inequities in health status associated
> with, for example, poverty, inadequate housing, lack of

employment opportunities, racism, and powerlessness has led to calls for a renewed focus on an ecological approach that recognizes that individuals are embedded within social, political, and economic systems that shape behaviors and access to resources necessary to maintain health. Researchers and practitioners alike have called for increased attention to the complex issues that compromise the health of people living in marginalized communities for more integration of research and practice, for greater community involvement and control, for example, through partnerships among academic, health practice, and community organizations; for increased sensitivity to and competence in working within diverse cultures; for expanded use of both qualitative and quantitative research methods; and for more focus on health and quality of life, including the social, economic, and political dimensions of health and well-being.

An important factor influencing public health recently is the recognition that macro social forces have powerful effects on the public's health (for example, Evans and Stoddart 1990). This understanding contrasts with most existing public-health programs, which focus on micro-level processes such as individual and group behavior. Moreover, it has been known for a decade that medical care has only a minor effect on the health of the public (Frank 1995). We can move beyond these more individually oriented health services to examine levels of causes of population ill health. One level of cause, and the best known, is communicable disease (well handled by medicine until now, as a variety of diseases have become drug-resistant). Another level includes the immediate precursors to chronic disease and injury, such as diet, smoking, and use of seat belts—factors that are the focus of many public health projects. A third level includes much broader social factors that affect population health. These "social determinants of health" (Marmot and Wilkinson 1999) include poverty, low access to education, substandard housing, and toxic waste. Some public health projects are working on finding remedies to these problems that must be handled on a national level. In addition, President Clinton's race initiative has had an effect on the actions of public health. Now there is a national effort to follow the mandate of Healthy People 2010

(2000) to eliminate racial and ethnic disparities in health status and health access.

Partnerships, coalitions, and other system-level approaches are required to address the social determinants of health. For example, projects to mobilize communities around the issue of substandard housing necessitate the serious involvement of various institutions and groups—environmental justice organizations, the municipal housing authority, the local health department, tenant unions, real estate representatives, builders. Of course, community agencies and activists need to be involved. Coalescing diversity such as this in an action-oriented coalition requires great skill by the leadership. Moreover, without accurate and convincing qualitative and quantitative descriptive data about the problems and their health effects, the best of leaders will have a difficult time.

Scientific and political attention to the factors that severely compromise the health of America's poor people of color is nearly revolutionary for a public health infrastructure that joined medicine in victim blaming for decades. Funding for community health projects that focus on racial, ethnic, and economic disparities, on the social determinants of health, and on community participation offer opportunities for applied anthropologists, especially given our theoretical and methodological abilities, to work at both micro and macro levels. We are able to bring two important sets of tools to these endeavors: our conceptual focus on culture and community and our methodological skills in ethnography.

CULTURE AND COMMUNITY

A major contribution that applied anthropologists make to community health is conceptual: ideas about culture and community. Although not unique, the anthropological perspective on these phenomena can be extremely helpful to community health practitioners. Public health, and health care practitioners more broadly, have a difficult time with the concepts of culture and community because these contrast so strongly with the theoretical center of health practice. Health practitioners use a biological theory to understand health and illness and are nearly blind to the dual contexts of culture and community. They construct human illness as pathophysiology that operates within the human body but is affected by outside forces in ways not yet completely understood by medicine. These factors, however, are the focus of the social and behavioral sciences (Anderson 1998). Public health projects tend to be organized around diseases that need to be prevented or controlled. Thus, this biological view of people takes center stage in public health. In fact, one of the biggest obstacles to any kind of sustained community work is "categorical funding" of disease studies, funding that ignores community desires for health change in favor of cancer or diabetes, for example.

Clinicians frequently interpret patients' beliefs and behaviors as inappropriate, misguided, or wrong when judged against orthodox medicine. Often clinicians react with frustration to "odd" beliefs and behaviors. This narrow perspective fosters public health practitioner perceptions that inappropriate or incorrect outside forces act on populations and inhibit the success of public health programs. Social planning programs are highly at risk because planners have limited contact with population members and extensive contact with epidemiological studies of biological phenomena. As a consequence, of course, the programs do not meet population needs or, worse, create more problems.

Applied anthropology can transform public health practitioners' views of culture to replace frustration with sensibility to the "odd" behaviors of people of color. With the growing understanding that heart disease and other lifestyle diseases, as well as related public health problems such as motor vehicle accidents and alcohol and drug abuse, comprise a major portion of the public health challenges today, we are attending more to everyday life. The ability to describe and analyze lives in the context of culture is an anthropological strength and is receiving greater recognition in community and public health. Yet, without the applied anthropologist to communicate ethnographic knowledge of various populations to health practitioners, that knowledge remains somewhere in the ivory tower.

Multiple roles exist for the applied anthropologist who introduces better cultural knowledge to public and community health workers. One of these roles is as a trainer (Chrisman and Schultz 1997). For example, I worked with a training business to educate health department managers about the importance of cultural competence in an overall community-level approach. My rationale for this knowledge is that unless practitioners can demonstrate their abilities to work in culturally appropriate ways with community members, they cannot create and sustain long-lasting relationships with community members. A second role is that of researcher and analyst (for both assessment and evaluation). These roles take advantage of our abilities to do ethnographic research. Through a process of highlighting and explaining cultural practices that affect health and receptivity to health projects, the anthropologist as mediator or facilitator also improves the abilities of team members to work cross-culturally.

Community-based projects that include a focus on local customs and beliefs about how people should relate to one another, on leadership styles that are appropriate, and on the group's religious or nutritional beliefs, for example, are much more likely to succeed because community members can be comfortable with the plans and activities. Such cultural knowledge is essential if practitioners follow the dictum common in community organization to "start where the people are" (Minkler and Wallerstein 1997:43). In fact, my depiction of one way to think about key processes in community building depends heavily on accurate, continuing, and culturally appropriate assessment and evaluation processes to learn what people want and how a project is working.

Figure 7.1 illustrates how to conceptualize several key principles in community building (compare with the scheme offered in the introduction to this volume). The central piece of the puzzle is assessment and evaluation. This includes both a "health assessment" of disease and population distributions (classic epidemiological data) and a "community assessment" of social and cultural patterns in the context of political and economic realities. The latter assessment must also consist of community assets (Kretzmann and McKnight 1993; McKnight 1995) and members' felt needs from their own points of view. The community-building process is based on these felt needs (Goodenough 1963) and assets. It is much easier to mobilize community members to participate in a change process that recognizes and builds on community strengths and will lead to outcomes they seek. We should distinguish between felt needs and needs determined by classic epidemiological assessments that identify problems as defined by public health. The former are the desires of community members, not a list of community deficits. Moreover, the deficit approach frequently alienates community members, reducing their desire to work together.

One outcome of the mobilization process can be participation.

Community Partnership:
Interlocking Dynamics

FIGURE 7.1

Community partnership: interlocking dynamics.

Rifkin, Muller, and Bichmann (1988:933) suggest that participation is "a social process whereby specific groups with shared needs living in a defined geographic area actively pursue identification of their needs, take decisions and establish mechanisms to meet these needs." In contrast, Arcury and others (1999) view participation more concretely as a set of dimensions that describe joint activities. In any event, participation is a vital goal in the community organizing process (for example, Minkler and Wallerstein 1997). As Linda Stone (1992) points out, however, participation as a goal reflects a Western European cultural perspective on self-reliance that is not true for all cultures. The applied anthropologist can help clarify such subtle cultural processes, whether as consultant, evaluator, or community organizer.

When the community organizer assists community members to plan and implement a program that proves successful, jointly experienced success may lead to feelings of empowerment, both on the individual level and, more important, at the community level. Chrisman and colleagues (2002:8) suggest that empowerment is "the group's belief in its capability to succeed in future actions." Here again, there will be cultural understandings of which experiences lead to a joint feeling of success. Finally, the concept of community competence is a singularly important goal for the community organizer. This concept is usefully conceived at three levels: individual perceptions and behaviors, social networks with accompanying social support, and services and policies at the institutional level. Thus, multiple levels of intervention are required for development and maintenance of community competence and health (Eng and Parker 1994). A competent community can define its goals in ways appropriate to its culture, organize to act on those goals, and maintain sufficient support among community members to resolve problems. The role of the applied anthropologist is to work with others on the intervention team to prepare culturally appropriate, capacity-building programs such as English as a second language, citizenship, and nutrition classes.

Anthropological theoretical perspectives on the meanings of community are also useful to public health practitioners. Community interviewees in the Seattle Partners for Healthy Communities (SPHC) study discussed below were clear that community—whether ethnic or local—includes relationships and jointly held values and beliefs (Kone et al. 2000; Sullivan et al. 2001). This view is congruent with anthropological theory and contrasts with the mistaken use in public health of the term *community* instead of the term *population*. Public health interventions have traditionally been designed for populations, groups of people who share little but a common health problem. Although this is a productive target group for top-down health projects, it is not designed to engage or empower people. *Community involvement, mobilization, participation,* and other buzzwords refer to working with the goals and relationships of community members. When *community* refers to population, the supposed relationships are not present, and mobilization efforts may fail. A significant anthropological tradition, typified by the work of Robert Redfield (for example, 1955), stresses the interconnectedness and interrelationships of communities.

Like the concept of culture, the concept of community is difficult to specify; it is ambiguous. In useful reviews of the concept, Bell and Newby (1971) and Lyon (1989) describe how unclear the idea is. The utility of the concept does not derive from a specific and single definition, for no such thing exists. Therefore, it is helpful to know the history of the concept and its varying meanings in different situations in order to determine which aspects of this complex concept are relevant at a particular time. For example, early contributors to ideas of community were Robert Park (1952) and the ecological school at the University of Chicago. Their set of ideas attunes us to looking at relationships among people and institutions in a common space. The classic work by Ferdinand Tönnies (1963) on *Gemeinschaft* and *Gesellschaft* promotes insight into the nature of community ties rather than making assumptions. I use a definition derived from a paper written by a group of sociologists and anthropologists who were designing a community intervention (Kinne et al. 1989): *community* is a system of people with common values and institutions, who share a common identity, and who *might* live in a common area.

In spite of the clear need to place culture and community in the center of public health research and interventions, applied anthropologists face great challenges as we attempt to convey both the meaning and importance of these two concepts to researchers and practitioners. The notion that multiple definitions can be an advantage is difficult to grasp when consensus on a single definition has been rooted in public health practice for years. Moreover, the tradition of reductionist thought in public health, derived from its close relationship with medicine, conflicts with the broad-based systems thinking required of the culture and community concepts. Two possible approaches to these challenges are to use examples—always a strength of anthropology—and to build on experiential information possessed by public health personnel. For example, exposing practitioners to multicultural projects in which common-sense, but culture-bound, ideas are unsuccessful gives the anthropologist a chance to show how a well known culture pattern fits into a larger cultural system. Fatalism, another example, has become a popular topic in public health; it seems to refer to a cultural pattern that presents a barrier to taking preventive action. Understanding this pattern in context so that its meaning is expanded can help practitioners make sense of the idea. Practitioners could be helped to understand how religious and family beliefs and values are complexly interrelated among people who are fatalistic. They could also discover that the phenomenon differs from culture to culture. Similarly, "community" exists as a common-sense idea, but hearing community partners discuss their experiences of their own communities may introduce health scientists to the complexity of the concept.

A third challenge will be to help public health personnel think and act at the systems level. This topic emerges from both culture and community. Systems thinking is extremely important in contemporary public health for two reasons. One is that multiple levels of intervention are needed to facilitate community change. An existing approach already popular in public health is the ecological model (for example, McLeroy et al. 1988). Anthropologists can build upon various ecological approaches to strengthen inclusion of culture and community in the models. Second, the construction and maintenance of successful coalitions and other social organizations to link with the community require the ability to juggle multiple agendas. This ability is greatly enhanced when the researcher or practitioner has an accurate picture of how the whole system works.

ETHNOGRAPHY

A second major contribution by applied anthropology is methodological. We are able to augment the work done in traditional public-health research. Public health researchers and practitioners face an obstacle in the design of prevention and control programs: the nature of their basic sciences, epidemiology and biostatistics. These disciplines, which supply the methodology for work on population health, are largely organized around diseases conceived in a biomedical fashion. The success of biostatistics and epidemiology (and they are very successful) lies in their capability to seek isolated variables or clusters of variables that correlate with disease distributions. All of us are familiar with epidemiological pronouncements that some everyday life activity is associated with the risk of a certain disease. To accomplish these studies, epidemiologists must decontextualize the individual. They conceive of the individual as a bundle of individual characteristics such as age, gender, "race," eating patterns, and smoking. Armed with these discrete factors, public health scientists can manipulate them statistically. Although this method was helpful in an age when infections were viewed as the outcome of an interaction among susceptible individuals in a specific environment and pathogen exposure, it fails in the examination of chronic diseases resulting from the ways people live their lives. What epidemiologists consider to be "attributes" of an individual are, for the social scientist, participation in social and cultural patterns. These patterns become associated with individuals through people's interactions with others in the same social and cultural groups—socialization and enculturation. Without the social sciences, epidemiology cannot conceptualize life at the supra-individual level except as artificially grouped variables. This makes it difficult for public health programs to plan projects to affect societal patterns. Anthropologists are capable of working at these more macro levels.

The challenge facing the applied anthropologist, however, is to discover ways to convince epidemiologists and other public health professionals of the "reality" of social and cultural patterns. The core of the problem is measurement. For many epidemiologists, a phenomenon is not real until it can be measured in some sort of numerical fashion. As anthropology becomes more quantitative, I think that we will have a better chance to communicate in productive ways with these other scientists. Meantime, the epidemiologists are learning something of qualitative methods. (Unfortunately, many continue to regard qualitative data as inadequate quantitative data.) One approach that has been successful in interactions with epidemiologists is to show that qualitative data about social or cultural patterns complement epidemiological data. This can happen through pointing out that survey items can benefit from knowledge of what is important to the respondents and that a depth understanding of what the survey results mean is available through qualitative methods. Also convincing are quotations derived from interviews or focus groups that convey the real-life experiences of the people quoted.

Two useful methodological approaches to community work that are gaining credibility in public health are more or less straight anthropological research (Bernard 1995), such as ethnography, and a more participatory approach, such as PAR (for example, Whyte, ed., 1991) or CBPR (Israel et al. 1998). Our traditional reliance on ethnography pays off in community projects. Ethnography has emerged, in whole or in part, as a significant set of techniques to gather data for community assessment and mobilization, as well as for various types of evaluation.

This should not be surprising, given the importance of understanding culture and community; ethnography has been the method of choice for researching these topics since the early twentieth century. Currently, it is meaningful that more projects and funding sources seek to hire ethnographers, or at least qualitative researchers.

An important reason for ethnography's popularity is the mix of methods. Increasing numbers of public health researchers have learned the advantages of "qualitative methods" for working with small populations and for gathering the frequently subtle descriptions of how community projects work. For example, I am involved with two process evaluations for large community-building projects in Seattle. Research with Seattle Partners for Healthy Communities, where I work on a team, depended extensively on participant observation, semistructured depth interviews, and document analysis. The other project (where I also work on a team), REACH 2010 (Racial and Ethnic Approaches to Community Health), has used the same methods. In the second phase of this project, which began in 2001, we are using focus groups, key informant interviews, and unobtrusive observation in grocery stores and restaurants. In the coalition-building phase of the REACH project, I also used network analysis to document relationships among coalition members. Both projects have characterized their work as CBPR.

A second reason for this interest in ethnography is reminiscent of what I heard about anthropology in public health settings in the 1960s: "We don't know what you do or how you do it, but you get really interesting results." Given the slow but radical set of changes taking place now, normally conservative public-health researchers are turning to new research methods to match the new intervention plans. This does not mean that public health researchers are willing to give up on the randomized, controlled trial and experimental design as the standards, but these more elegant and traditional designs may not work in community projects and often are too expensive.

Ethnography has nearly a century of proven results but can be expensive to carry out. It is also time-consuming, and community health projects do not always have that kind of time. Including ethnography as part of PAR or CBPR, however, may fit better with the time scale of community health projects and with the increasingly popular objective to work with the community (Chrisman et al. 1999). In addition, because the researcher is working with community members toward their own change, they will more likely buy into the project. This can improve validity of the findings. Validity can also be measured in a more practical way in terms of program success when the program was based on a cultural analysis.

Ethnography, PAR, and CBPR create close ties with community members and organizations. The latter two approaches explicitly build on those ties to work together toward common goals. Although these relationships may not pay off in the short run for a specific problem—for example, screening or immunization—the longer-term consequences for communities can be positive. For example, communities and professionals can work on other problems facing residents, or practitioners can increase service delivery for other health and social problems. Ultimately, social ties that evolve over time can generate creative solutions to sticky problems. Practitioners may become more flexible when the anthropologist is able to convince them that culture is neither a "variable" like income nor seemingly immutable like history. To illustrate roles for applied anthropologists in community health, I will briefly describe some of my work.

COMMUNITY PROJECTS IN SEATTLE

Seattle Partners for Healthy Communities (SPHC) was a CDC-funded Urban Research Center (CDC 1998) with an original mission to evaluate urban community health projects. Because of its commitment to community building, however, that mission expanded: "*Seattle Partners* works to improve the health and quality of life of urban, disadvantaged Seattle communities by promoting activities which are effective in preventing disease, promoting healthy behaviors and environments, and influencing the underlying social factors which affect health, such as education, income, housing and economic development." SPHC learned from the Community Interview Project that several key principles needed to be in place.

The Community Interview Project (Kone et al. 2000; Sullivan et al. 2001) explored the perceptions of eighty-five people from sixteen ethnic groups in Seattle who had been involved with community-based projects in the city since the 1980s. Kone, Sullivan, and their colleagues found that these research participants defined community as an interactive, relational entity. Participants recommended that future projects recognize how communities are constituted. This knowledge enables researchers to work with the communities as they are rather than to rely on stereotypes. Participants also felt that communities usually were not adequately represented on community research projects. They differed, however, on whether to include agencies (which may promote only their own interests) or grassroots activists (who may not have the big picture). Their solution was that projects should "maintain close ties in the communities with which they intend to work by cultivating diversity among community representatives and by ensuring that the different voices of community members are heard in the collaboration" (Kone et al. 2000:245–246).

People interviewed in this study believed that community members should be included in project decision making, but they differed about the degree of influence community members should have. Some felt that an advisory role was sufficient; others felt that members should be full decision makers. Seattle Partners chose the latter approach. Stronger participation could bring community empowerment, depending on continued good will and hard work as researchers and community members collaborate. If community-based projects are to promote the active participation of community members (increasingly a requirement of funding agencies), communities and their members should reap tangible benefits. Too frequently, only researchers are seen to benefit, because they can acquire more grants, tenure, and growing reputations. Finally, respondents noted that even though projects were carried out in communities of color, the staff was usually white. They argued that people with similar heritage to community members be hired and that all staff act in a culturally competent manner. As Seattle Partners recruited its community board and began to plan projects, these research findings were crucial to its work.

SPHC was a coalition of ethnic health agencies, the Department of Public Health, University of Washington researchers, and community members. In 1996, the second year of the project, the Community Board (CB) developed and agreed to Community Collaboration Principles, based on the interview project:

- Community must be involved in plans and development *from the beginning.*

- Community partners have *real* influence on the center's direction and activities.

- Community is involved with specific projects in objectives and selection, implementation, evaluation, and interpretation and dissemination of research findings.

- The values, perspectives, contributions, and confidentiality of everyone in the community are respected.

- Research process and outcomes will serve the community by sustaining useful projects, producing long-term benefit for the community, and developing community capacity (training, jobs).

Seattle Partners engaged in two kinds of community-building activity: developing and finding funding for new projects such as Healthy Homes (Krieger et al. 2002), a top-down project to reduce asthma morbidity among low-income children, and the Domestic Violence Project in partnership with a refugee women's organization. In addition, SPHC invited existing community projects to use the evaluation services the center could provide, for example, Reality Check, a project to document how welfare reduction plans were working in the county. The collaboration principles were expected to apply to all projects. In the second funding cycle, which began in 2000, Seattle Partners focused explicitly on the social determinants of health, hoping to improve societal-level influences on health disparities such as poverty and education.

Two key members of the process evaluation team for Seattle Partners were anthropologists. We developed an evaluation plan that used ethnographic methods exclusively and a theoretical framework that drew from literature in public health (Chrisman et al. 2002). We accumulated much data that satisfied our research goals, but we did not help the Community Board improve its performance. We then developed a much less data-intensive approach to address CB questions specifically. Ethnographic methods, however, provided an intimate picture of how the center operated for its first four years. Through interviews, participant observation, and document analysis, we were able to describe the time-consuming process of building trust among members of the board. In addition, we were able to highlight and bring back to the board the problems that continually vexed them. For example, a debate that occurs in most community projects concerns the amount of time spent on relationship building among coalition members (Israel et al. 1998). Professionals and community activists are committed to accomplishing the goals of the organization. Yet both groups recognize that unless time is spent developing and sustaining trust, the whole endeavor may fall apart. The evaluators with Seattle Partners twice stimulated these "process versus product" discussions during Community Board retreats, with no resolution. People continued to feel the tension and, for the most part, decided to live with it.

The second project is REACH 2010. I worked alone during the planning year to document the inception and growth of the coalition. Now I work with a team of evaluators on both the process evaluation and the impact evaluation. In contrast to SPHC, REACH began with an explicit health problem to address: diabetes. Epidemiological data from Seattle and King County demonstrate unacceptably high disparities in the incidence and prevalence of diabetes between European Americans and the four other major racial/ethnic groups in the county: African Americans, Native Americans, Latinos, and Asian Americans/ Pacific Islanders. After the Request for Proposals from the CDC was published, ethnic and community groups became very active in deciding who should be involved and, most important, who should take the lead and be the fiscal agent. Ultimately, Public Health-Seattle & King County took the leadership position, and agencies working with all groups but the American Indians (who had a diabetes project in place) joined in the proposal. Also, the University of Washington School of Public Health and School of Nursing were involved, as were both university hospitals. Other early participants were a quality assurance firm, an agency whose mission is to foster more culturally appropriate care for county residents, and a consortium of clinics serving low-income families throughout the county.

The project began in November 1999. The early participants, relying on their contact networks, invited a wide range of people to the initial meeting. Attending the first meeting were a representative from the Washington State Department of Health in charge of diabetes work, the director of a large health-promotion/disease-prevention project from the university, the director of a second African-American community health agency, a representative from the American Diabetes Association, and additional people from the large institutional partners (the health department and the university), as well as representatives from all the initial partners. This meeting and later retreats were facilitated by well known community activists in order to minimize feelings of the "white doctors" taking over. Throughout the first year, however, people continued to comment about the doctors and other university people.

In my role as process evaluator, the ethnographic skills I brought to the project were useful. I engaged in participant observation, interviews, and document analysis (of coalition and executive committee minutes). I attended and was active in nearly all coalition meetings, took notes, and interviewed about 75 percent of the coalition members. My visibility and formation of social relationships with other coalition members may have reduced my traditional anthropologist position as an "outsider" and increased trust. I have produced six short reports to the coalition, one of them just in time for our application for a renewal for the four years of Phase II in 2000. I submitted the fourth report to coalition members in early 2002. Through analysis of interviews (fifteen semistructured interviews) and of participant observation, I discerned some underlying tensions among three major perspectives on what the project is. Diabetes experts see the project as one to help diabetics, and they wonder why we don't just "get to it" rather than do all this community work. The people from agencies are dedicated to helping their communities and wonder why money is being spent on activities other than service provision. The public health practitioners are interested in tracking the progress of the project and worry that there will not be enough money to carry out the evaluation. This report and the issues raised became the subject of a coalition retreat a few months later. The data-gathering efforts underlying the reports allow people to comment anonymously on how the coalition is doing. In addition, I compare activities of the REACH coalition with literature on other coalitions so that the group can see itself in relation to similar community projects.

My approach to the REACH project (as to Seattle Partners) includes a version of participatory action research. I participate consistently in coalition meetings and report informally and formally on how the evaluation is going. I also make public the conclusions I am drawing and suggest directions in which the coalition might want to grow. Also, the two researchers carrying out the outcome evaluation (a quantitative researcher and I) work on a committee of coalition members to carry out the evaluation.

In the current phase (II), I work with a team and continue with the coalition evaluation, in addition to overseeing the qualitative data gathering for the outcome evaluation. This phase presents two significant challenges. One is to train and supervise community members to carry out the interviews, focus groups, and participant observation as we investigate whether and how the intervention plans (mostly education and self-help groups) are working. I did some of the work to discover the likely dimensions to be sought and then provided a day-long methods workshop, with one follow-up session, to prepare community members to facilitate focus groups. The focus group training took place in mid-2002 for twelve facilitators and co-facilitators of focus groups to be carried out with former participants of our educational intervention groups. The groups required facilitators bilingual in Mandarin, Cantonese, Vietnamese, Korean, and Spanish. African Americans facilitated their groups in English.

The second challenge is to continue the coalition process evaluation under considerably more complex circumstances. That is, REACH is a coalition of the three racial/ethnic agencies, the health department, the university, and other related organizations. A common intervention plan is supervised by the coalition and is carried out by the three agencies. This means that the style in which the intervention is carried out is tailored to the particular ethnic groups selected by the agencies. The difficulty is to assess the degree to which the coalition can receive and contribute information and advice that will enable coalition connections to be maintained and to be productive, and for consistency across the agencies as they carry out the intervention. I keep these questions in the foreground of my observations and interviews and attempt to set up mechanisms whereby the community researchers will also provide information to answer the question. One research question concerns the degree to which culture is making a difference in the delivery of the intervention.

CONTRIBUTIONS FROM APPLIED ANTHROPOLOGY

I have suggested in this chapter that applied anthropology is well positioned to help with community building in public and community health. We have important theoretical strengths—a long tradition of basic and applied field research on the concepts of culture and community. As public health is discovering that cultural competence is key to working with diverse communities, anthropological insight can be helpful. In parallel, as public health is discovering the need for community-based participatory research and other community approaches, our knowledge of how communities are constituted and constructed will be helpful. Culture and community, however, are complex concepts to grasp. Anthropologists have a difficult, but surmountable, challenge to convey these ideas to public health researchers and practitioners.

We also have important methodological strengths. For example, ethnography can offer much to public and community health through its focus on the way people live their lives. This is particularly important for current public health projects that are trying to change people's everyday, health-related behaviors. Moreover, ethnography tends to use both qualitative and quantitative data-gathering and analysis approaches. Public health has begun to attend to the rich descriptive data issuing from interviews, participant observation, focus groups, and document analysis. These data help to answer the how and why questions so elusive with quantitative analyses. Yet there is a challenge in this area as well. The randomized, controlled trial and experimental design are well established in the minds and hearts of public health researchers, and other approaches are seen to lack power.

CONCLUSION

In this chapter, I have raised issues that I think will attract anthropologists to work in community building for health, to push the limits of our knowledge and skills for helping practitioners and community members to eliminate disparities in health. First, we must enhance or develop methodologies to document community projects in ways that are convincing to public health practitioners and helpful to community members. Second, we need to understand and describe culture in ways that reduce health practitioners' culture blindness and facilitate using culture more centrally in community projects for the good of population health. Developing notions about culture that can be communicated to public health practitioners and researchers should also produce new anthropological understandings of culture. Third, we must exercise our long-standing abilities in systems thinking and acting to link the need for micro-level projects in health services delivery with the need for macro-level work to affect the social determinants of health. And fourth, anthropologists must learn how to conduct all the preceding activities to effect a balanced recognition of both population health needs and community assets so that communities can be mobilized to work on their own projects and to empower themselves to an end of community competence.

These challenges are daunting but can motivate members of our discipline to make substantial contributions to anthropology. More important, we can make contributions to the nation's health. In the end, however, much of the satisfaction in community work is the fun of being in the field and making a difference.

Notes

1. These two terms, *public health* and *community health,* are nearly synonymous in that both refer to health promotion and disease prevention activities outside clinical settings. *Public health* implies that the activities are part of a mandate to preserve and protect the health of the general public. For me, *community health* encompasses public health and refers more to work in and with communities.

8

Strengthening Communities through Research Partnerships for Social Change

*Perspectives from the Institute
for Community Research*

Jean J. Schensul

In constant dynamic flux, communities rebuild and redefine themselves without the benefit of social science consultation. Despite community-level agency, however, larger processes of social change—migration, innovation, renovation, gentrification, renewal, rebuilding—are not always transparent to individuals or to communities (Cowley and Billings 1999; Denner et al. 2001; Stevenson 1998). Furthermore, when national systems are in rapid transition, governmental and external interests step up the process of reframing information and redefining "communities" to meet the demands and constraints of national and international priorities (for example, welfare reform regulations and policies guiding the demise of public housing in the United States). Some communities, such as those in exile, face sudden cultural transitions and extreme cultural losses. To redefine themselves, they struggle to reshape their own national and cultural identities (Williamson et al. 1999). Others confront the suffering associated with potential demise and reconstruction: for example, communities that have experienced natural disasters or the psychological and physical destruction of repeated wars; ethnic, class, race, or religion-based genocide; and other forms of social violence (Kleinman, Das, and Locke, eds., 1997). Communities not privileged with information on how global or national economic and social policies may be affecting them are forced into reactive rather than proactive positions. Socially and informationally marginalized communities may seek all the tools necessary to express agency but may have no access to them (Flint 2003; Rankin 2003). By *agency*, we refer to a community's identification of needs and sociogeographic and cultural boundaries, as well as its defense of identity in place and space. *Agency* also means the capacity for authentic representation to the public and the ability to assert and negotiate plans for the future (Baker and Brownson 1998; Barnsley and Ellis 1992; Brydon-Miller 1997; Gaventa 1991, 1993; and Steckler et al. 1993).

The field of anthropology is rooted in research based in local communities—the contexts within which individuals and families live their everyday lives. Most anthropologists work at the interface of changing local communities and national and international systems (Simonelli 2003). It makes sense, therefore, to ask how research conducted by anthropologists and other social scientists can not only describe local community capacity to promote and sustain community, but also strengthen it. How can our research improve the survival of families and individuals, the growth of their communities and quality of life, and their social, cultural, and economic well-being? (See Hyland and Bennett, introduction to this volume; Brown and Tandon 1983.)

Even though anthropologists work in communities, they have generally not used the words "community building" to conceptualize their work. There is a considerable literature on community development (see van Willigen, chapter 2 of this volume). There is also a growing public health and community psychology literature on participatory action research (PAR) generally directed toward individual and community- or organizational-level change (Minkler 1997; Minkler and Wallerstein 2003). Some of the earlier work of Stephen Schensul (1974), Barger and Reza (1989), and a handful of other anthropologists working in partnership with immigrant, exiled, or impoverished communities (Arcury, Quandt, and McCauley 2000; van Willigen, Rylko-Bauer, and McElroy, eds., 1989; van Willigen 2002) comes close to the notion of community building (S. L. Schensul and J. J. Schensul

1978; S. L. Schensul and Borrero 1982). This tradition, sometimes referred to as "advocacy anthropology," involves the use of research and intervention methods to create and render operational new community institutions framed around ethnic/cultural identity. Meeting residents' material and social needs and addressing social injustice stemming from inequitable resource distribution and discrimination are also goals. For the most part, however, anthropologists have been less concerned with theories of community building (Minkler and Wallerstein 1997; Stafford 2001) and more interested in local communities (places) as locations where problem-oriented research and practice are conducted (see Cook and Taylor, eds., 2001; McElroy et al. 2003).

Community building entered the social vocabulary of American social scientists, policy makers, and social change agents with the Ford Foundation's funding of community development corporations in the 1960s. As US government policy shifted in the 1980s, more private foundations stepped in to replace lost public-sector service. Their approach emphasized privatization of services through the nonprofit sector and improved interagency coordination of services. Foundations gave more attention to "community assets," social capital, and resident engagement in community planning, development, and evaluation processes (Chaskin et al. 2001; Lepofsky and Fraser 2003). Internationally, the demise or decentralization of centrally organized governments also had the effect of reducing government funding for basic social infrastructure. Bolstered by bilateral or multilateral funding, the nongovernmental organization (NGO) and voluntary sectors privatized services, supported social entrepreneurship, and promoted social change. In some cases, they offered options for circumventing corrupt governments to deliver services to the local population.

A variety of social philosophies and theories undergirded this approach. These philosophies were operationalized by sector: infrastructure (housing and economic development), services (service delivery to families and children in health, mental health, and social welfare), the arts, and information. Significant literatures describe community building through housing, health planning, the arts and technology, and spiritual development—as do many websites, for example: Building Better Communities (http://www.bettercommunities.

org/), Foundation for Community Encouragement (http://www.fce-community.org/), and National Community Building Network (http://www.ncbn.org/). Comprehensive community building was conceptualized as coordinating across all sectors, with citizen participation in decision making at all levels. More recently, we have seen the growth of community building through information technology and the Internet, but communities have differential access to this technology. Whether the Internet will reduce or increase class and ethnic disparities remains to be seen (Alaedini and Marcotullio 2002; Rheingold 2002; Weinberger 2002).

Tools for grassroots and other forms of community building range from strategic planning and community organizing manuals to methods for assets mapping and participatory planning and evaluation (Gibbon, Labonte, and Laverack 2002; Mauro 2002). Some community-building efforts pay more attention to research and evaluation but are framed primarily as tools for guiding needs and assets (community resource) assessment and for evaluating outcomes against a community plan, rather than as information exchange and technology transfer (The Community Tool Box, http://ctb.ku.edu/). Most of these tools do not include the array of qualitative and quantitative research methods typically used by anthropologists (Barnsley and Ellis 1992; J. J. Schensul and LeCompte 1999). Nor do they discuss how a participatory process for using these research methods can guide data collection, increase knowledge, strengthen community resources and assets, and build critical social capital at the same time.

The purpose of this chapter is to describe specific approaches by a group of social scientists (anthropologists, psychologists, and sociologists), community researchers, and cultural workers who use research to benefit the communities in which they live and work. The institution that provides a base for these approaches is the Institute for Community Research, formed in 1987 to conduct community-based partnership research for social change. To situate the institute and its work, this chapter first defines *community*. Next, it suggests community strategies for survival and growth that are amenable to strengthening through the use of research theory, methods, and results and community research partnerships. The chapter outlines four approaches to community-based research that interface with community survival and growth strategies, illustrating them ethnographically with examples drawn exclusively from the work of the Institute for Community Research. It concludes with ways these approaches assist communities to combine critical analysis for transforming social and health disparities and institution building (see Erben, Franzkowiak, and Wenzel 2000) with bonding and bridging. The latter are Putnam's (1993, 2000) terms for the generation of social capital critical for survival and growth in a global economy.

DEFINING COMMUNITIES: LOCAL COMMUNITIES, NEIGHBORHOODS, AND NETWORKS

Anthropologists and social scientists interested in community "work" have seen the notion of community evolve over time, along with notions of world system and globalization (Amin and Thrift 1997; Kelly et al. 1993; Rankin 2003). Until the mid 1930s, anthropologists conceptualized communities as closed, bounded, local systems. Eventually, it became apparent that even the most local communities were linked to other communities and subject to regional and national economies and policies. As community boundaries became transparent, researchers began to consider community in the context of interaction with and response to outside forces. In the later twentieth century, notions of world system, center and periphery, and globalization began to emerge and become defined (Giddens 2001; Hutton and Giddens, eds., 2000). The migration of labor and capital and the expansion of communications technology now connect even the most isolated locations and support the formation of international networks and virtual communities of people who share a common national origin, culture, and identity—and these also increase disparities (Navarro 1999, 2002; Nguyen and Peschard 2003).

For purposes of this chapter, the communities of interest are geopolitical entities characterized by a common history, a recognizable status in national (or global) systems, a shared set of understandings about membership, and a vision and/or a plan for continuity. They may be geographically concentrated, dispersed (in *diaspora*), or both, and they may or may not constitute ethnic, class, caste, or religious groups in national systems. While the work reported here focuses on locally situated communities, all communities have links to local, national, and global networks, forces, and resources. These forces and resources change over time, and communities evolve and change with them.

With respect to informational capacity building, it is important to recognize that economically and social marginalized communities are also informationally marginalized by lack of research-related infra-structure and limited involvement in science-related policy (Ansley and Gaventa 1997; Center for AIDS Prevention Studies [CAPS] 2001). Generally, informational marginalization is a consequence of poverty, disinvestment, institutional racism or other forms of discrimination, forced migration, and other structural problems. Therefore, the changing status of communities in relation to acquiring, generating, and negotiating knowledge must be viewed in the context of attempt-ing to rectify these forms of power imbalance.

DEFINING COMMUNITY-INITIATED STRATEGIES FOR SURVIVAL AND GROWTH

Communities face several challenges to survival and growth. They must maintain physical and psychological well-being, sustain and con-serve their cultural resources, expand their community resources, and negotiate political change. Finally, they must generate and utilize infor-mation so that they can enter the global dialogue.

Communities experience stress when they are subjected to natural disasters such as earthquakes, floods, tornadoes, hurricanes, and fires. Erroneous public- and private-sector policies and human error also provoke stress responses when they cause or enhance disasters. The list of such disasters is long: diseases (such as HIV, SARS, and hepatitis C, which spread through poverty), changing environmental conditions, urban crowding, forced migration and relocation, rapid economic development, and outmigration of capital investment. Also, wars of attrition associated with terrorist acts provoke fear responses to normal situations. Disasters such as Bhopal and the Exxon oil spill pollute envi-ronments and degrade the social and mental health of the individuals in those environments. Communities in which disinvestment, develop-ment, and gentrification are occurring suffer stress that manifests in physical and emotional violence, hopelessness, and cultural loss.

These conditions destroy infrastructure and rupture relationships. They undermine cultural patterns, eliminating material and other forms of cultural production that reflect deeply rooted social and cultural meaning. Rebuilding communities that have undergone such destructive processes calls for reinstatement or reconstruction and sometimes redefinition of all these elements. First, we must understand the underlying factors responsible for these circumstances. Then, we must devise strategies to maintain property, define and institutionalize community identity, plan proactively, and stimulate new forms of local economic development, as well as other development (see Nguyen and Peschard 2003).

Communities maintain a strong sense of collective identity by sharing common cultural and historical experiences. Individuals and families play a valuable role in preserving and conserving stories and items that reflect the history and culture of their communities of reference. Many communities build institutions through which they pass on these traditions—schools, after-school programs, museums, historical societies, cultural performance organizations, and archives. Preservation and conservation efforts rooted in visual and oral/aural documentation and archiving are instrumental in maintaining historical and cultural continuity (Guan and Dodder 2001). They also form the basis for cultural resource development, that is, for the social co-construction and creation of new forms of cultural production—material, oral, and performance-based (Caro 1991). Communities often sustain a dialogue among these three dynamic processes (preservation, conservation, and creation/re-creation), with different sectors maintaining the relative importance of one over the others (Harding 2003). All three are necessary in supporting the production and reproduction of meaning in new sites and situations. They are crucial as communities undergo voluntary or forced diaspora or endure natural or human disasters.

Global disparities in economic, health, and educational status are increasing. Environmental degradation has disrupted the quality and availability of natural resources for subsistence and commercial production in many parts of the world. Fishing and farming communities struggle for survival without full knowledge of the source, extent, and consequence of their production problems. New or minority communities seeking recognition and stability in national or international systems rarely possess the resources necessary to provide sufficient constituent support for economic and social survival and growth. Gaps exist in physical infrastructure, in access to high-quality food, health care, and education, and in capacity for economic development and cultural expression. Shantytowns and slums in urban areas around the world must compete with other communities for scarce water, electricity, sewage disposal, food, transportation, and access to income generation, basic education, and health services. Communities best at expanding resources and access do better than others over time. The key enabling factor in resource expansion is the capacity to generate and obtain essential information to assess current conditions in national settings and identify potential solutions.

Social and political environments and government policies and regulations alter with changing governments and political trends. Government officials and other policy makers often make decisions that affect communities in unpredictable ways. Communities must be able to respond to these changes in a proactive, informed manner that protects their interests. Communities that are politically and informationally marginal or marginalized are especially ill equipped to do so. Research can help local communities gain information to improve their understanding of the structure of power, economy, and social policy. Fully informed, they can prepare effective responses and enhance their capacity for dialogue and negotiation.

Information technology guides development in most parts of the world. The Internet and electronic communication enable even the most isolated communities and organizations to communicate with one another rapidly and efficiently. Cyber cafes exist even in small towns in Siberia, Honduras, and rural India. Businesses and residents find it cheaper and more efficient to use cell phones and satellite communication systems in developing countries such as China and India, where public telephone infrastructure cannot meet demand or is restricted. Literacy rates have improved in many parts of the world, making Internet and satellite communication systems feasible. At the same time, the costs of such systems have decreased. Marketing on the Internet is now possible for even the most remote communities, with the proper equipment. For many communities, local development depends on ability to penetrate the world market. Computer and Internet literacy, though not a solution for economic disparity, is critical for participation in local and global development (Castells 2000; Dickens 1998; Hill, Raven, and Han 2002). Social science research can enhance both.

In sum, social science research has the power to assist communities and their members to sustain themselves, to solidify cultural and historical identities, to recognize and address sources of disparity, and to see themselves as globally connected. How research can contribute to these complex processes, and through what infrastructure, is the subject of the next section of the chapter.

DEVELOPING THE SOCIAL INFRASTRUCTURE FOR COMMUNITY RESEARCH PARTNERSHIPS

To make social-science research technology available and helpful to communities calls for identifying appropriate social and technological infrastructure for technology transfer and knowledge exchange. Various forms of research partnership are the primary means through which these exchanges can occur. Who, then, might be the "partners" in these research partnerships? Marginalized sectors of local communities are usually represented by community-based organizations (CBOs), nongovernmental organizations (NGOs), alliances and coalitions, informal or unincorporated networks, and organizations such as parent-teacher organizations, block clubs, and advocacy groups. These organizations play a critical role in community-building strategies by ensuring survival and promoting growth. They advocate for access to scarce resources, further the development of communications technologies, and act at the forefront in negotiating sociopolitical survival in changing political environments.

Community-based organizations constitute the local social backbone of many communities. Composed of local residents (often volunteers) concerned with local issues and confronted with financial challenges, CBOs perform many important functions. They provide health care, housing, supplemental food services, child care, tutoring, mentoring, literacy programming, and services to victims of violence. CBOs organize local political agendas and foster cultural identity, cultural conservation, and cross-ethnic bridging opportunities. Finally, CBOs advocate for community needs, using whatever tools they perceive to be useful, such as fairs, telephone and community informational campaigns, meetings with policy makers, community tours, site visits, marches and demonstrations. The capacity of CBOs to respond to local needs depends on the availability of financial, human, and other resources. Many CBOs are short-lived because they lack access to resources. With better informational capacities and the skills to use them, they could endure and could improve their effectiveness in solving the community problems that constitute the reason for their existence in the first place.

Other nonprofit, nongovernmental organizations in communities fulfill a variety of community service functions. Such organizations, referred to internationally as "NGOs," are usually "more than local." They may be networks, alliances, or hierarchical organizations with central offices and chapters (in the United States, for example, Boys and Girls clubs, the National Urban League, AIDS projects in various cities, and Aspira of America). They may be quasi-public, representing infusions of private and public resources for service, education, or advocacy purposes (for example, area agencies on aging). They often come into play when the public sector no longer functions well (as in China or Russia) or when the public sector actively promotes privatization of services (as in the United States). NGOs may be driven by a social-change agenda (for example, the Center for Community Change in Washington, DC, the Applied Research Center, or Project South). They may provide specific forms of technical assistance or build organizational capacity. Many NGOs recognize that research, especially evaluation, is important in their work. Although they do not usually offer training and technical assistance in research methodology, they can be strong allies in promoting the use of research for development, social change, and social justice.

SUPPORTING COMMUNITY RESEARCH CAPACITY

Many efforts to advance social-science research capacity have concentrated on improving the research capacity of universities in developing countries (Trostle and Sommerfeld 1996). This process can have a "trickle-down" influence (or could promote technology transfer) if universities link effectively to local communities and their social infrastructure (Altman 1986). A handful of programs have aimed at improving, or promoting the improvement of, research capacity in the nonprofit or community sector. Several have been university-based: University of California, San Francisco's program of public-private partnership research in HIV (CAPS 2001), the CDC-supported Urban

Research Centers (URCs)—university-community partnerships for health improvement in cities such as Seattle (Eisinger and Senturia 2001; Higgins and Metzler 2001) and New York (Columbia University and a Harlem-based coalition)—and PRCs (prevention research partnerships), which link universities and communities for the improvement of prevention through prevention science. Although these efforts build on universities' research strengths and communities' programmatic and prevention needs, they do not always focus on building community research capacity.

Universities provide research services to local organizations in many ways, through undergraduate service learning programs, undergraduate research, and applied-research graduate internships or science shops (Mayfield and Hellwig 1999). As yet, these programs do not view their mission as community capacity building through research. Rather, they see the results of their research as contributing to community development efforts. There are some exceptions. Perhaps the most significant experiments in community capacity building through research are Canadian Government Community-University Research Alliances. These alliances fund programs that link communities and universities across the country in applied, community action–oriented health, environment, and cultural conservation efforts (Canadian Community University Research Alliance, 2004, http://www.sshrc.ca/web/apply/program_descriptions/cura).

Other efforts have been undertaken to strengthen NGOs' research capacity directly. In small universities and NGOs in urban areas of India, the Ford Foundation sponsored a ten-year effort to develop medical anthropology that concentrated on building research capacity on sexuality (Verma et al., eds., 2004). For this effort, Pertti J. Pelto received the Society for Applied Anthropology's Malinowski award in 2002. The International Center for Research on Women's international program of HIV-related research and development instituted projects in more than fifteen countries, with the help of USAID funding. NGOs and universities conducted formative research and intervention studies addressing the role of gender in HIV prevention (ICRW 2004).

All such efforts achieve a measure of success only when they fulfill specific criteria. Partnership programs must

- Establish long-term relationships in and with communities.

- Promote the value of research to organizations that doubt its use or distrust its users.

- Choose organizational bases interested in using research to improve health or other conditions in a community.

- Help organizations become research-ready.

- Introduce cost-sharing mechanisms, such as subcontracting or hiring community staff to reinforce relationships between institutions and the community.

- Identify politically committed, trained researchers who are interested in serious community partnerships and can adapt research methods and tools to community needs and constraints.

These criteria are fundamental to good partnerships. Fully participatory community research partnerships, however, add technology transfer and knowledge exchange to build the community's research-based problem-solving capacity. This means co-constructing meaningful, researchable questions and issues and conducting rigorous partnership research so that communities can generate knowledge and use it to serve their social, policy, and science needs. The guidelines for partnership research and capacity building are summarized in several locations (Labonte and Laverack 2001; Minkler and Wallerstein 2003; J. J. Schensul, Weeks, and Singer 1999).

In the next section of this chapter, we describe the research capacity-building program of the Institute for Community Research (ICR). By partnering with CBOs, NGOs, alliances, community residents, and informal community networks, the institute endeavors to support basic community needs for survival, adaptation, advocacy, and growth through social science research. Examples are drawn from ICR's work since its inception in 1987.

DESCRIBING THE INSTITUTE FOR COMMUNITY RESEARCH COMMUNITY CAPACITY-BUILDING MODEL

The Institute for Community Research is founded on critical social-science and education principles and participatory and partnership action research methods. Its mission is "to conduct research in collaboration with community partners for the promotion of justice and equity in a diverse, multiethnic world" (http://www.incommunityresearch.org). A deeply held ICR belief is that theory, research methods, and results (the tools of research) can give communities and organized groups of any age greater control over their future. ICR forms research partnerships with communities to provide for survival needs, conserve cultural heritage, develop cultural resources, improve educational and health access and quality of care, develop strategies for short-term and long-term sociopolitical change, and achieve access to information resources and technology. ICR's staff comprises more than sixty full-time social science research, health education, and advocacy personnel, including anthropologists, psychologists, epidemiologists, and urban planners. The staff also includes part-time arts management coordinators throughout Connecticut and twenty to forty youth action researchers who conduct their own action research projects in communities and schools or assist adult researchers who are studying youth culture.

From its inception, ICR saw its role as demonstrating the efficacy of research in furthering the goals and outcomes of economically and socially marginalized communities. ICR remains committed to the democratization of research through sharing social-science research methods, co-constructing local knowledge, presenting exiled, invisible, or hidden communities, and critiquing social, economic, and health disparities locally, nationally, and internationally. The involvement of all research partners, including those not formally trained in the conduct of social science research, in the process of conducting research, from beginning to end, is critical to effective use of research results. ICR also believes that the process of conducting research—structured inquiry, face-to-face interaction through interviewing and other forms of data collection, and hypothesis testing (openness to alternative explanations)—is empowering because it reinforces intersectoral relationships, confronts power structures, and questions the status quo (Flaskerud and Nyamathi 2002). Finally, partnership research as ICR practices it requires long-term commitment to community partners, ongoing engagement and conflict resolution with community partners, equitable cost sharing, and hiring and training of local staff from local communities. By erasing research disparities, it addresses economic and health disparities.

ICR has viewed its role in developing community research partnerships in several ways. By democratizing research, we enable marginalized or underserved communities to access the social sciences for their own development (J. J. Schensul 2002). Partnerships are our primary means of ensuring the utilization of research results for community change (J. J. Schensul and S. L. Schensul 1992). Our research partnerships transcend cultural, social, economic, political, and racial boundaries by identifying and addressing structural disparities common to all groups (J. J. Schensul 1994). In 2000 we responded to the challenge to identify anthropologists' approaches to community building by subsuming these commitments under the rubric of capacity building (J. J. Schensul 2001). We defined community capacity as the means to survive, grow, compete for resources, negotiate place, and gain information for strategic planning through research. As a capacity-building NGO, ICR partners with communities and the organizations that represent them and uses social-science research technology for community survival and development in stressed global economies.

Four main, mutually supportive research strategies engage communities and CBOs: building basic and intervention research partnerships, teaching "research methods for social change" through participatory action research, and documenting, archiving, and ensuring cultural conservation.

Building Basic and Intervention Research Partnerships

Most "basic" anthropological (and community psychology) research is conducted in community settings. Even if the intention is to provide the basis for interventions, the inclusion of community partners in basic or formative social-science research is still uncommon. The exclusion of those for whom an intervention is to be formulated reinforces existing social hierarchy unless great care is taken to disseminate the results in ways that make them useful to community constituencies (Sohng 1995). Despite the attention paid to these factors, many community-based organizations do not have a clear vision of how local knowledge gained from basic research can further their organizational and conceptual development and increase their intellectual capital. In addition to the university-community models mentioned earlier, important alternatives to address this issue are community research institutions such as the Institute for Community Research, the Applied Research Center, Project South, the Southern Poverty Law Center, and the Hispanic Health Council. All are independent, nonprofit, activist research organizations that share similar conceptual and political origins in action research and critical theoretical approaches. Because community research staffs are committed to improving the quality of life for local people, community research institutions can readily link with other community organizations and embed research activities in their daily life.

Engaging community organizations in partnerships is less difficult when a study has an intervention component that is viewed as a service. This is because many CBOs are committed to service. Intervention research partnerships have four objectives: (1) They build research and evaluation infrastructure. (2) They introduce new interventions or improvements to existing interventions in service, case management, education, health promotion, and cultural development. (3) They create opportunities for closing the gap between research and practice by reframing the narrow concept of "communities of practice" to include reflection on both personal experience and research and evaluation. (4) They encourage communities and community agencies to play an active role in conceptualizing (theorizing) and operationalizing new approaches to service that come from local knowledge and experience. These activities bring providers, educators, and activists into the world of research and policy and elicit greater direct involvement of researchers in service provision and educational activism (see Stevens and Hall 1998).

Partnership intervention research can vary in the degree to which partners play a role in each phase and in the degree of support for research versus service. Ideally, partnership would include all partners in all phases of an intervention research process. In reality, partners co-construct their roles based on resource constraints (time, money, personnel) and trust. To evaluate an intervention, however, full partnership is critical in the conceptualization of the intervention and the operational steps implementing it so that it can be evaluated. Otherwise, the intervention can "fail" from a research standpoint, because it lacks fidel-ity and social validity. Further, the research design can fail because partners may not recognize the importance of systematic collection of evaluation data with appropriate instruments (J. J. Schensul n.d.).

Conducting Training in Participatory Action Research for Social Change

Participatory action research (PAR) training helps community members develop local knowledge (theory, data, and results). Local knowledge embodies the conflict between the truths local residents gain through their own observation, knowledge co-construction, and experience and the truths from privileged scientific knowledge. Local knowledge is more than simply an "emic" perspective (Sohng 1995; Pelto and Pelto 1978). It places lay and scientific knowledge on an equal plane and provides the infrastructure for local agency, or self-efficacy. Local knowledge generated over decades, even centuries, is important. Armed with valid local knowledge, communities can confront government policy makers, scientists, and others who use often incorrect or inappropriately collected and interpreted scientific knowledge to persuade them to make certain social, economic, or ecological decisions.

Documenting, Archiving, and Presenting Culture

Substantial literatures on dynamics of social change and migration, as well as many personal narratives, illustrate the emphasis that communities place on reconstructing cultural institutions as they relocate. Cultural institutions (clubs, religious institutions, burial societies, restaurants, cultural centers, traditional celebrations) unite communities and give them a strong sense of identity and place, even under conditions of forced migration, refugee status, exile, and natural disasters. Through these institutions, communities can state, re-instate, and redefine traditional symbols, narratives, history, and place and can situate themselves in local and national systems.

Separately or in combination, these four strategies have proven successful in helping communities to gain local knowledge and expertise through the use of scientifically sound research. Armed with that knowledge, they can enter in a dialogue with scientists and policy makers who have decision-making power over their lives. Table 8.1 interfaces ICR programs and projects, approaches to research, and community capacity. The remainder of the chapter addresses how the ICR utilizes these four research strategies to contribute to community survival and growth.

SURVIVING UNDER STRESS

HIV/AIDS threatens the survival of many communities in the United States and elsewhere in the world. In 1988 ICR took the first steps toward basic research partnerships by forming a group of organizations in Hartford, the AIDS Community Research Group, interested in beginning a comprehensive program of AIDS prevention/intervention. This partnership included ICR, the Hispanic Health Council, the Urban League of Greater Hartford, and the Hartford Health Department. Each organization contributed resources and obtained resources through cost sharing. The consortium designated specific roles and responsibilities, establishing a prototype for other consortium work in the future (AIDS Community Research Group 1988). ICR managed the project, coordinated the interviewing process, trained and monitored research, and managed data entry and quality control. The Hispanic Health Council led in data analysis, the Urban League conducted qualitative data collection and analysis, and the Hartford Health Department was assigned a dissemination and monitoring role. The project employed community interviewers who represented the diversity of the city's population and the neighborhoods where the study was conducted. All organizations participated in data analysis and interpretation, report writing and finalization, and dissemination.

This formative work led to a long and continuing history of HIV/AIDS research and intervention in which the original consortium grew, changed, and shifted over time to sustain a coordinated, citywide approach to HIV prevention and risk reduction. For example, from 1992 to 1998 the Community AIDS Action and Prevention (CAAP) consortium integrated multiple citywide approaches to AIDS research and intervention, case management, individualized and group education, and policy change (Himmelgreen et al. 1994; Weeks 1991; Weeks, Grier, et al. 1998; Weeks, Singer, et al. 1998). A second, the AIDS Research Consortium, combined the AIDS community research, outreach, and intervention research resources of ICR and the Hispanic

Table 8.1

Interfacing collaborative research approaches with strategies for survival and growth.

	Basic/Formative	Intervention	PAR	Cultural Research and Presentation
Survival under Stress	Aids Community Research Group	CAAP Consortium	Urban Women's Development Project	Tibetan Program
				Taino Program
		AIDs Research Consortium	Children First Parent Initiative	
Expanding Community Resources	Mental Health Consortia; depression in older adults	Improving mental health care for Southeast Asian families	Rapid Sociodemographic Assessment (RSA)	
Negotiating Change	Microbicides Acceptability Study; female condom study	Hartford Needle Exchange Project	Upper Albany Neighborhood Collaborative Survey; resident engagement through PAR	PR series; apprentice-ships
Expanding Information Technology	All basic research partnerships	Encontrando el Poder Dentro de Ti	All PAR projects	Interactive archival work
				Preparing marketing materials

Health Council between 1996 and 1999. As participating organizations expanded their own HIV prevention and research resources, these large consortia reconfigured into smaller working groups. The relationships among groups continue and come into play as new HIV-related problems and opportunities present themselves. This history illustrates a new mode of sustainability based on building research and intervention infrastructure, in contrast to more traditional notions of sustainability that depend on knowledge or model transfer. These consortia have addressed critical questions in HIV and substance use–related research:

- Are culturally targeted interventions more effective than standard interventions for reducing HIV risk in injection drug users? Are "standard" versus "enhanced" brief interventions more effective with the same population? (Dushay et al. 2001)

- What is the effect of needle exchange on HIV risk? (Himmelgreen et al. 1994; Singer 1994; Weeks, Grier, et al. 1998)

- What are the associations among violence, poverty, drug use, and HIV? (Weeks, Grier, et al. 1998)

- What do the conditions of "setting" have to do with enhancing or reducing risk of exposure to HIV among injection and crack users? (Weeks 1999)

- How does gender intersect with violence and drug use to heighten risk in women of color? (Weeks et al. 1999)

- Does Outreach Intervention make a difference over time?

- What drug use pathways lead to hard drug use and injection among young adults?

- What factors expose older adults in senior housing to HIV/AIDS? (J. J. Schensul 2000; Schensul, Levy, and Disch 2003)

- Are microbicides (a female-controlled form of protection against HIV) acceptable to women at high risk of exposure to infection? (Weeks et al. 2002)

- Can active drug users act as peer health advocates, reducing risk of HIV exposure in their peers in the locations in which they are using drugs? (Weeks 2002)

Participatory action research (PAR) can empower communities to withstand the impact of legislation detrimental to women and children. In 1990, with federal and later state and foundation funding, ICR formed a consortium of organizations, the Urban Women's Development Project, to engage neighborhood women without a voice in city decision making in research on issues that concerned them directly. Following the steps of PAR, four cohorts of women representing Hartford's marginalized neighborhoods addressed issues such as the absence of demographic data on women, abuse of women, noncompletion of high school education, and gaps in early childhood resources and neighborhood/environmental infrastructure (J. J. Schensul and S. L. Schensul 1992). With the help of the partner organizations, women in these cohorts gathered and interpreted data and presented it to city and state officials and to local and state permanent commissions on the status of women. They also joined advocacy groups advocating on behalf of women against violence, for early childhood education, and for educational and workforce entry opportunities allowing young women to complete high school, enter college, and gain mobility in their jobs.

This model was reinvented to combat the premature definition of "school readiness" as a means of screening out poor children and those whose parents believed that social development was more important than the reading, writing, and mathematics preparation required to meet federal mandates. With help from ICR facilitators, parents who were part of a statewide Children First initiative developed an extensive survey examining parental socialization beliefs and practices. They administered it to a sample of more than three hundred parents of mixed ethnic and class backgrounds. The research team (ICR and parents) found that, contrary to the perception of professionals, parents had high aspirations and expectations for their children in specific areas that were congruent with federal mandates. This discovery prompted professionals to develop a more positive and supportive view of the children and their families (Berg 2001a).

Cultural conservation efforts enable communities in exile to survive in new and unfriendly surroundings. In 1999 and 2000, Tibetans in the northeastern states (Connecticut, Rhode Island, Massachusetts, and upstate New York) numbered forty families who were recently arrived from India, resettled, and disconnected from their heritage, their new locale, and one another. Together with ICR's Cultural Heritage Arts Program, a small group of new arrivals created a program of participant observation, documentation, and identification of ritually and culturally significant objects. A *chorten* (Tibetan stone altar) was constructed and exhibited along with weavings, woodcarvings, and religious paintings in the ICR gallery. A bazaar outside the gallery created a space where people could meet one another and sell their products. Finally, monks released from prison, as well as community and university scholars, gave a series of talks that served to connect families. The Tibetan community thus began to establish its Connecticut base in exile (Williamson et al. 1999). A similar program raised widespread awareness of the continuing presence of Taino culture and language in Puerto Rico and the United States. The Taino culture was commonly believed to have been lost as a consequence of the Spanish invasion of Puerto Rico.

EXPANDING COMMUNITY RESOURCES

To convince community residents and service or advocacy organizations of the benefits of research without the promise of immediate service delivery, we must make a short-term promise to develop critical informational, technical, or advocacy skills. We must also make the longer-term commitment to use our research results to bring about change. ICR's research on HIV/AIDS attracted attention to this poorly addressed problem. Research partners were then able to obtain independent funds to expand their service programs. As a result, a comprehensive network of service, case management, prevention, and harm reduction programs developed (Weeks 2002).

In the area of mental health, two research consortia were involved in identifying gaps in mental-health service delivery to older adults[1] and to Southeast Asian families and children in Connecticut.[2] These studies have presented multiple opportunities to promote the development of mental health services to these two populations. For example, highlighting depression in older, culturally diverse, low-income adults has resulted in the delivery of mental health services directly to residents in senior housing (Schensul et al. n.d.). Basic research with Southeast Asian families through Asian Family Services is leading to service interventions and health care infrastructure that expands the service resources of this new and growing community in the central Connecticut area.

Participatory action research can also serve to expand community resources. From 1990 to 1992, ICR embarked on an ambitious program that involved more than eighty agencies and community groups in the collection of community demographic and other data. The goals were to build capacity to critique and use census data for planning; to transfer survey research technology to community agencies; to provide an independent, neighborhood-specific database for community use in proactive planning; and to bridge neighborhood diversity and division by integrating a broad spectrum of organizations and individuals in a critical inquiry process and resulting action (J. J. Schensul and S. L. Schensul 1992). In this project, the Rapid Sociodemographic Assessment (RSA) project, neighborhood historians produced neighborhood histories. Trained neighborhood researchers gathered, interpreted, and reported data that were used for neighborhood reports. The project developed a process for the dissemination and use of neighborhood data files. "Hub" agency staffs were trained in the use of the data files and learned to compare and contrast data files with the 2000 census. A consortium of agencies and informal organizations in the city neighborhood chose "special issues" that appeared in individual neighborhood reports.

The process of working with community agencies in the formulation, collection, analysis, interpretation, and use of data and data sets embodied PAR best practices. The data and the community histories have been used to argue for family resource centers, neighborhood school growth and improvement, and a variety of community services. The materials continue to be used by community agencies and local historical archives and provide a backdrop for proactive organizing around invasive development and gentrification.

NEGOTIATING CHANGE

Several ICR examples illustrate how research partnerships can assist communities to navigate the changing policies of government and other agencies. For the past decade, welfare policies have increasingly privatized employment and employment training for women on government assistance and have reduced government aid for impoverished women. In the process, the resources and capacities of poor women to protect themselves and their families have decreased. The sexual risks to which they are exposed have increased, as witnessed by rapidly accelerating rates of STDS and HIV infection among Black and Latina younger women.

In the domain of health, one way of addressing these changes and enhancing understanding of women's protective resources is to conduct research on female-controlled sexual protective measures (microbicides and female condoms). A partnership study of microbicide use and acceptability, which linked ICR with the HIV Action Initiative (a policy and advocacy coalition), illustrated widespread acceptance of microbicide products among women and their male partners. An ICR-sponsored conference in June 2003 disseminated results to national policy makers (Weeks et al. 2002). Microbicides are not yet available. This study, however, illustrated some conditions for sustaining the use of female condoms. Female condoms are not available either, primarily because of their cost. ICR will now embark on a study of factors sustaining female condom use. The intent is to make female condoms widely available and then to demonstrate that availability plus other factors facilitate widespread use. Joining the national push to promote female-controlled protection methods should result eventually in reducing the cost of female condoms and increasing their acceptability and use.

In the area of intervention research, a similar process, in which ICR and other agencies negotiated policy and community ambivalence toward needle exchange programs, resulted in the introduction of the Hartford Needle Exchange Program in 1996. The Hartford NEP has successfully sustained activities in the face of national controversy and community opposition to NEPs in other parts of Connecticut, helping to reduce new HIV infections in a resistant infection network (Himmelgreen et al. 1994; Singer et al. 1995).

Participatory action research lends itself to negotiating policy changes, as two ICR examples illustrate. In both, community residents participated in action research for improved economic development and quality of life in the face of gentrification and centralized development. The first, funded by the Ford Foundation as part of a four-city community-building effort, enlisted community residents in Hartford's North End in the conduct of a baseline evaluation survey. These residents, however, were not simply data collectors. A consortium of community organizations including ICR, the Center for Urban Research and Training, and the University of Connecticut School of Social Work trained the residents as survey researchers and activists. Confronting national evaluators, they demanded input into the survey process. As activist researchers, they implemented their survey and used it as the basis for identifying candidates for community organizing around economic development, health, and other topics. Upon completing the survey, they requested participation in organizing community residents to interface with externally driven economic-development strategies. This small PAR program drew the attention of researchers to the need for political activism in response to imposed change.

A second, similar project currently in the field is part of the Annie Casey Building Bridges initiative, designed to link indigenous economic development with family strengthening. Groups of residents in different parts of the city receive PAR training for group-initiated change efforts. After gaining expertise on their chosen topic, members join forces with other groups in the city to address and, if necessary, object to economic development policies that threaten sense of community in their neighborhoods (Berg 2001b; Williamson 2003; Williamson et al. 2003).

EMPLOYING INFORMATION TECHNOLOGY

Information technology refers to computer and Internet use and also to the use of research technology to obtain, disseminate, and apply social science data and results. Basic research and intervention research, as conducted in the studies mentioned earlier, facilitate research technology transfer and information exchange when all partners help design the research. Designing participatory studies should always bring together the knowledge base of the community partners with the technology base of the researchers. The net result is the production of locally situated, culturally specific research designs and data collection techniques and instruments, as well as an analytic procedure that brings authenticity to the interpretation of research results. Moving beyond requires time from researchers to give technological training (in the use of computers, software, and data management and analysis procedures in programs such as SPSS and Atlas Ti) and time from community partners to teach researchers about their communities in a systematic way (through participatory observation and analysis).

Several examples of ICR work exhibit these exchanges. In the area of intervention research, ICR researchers have utilized this process with a local Latino early-childhood education center to develop substance-abuse prevention programs for young children and their parents. In the project titled "Encontrando el Poder Dentro de Ti/Finding the Power within You," Latino (Puerto Rican and South and Central American) parents and staff developed their own conceptual model for risk prevention, identifying risk and protective factors associated with early indicators of substance use. Parents then conducted exploratory and confirmatory research with other parents in the same community, thereby drawing them into the process of critically analyzing early childhood education and parenting skills. After analyzing the data, they chose components of existing national or state prevention programs that met their own community/constituency needs. With ICR research partners, they evaluated their program. The process resulted in program ownership, and these same parents disseminated their successful program to other Latino child care centers across the city.

ICR youth researchers have shared their culture through the development of conceptual models and data collection and analysis. In return, they have received social science research, data entry, and analysis skills; library and Internet search skills; interpretation and writing skills; and communication skills. These youth prefer to develop their own prevention or education strategies, rather than borrow from national sources. Their approaches range from prevention fairs, to educational materials, to advocacy efforts with legislators (Berg and J. J. Schensul, eds., 2004; J. J. Schensul and Berg 2004).

ICR's cultural research and presentation programs (such as the Folk Arts program and the Urban Artists' Initiative, a training and advocacy program for emerging urban artists) offer numerous opportunities for new or heritage artists and their communities. They gain technological skills in graphic arts and have their work represented. They learn how to label and present materials. Artists are trained to conduct Internet searches and to develop websites for portfolios and community history. They establish connections with other artists and members of their communities in diaspora.

CONCLUSION

This chapter discusses multiple, complementary approaches to using research partnerships to support various dimensions of community building, illustrated by the projects of the Institute for Community Research. Partnership research offers communities opportunities to access new information related to survival issues. Methods training, by itself or through collaborative projects, diffuses collective research technology for assessing, analyzing, recording, and re- and co-constructing components of cultural identity and social issues. Partnership principles unite people and organizations around a common set of questions, problems, and issues related to addressing disparities in power and resources; thus, partnership research processes parallel desired outcomes, producing systems consistency (J. J. Schensul 1985). Partnership research provides the basis for identifying local ways of conceptualizing and defining problems, needs, and resources; it clarifies local ecological knowledge and local theory. Engagement with cosmopolitan theory and knowledge is important because it reveals the differences and the similarities in what social scientists, indigenous scholars, and culture bearers know. Addressing these from a community perspective is empowering for residents and community agencies. The perspective of the community gives its social-scientist partners an informed basis for critique, resistance, and redefinition and for political and scientific advocacy. The process of sharing and building knowledge and social science methods and theory democratizes science and access to science technology.

One set of theoretical approaches to enlarging community capacity through research partnerships frames social-science research partnerships as an attempt to address persistent structural inequalities stemming from economic, political, social, and cultural marginalization in national and global systems. Research partnerships with activist-oriented community agencies and residents use science technology more effectively as a tool for advocacy, mobilizing disenfranchised people to find a voice in claiming more equitable distribution of scarce resources.

A second set of current theories suggests that community research partnerships build social capital, which many social economists now view as the critical missing component in local community development (Hyman 2002). Bonding and bridging, two core processes that facilitate social capital, are implemented in community-based partnership research. *Bonding*, as operationalized in ICR partnership research, means solidifying relationships between like people. For example, ICR has formed sexual minority youth groups for participatory action research. ICR partners with community organizations in Puerto Rican and African American areas of Hartford to engage residents in PAR for community development and family strengthening. We support presentations and programs of Tibetans, Cape Verdeans, first-generation Polish migrants, Laotians, Cambodians, and other Southeast Asian nationalities. To reinforce cultural identity and ethnic and interethnic pride, we build culturally specific interventions.

Bridging means crossing social boundaries to forge new relationships for social and instrumental purposes. Social boundaries can be defined by geography, culture, sexual preference, neighborhood, school, gender, ethnicity, class, and age. ICR and many ICR research partnerships support bridging. For a common purpose, they bring together people from different communities, ethnic groups, ages, and experiences to find common ground through research. These partnerships offer opportunities to develop new links, obtain new resources, forge new concepts of community, and blur the boundaries that, sometimes intentionally, separate organizations, neighborhoods, groups, and individuals from one another.

Combining an activist research approach with the generation of social capital gives communities the advantage of using research tools and results as a critique and counterpart to existing social paradigms and programs. The rewards for community building are multiple. Enduring relationships continue to foster community research partnerships over time, which, in turn, transform persons, partnerships, and communities. Participation in projects from the very beginning and the sharing of costs entail the location and training of research staff in partner agencies, the building of research knowledge in neighborhoods, the improvement of overall activist-research capacity, and the ability to draw strategic research and other resources into communities. Translational research is an approach that federal funders now favor because research results have not been effectively diffused into user settings. Translational research finds a home in communities that are research-ready, that is, prepared for utilization of research results for better service delivery, advocacy, and prevention programming.

Positive partnership experiences encourage community researchers to gain research degrees, increasing the diversity pool in the social-science research world. Artists, organizations, educators, researchers, youth workers, and youth as cultural workers think critically and co-construct new community models and realities—through partnership. Community partnerships endorse diversity and encourage informed public opinion and dialogue. More "open spaces" appear in a segregated society. More people move together, from the margins to the center.

The Institute for Community Research represents a collection of approaches to collaborative research and intervention that have as their common mission community building in health, human services, housing, and environmental improvement. These approaches involve the critical components of community-based PAR—partnership in all phases of the research project; inspiration and guidance from community-identified needs; technology transfer and resource sharing; joint utilization of research results for continued local community intervention; and a commitment to scientific dissemination and generalization. Some ICR work is rooted in anthropology; other projects are interdisciplinary or stem from commitments in community psychology, environmental advocacy, community development, folklore, and public health. In the end, the discipline guiding research partnerships is irrelevant. More to the point are the political vision, deep research skills, and long-range commitment to local-level social change that motivate scholar activists to join community research partnerships that make a difference.

Notes

1. This consortium includes the Institute for Community Research, the North Central Area Agency on Aging, the Braceland Center on Mental Health and Aging, the Institute of Living, and the Hartford Housing Authority.

2. This partnership includes the Institute for Community Research, Asian Family Services, and a network of clinics and health care providers that serve Southeast Asian families.

9

Community Building in the Twenty-First Century

Implications for Anthropologists

Stanley E. Hyland

Contributors to *Community Building in the Twenty-First Century* have provided unique insights into the history, current status, and future promise of applied social science in community-building endeavors. To conclude, we briefly summarize the main implications for community builders from each chapter. Immediately following each summary are the author's reflections on how participation in this project has affected his or her understanding of community building in the twenty-first century, as well as his or her mentoring of the next generation of social scientists. Finally, we end with some overarching implications for the future of engaged scholarship and community building.

CHAPTER 2 SUMMARY AND REFLECTIONS

Van Willigen encourages community builders to think of community assets in terms of the culture and history of a community. Just as important, the differences between community development and community building should be contemplated with respect to the way assets are discussed and mobilized. According to van Willigen, it is essential that anthropologists recognize the advantages of identifying and using internal resources, because these assets can be mobilized more quickly and efficiently and have a positive effect on community capacity. "External resources can overwhelm." Nonetheless, when introduced properly, external resources do have their place in the process of community building. Van Willigen advocates that anthropologists be more comprehensive in their understanding of the community and more critical and reflective in identifying and using assets and external resources for community development. Because community assets have a substantial impact on community development and community-building activities, anthropologists must continue to research this area, to explore the relationship between "the resource allocation process and the cultural and social appropriateness of the development plans."

John van Willigen: Chapter 2 reflects my core experience in comparing "ways of thinking" about development resources—juxtaposing concepts that were important to me in applied work earlier in my career with contemporary ways of thinking.

The comparison reinforced my view that "new" ideas are often expressed without reference to earlier, similar conceptions. That is the case with my reading of Kretzmann and McKnight. Their approach is sound but does not take advantage of the useful ideas developed by earlier writers in anthropology. An intellectually richer and more practical approach can be constructed by combining the valuable aspects of earlier ideas with contemporary expressions. Kretzmann and McKnight's community assets model ignores precursors and promulgates a kind of intellectual rootlessness. In brief, their model would be improved by the incorporation of culture as an important class of community resources.

It seems as though a basic set of truths (that is, some workable propositions) cycles in and out of style, expressed in new ways but not necessarily improved. I think that accumulation of conceptualization contributes to the utility of these truths. The limitation in the accumulation of theory plagues the literature on the practice of development. Also, there is little empirical verification beyond that of intellectually rootless case studies.

The production of a more comprehensive and accumulative contemporary statement on community-based development would be a worthwhile endeavor—something that would look across disciplines more aggressively. Within the context of that work, I think that future research should focus on how the nature of development resources affects the outcomes of the development process.

CHAPTER 3 SUMMARY AND REFLECTIONS

Oliver-Smith stresses the ever-expanding role of anthropologists in work with uprooted peoples of the world. According to Oliver-Smith, anthropologists are now actively engaging in applied research, policy formation, theory building, evaluation, planning, and resistance in their work with communities. Besides evaluation, Oliver-Smith states, "anthropologists have carried out the applied research necessary for informed planning and the implementation of humane and developmentally oriented resettlement projects." Anthropologists must be prepared to be agents on behalf of these communities. Advocacy and leadership roles are taking on an increasing importance as uprooted communities relocate and establish or re-establish their cultural resources to find a meaningful place in the world. In performing the role of agent, anthropologists must recognize that local cultural resources and cultural traditions have the power to mobilize uprooted peoples. Oliver-Smith emphasizes that the substance of a culture and its traditions must be investigated. These should be articulated and acted upon by the people themselves during the recovery and reconstruction process. Anthropologists today need to do what they can to improve policy that recognizes and maintains these resources. Finally, Oliver-Smith states that much is to be learned from uprooted communities: "The displaced reveal to us the adaptive capacities of individuals and peoples and also the centrality of the grounding concept of community to the human sense of self and society."

Anthony Oliver-Smith: As an anthropologist who has been concerned for more than thirty years with the impacts of "extreme" events or crises on the survival of communities, my research and practice have consistently obliged me to confront fundamental questions about the nature of community. The circumstances of social and material destruction experienced by many communities around the world test the resilience of their social relations and the capacities of those who would assist them. In working with afflicted communities, we continually encounter consistent patterns and innovative responses as people come to grips with these challenges. The task for applied anthropologists is to help these people to make the best informed choices under very difficult conditions and to develop options for realizing the outcomes they elect.

The School of American Research experience has convinced me more deeply than ever of the importance of linking theory with practice. The various positions on and constructions of the concept of community, as well as the wide array of contexts in which it was explored in the seminar, graphically demonstrated that our efforts to support people in meeting the challenges to their individual and social well-being must be grounded in a solid understanding of social and cultural theory. By the same token, the efforts of all the participants in the seminar who are in the field of application tested and helped to refine, in innovative ways, the validity of certain theoretical constructs. The conversations and the papers by seminar participants underscored the importance of both explicit and implicit theoretical assumptions, as well as deep contextual knowledge and experience, in guiding significant applications in anthropology.

CHAPTER 4 SUMMARY AND REFLECTIONS

Kemper and Adkins promote the exploration by anthropologists of faith-based groups in the community-building process for several reasons. Primary among these is that any community has a soul or a spirit that needs to be recognized and respected. Quoting Ronald J. Hustedde (1998:155), they suggest that soulful practices incorporated into community development projects help "respect the diversity of the peoples we serve." They add that "soul can make sense out of paradox" (Hustedde 1998:160), which is so often a confounding factor in community. Basic to this idea are the foundational nature of human relationships and their power to sustain community in the face of challenge and change.

The work of anthropology—theories, methods, and practices—is valuable for understanding and implementing faith-based efforts in community development. In addition, involvement in such efforts holds a value for anthropologists. To those who are open to the possibility, such engagement offers opportunities for self-transformation and disciplinary development. Kemper and Adkins argue that community change is not merely a material matter, but also spiritual. If anthropologists and students of anthropology are to be agents of change, they must understand that establishing relationships and building local bases of political and economic power will be worthless if they do not also engage the community spiritually. Ultimately, effective community development "depends on being in communion, being together with others who see the world as it is and share a vision of and commitment to the world as it should be."

Robert V. Kemper and Julie Adkins: We became involved in this project through the back door. Kemper and Stanley Hyland, friends of long standing, happened to encounter each other at the book exhibit at the 2001 AAA meetings. Standing amid the crowds of book buyers, Hyland told Kemper about the SfAA session in Mérida and the goal of assembling those papers into a book to be published with the SAR Press. After hearing about the various chapters, Kemper asked, "And what about 'faith-based' community development?" This led to an invitation to participate in the book project—pending agreement with the other authors (who would be gathering at the SfAA meeting in spring 2002). Soon after the SfAA gathering, Hyland informed Kemper of the group's enthusiastic response to the idea of including faith-based community development in the book—and added that a draft of the chapter was needed within sixty days!

Immediately, Kemper began working on the chapter with his colleague, Julie Adkins, a Presbyterian minister who was just beginning her studies in the SMU anthropology doctoral program. Our work together on the chapter stimulated further work on faith-based organizations, part of which was reported in a paper read at the SfAA meeting in Portland in spring 2003 and more of which was reported in papers contributed to a session we co-organized at the spring 2004 SfAA meeting in Dallas.

In early fall 2002, Kemper posted the chapter on the website for his course "Culture and Diversity in American Life." During the academic year 2002–2003, the nearly one hundred students enrolled in that course read the chapter. In addition, several people at other colleges and universities contacted Kemper to ask permission to cite the paper in their own work, involving bachelor's theses and doctoral dissertations.

In sum, the opportunity to bring the theme of faith-based community development into this community-building book has had important spinoffs in our research, in our teaching, and in the work of others elsewhere. This proves once again the importance of the casual conversations we have, standing around at the book exhibit at AAA meetings.

CHAPTER 5 SUMMARY AND REFLECTIONS

Community building in the twenty-first century requires access to information. Computer mapping and technology is critical not only to multinational corporations and the global city but also to inner-city residents. Helping them to bridge the digital divide has become a complex, integral part of community building and development, calling for multiple, simultaneous strategies.

Hyland and Owens promote certain methods that enhance the effectiveness of technology and community building in targeted areas. They state that it is essential for the community-building process that anthropologists keep assembling this vast array of methods. For anthropologists, their ability to be effective agents of change, to move beyond description into action and to strengthen community capacity, is the challenge. Primarily at stake is the future training of engaged scholars and practioners, specifically in preparing computerized data systems, collaborative approaches, engaged scholarship, and policy-oriented publications. Hyland and Owens maintain that the discipline of anthropology in the twenty-first century must produce students capable of community building, not just community development.

Stanley E. Hyland and Michelle Owens: Working on this book with the other contributors has definitely affected our approach to community-building projects in two very specific areas—the importance of engaged scholarship to the future of the social sciences and the challenges of teaching anthropology to the next generation of scholars and practitioners in community building. Concerning engaged scholarship, it is increasingly evident from the variety of exciting research agendas presented by the contributors that each community member (however defined) must engage in the conceptualization, design, and execution of research. Each contributor makes a case that, as part of research and analysis, engagement means making a sustained commitment to the community, maintaining trusting relationships, and pursuing dependable resources. It is not enough anymore to set up and observe; intervention, facilitation, and engagement are the new mandate. Not only do we need to bring all the pieces to the table, but we also need to help assemble them. They do not just come together and fall into place.

Hyland's newest project, designing an urban kiosk for inner-city youth, has very much been affected by the perspectives presented in this book. Each author, by virtue of his or her command and analysis of unique cultural contexts and community relationships, has presented questions and challenges Hyland could not see in the daily flow of his community-building research in inner-city Memphis.

Similarly, in presenting these new perspectives about community building to students in a graduate applied anthropology course, Hyland simultaneously realized that most of our teaching paradigms are restricted to traditional classroom settings. Each contributor illustrated in his or her array of case studies of community building that every partner brings something to the process—assets, issues, or baggage. An understanding of what is brought to the community-building process is part of the engaged scholarship challenge. Students and the learning process are no exception. How we educate the next generation of students to become effective scholars and practitioners in this changing world of engaged scholarship needs to be rethought along the lines of Schensul's chapter 8. It is one thing to train students in the classroom, using principles of community building and case studies, but it is quite another to engage them meaningfully in the various settings described by the authors of this book. In responding to students and their issues, we need to revisit service learning courses, study abroad programs, and internships/practica in the context of engaged scholarship. We need to be thoughtful and deliberate in developing curricula and internship opportunities that value the student as a community-building partner, as much as the principles and skills of community building.

CHAPTER 6 SUMMARY AND REFLECTIONS

Baba challenges us to envision community building beyond the traditional concepts based on social and physical characteristics of community. By describing a virtual work community, Baba enables anthropologists to look more closely at the "processes of building human relationships through which people work and live," to find the ways in which community can grow out of "shared experience in a common environment, but not necessarily a common physical environment." The results of her case study on a global, corporate, virtual work community provide new insight into the role of global organizations in society. Baba states that the global corporation, because it is the workplace of the future, with implications not yet understood, warrants future anthropological investigation. Furthermore, anthropologists must re-examine traditional ways of looking at global corporations. To be fair, global corporations must be discerned as a resource, not just a risk. Baba makes the case that, with facilitation, global corporations can provide a "globally relevant framework of meaning" that supercedes competing local meanings, which divide people, create conflict, and prevent cooperation. Part and parcel of this context is the role of technology. It behooves twenty-first-century community builders to recognize how the use of technology can support collaborative work.

Marietta L. Baba: Participation in this experience broadened my thinking about the role of corporations in building communities around the globe. In North America, as in other parts of the world, corporations often have been viewed as forces of industrialization that bring destruction to traditional communities. They have been portrayed in a negative light by some in our discipline. Witnessing the struggles of my informants to build a virtual community within a corporate setting, however, gave me quite a different vantage point. In this context, the corporation provided some of the most important resources for community building, without which the individuals would not have been able to connect with one another. I speak not only of hard assets such as technology but also of motivational forces that encourage people to work collaboratively with people who are not like them. Plainly, this motivating force derived from the corporation's search for foreign markets. Whether or not we ourselves may celebrate this motive, we should recognize that it is a new kind of community-building force. And it is one that my informants were eager to embrace, once they had transcended the destructive force of localized culture and its tendency toward factional strife. Indeed, the more traditional community forces in this saga were not the ones to applaud. This is an emerging social reality that, I believe, increasingly will influence anthropological theory and practice in the decades ahead.

CHAPTER 7 SUMMARY AND REFLECTIONS

Chrisman narrows his focus on community-building activities to those related to community health, an integral part of any community's well-being and growth. Lifestyle diseases and other public-health problems, such as alcohol and drug addiction and substandard housing, are significant issues in most aspects of community work. In addition, because new views of public health are being introduced, anthropologists have more opportunities than before to engage in community building in multiethnic settings. Anthropologists, given their theory and methodology background, are poised to impact public health. They already understand the importance of cultural competence when working with diverse communities. As part of community building in the twenty-first century, Chrisman recommends that future anthropologists introduce better cultural knowledge to public and community health workers; facilitate partnerships, coalitions, and other system-level approaches required to address the various social determinants of health; and expand leadership to organize diversity into collaboratives dealing with health issues. Anthropologists need to assist in the balancing of "both population health needs and community assets so that communities can be mobilized to work on their own projects and to empower themselves to an end of community competence."

Noel J. Chrisman: Like many, if not most, applied anthropologists, I do not work in an anthropology department. Thus, mine is a lonely business. For more than thirty years, my applied work has been in a health science center, with bright and engaged colleagues committed to the use of research to enhance practice. I have fit in well, bringing the strengths of anthropology to bear on their issues and the health of the public. But, except for anthropology meetings and journals, anthropological colleagues are largely missing. It was in this context that I began my community-building work in the mid-1980s. My solid foundation was the history and principles of applied anthropology as I had learned them. Although my work was contributing to nursing and to public health, I did not have a sense of its position in anthropology.

This was much the same situation that Thomas Maretzki and I (1982) wrote about when we edited Clinically Applied Anthropology.

The School of American Research experience re-established my personal and intellectual links with other applied anthropologists. I was astounded and delighted to learn that others, who interact with different topics and problems, had moved in the same directions. Action and involved leadership over time are key ideas. The development of community-based participatory research in public health has been facilitated by anthropological thought and research. Now I understand that there are parallel developments elsewhere. This is an important understanding. Not only does it make my life less lonely, but it also allows me to see how my work contributes to anthropology, as well as to the health sciences.

CHAPTER 8 SUMMARY AND REFLECTIONS

Schensul promotes anthropologists' use of research partnerships to support community-building strategies. The value of partnership research and partnership principles is that they form "the basis for identifying local ways of conceptualizing and defining problems, needs, and resources." They clarify "local ecological knowledge and local theory," giving residents the ability to speak from their own knowledge base. For Schensul, community building is about confronting inequalities, and the role of anthropologists is to engage in community strengthening or the attenuation of these inequalities. When anthropologists engage in research collaboratives, they are addressing persistent structural inequalities; more effectively using science technology as a tool for advocacy, mobilization, and organization; and building social capital. By developing organizations such as ICR, anthropologists can also draw on interdisciplinary knowledge and experiences, better equipping and situating them to address three important issues in building and rebuilding community:

- to preserve and/or promote relationships, as well as the cultural and material infrastructure that give community meaning;

- to assist communities in the negotiation of sociopolitical changes so that they not only understand the changes but also can engage the process to put forth their own interests;

- to generate and use information and technology in ways that keep communities globally informed and connected.

Schensul also challenges anthropology curricula to prepare students for engaging in these partnerships, by including research, community organization, networking for resource development, and group facilitation as part of its content. Furthermore, she adds, anthropologists need to address the many ethical issues that arise out of the necessity to act immediately, specifically with respect to discovery, analysis, and interpretation of inequalities, discrimination, stigmatization, and marginalization in any form.

Jean J. Schensul: The concept of community building as we have discussed it throughout the life of our book project forces us to address the meaning of *community* in a globalized world. It also calls upon us to consider the multiple and sometimes conflicting ways in which social scientists and other constituencies define community. Which communities an anthropologist or other social scientist chooses to associate with, and the reasons for these choices, will depend on personal values, group dynamics, political contingencies and convictions, and economic assets and constraints. Choice is also directly relevant to our selection of the community processes we study and the communities in which we intervene and to the way we define our interventions.

Despite our preference for local, anthropologists can no longer imagine communities in isolation from the broader social, political, and economic influences that shape current conditions. These influences all too often serve to diminish or even to obliterate community identity, history, interaction, and meaning. Even in the worst-case scenario, however, people are resilient, somehow managing to reconstruct and renew their identity and place. They have agency. For this reason, *community building* continues to strike me as a somewhat arrogant term. I still prefer the term *community strengthening*, especially because we, as social scientists, generally work with existing communities or with community constituencies where we do not have indigenous membership. Our role involves deepening the dialogue that decides which cultural, political, economic, spatial, symbolic, ritual, and relational elements to retain, reduce, enhance, replace, or change altogether in a transformational process that enhances community agency. Is this old wine in a new bottle? Research and community strengthening are an uneasy marriage. Working on this project has enabled me to come to terms with the challenges and contradictions that emerge when using research as a strategy for community strengthening, which is the mission of the Institute for Community Research, a community-based research organization.

IMPLICATIONS FOR ENGAGED SCHOLARSHIP AND COMMUNITY BUILDING

The conceptual framework underlying this project questions conventional assumptions about the training and education of future generations of applied social scientists who intend to conduct research and serve as practitioners in the domain of community building. First, these chapters suggest a reconsideration of appropriate and necessary roles and strategies for researchers and practitioners working in community building. No longer is it sufficient to enter a community setting, bring our expertise to bear on its problems, and then leave after attempting to resolve some of those problems. Rather, we must engage affected community members and academic personnel in the identification of research questions, variable definitions, and data interpretation over an extended period of time. In short, we must establish and maintain relationships with members of the community. Thus, we are transformed into truly engaged scholars and practitioners.

This understanding of the role of applied social scientists in community building fits well within the national movement toward developing meaningful, reciprocal, and profitable connections between universities and communities. Typically referred to as "engaged scholarship," such work builds upon disciplinary theoretical frameworks, addresses questions inspired by practical needs, employs suitable methodologies, and results in practical outcomes. Essentially, such scholarship in building communities is based on both an intellectual and public purpose.

In this sense, our venture into community building is a good fit between the School of American Research's initiative on contemporary issues and the Society for Applied Anthropology's mission and objectives. In 1999 SAR President Douglas Schwartz took the position that "the School has a responsibility to use some of its resources to help identify those major problems of national and global significance that define our times" (SAR website, http://www.sarweb.org/Contem poraryIssues/ProgramDescription). Therefore, we undertook this project. Similarly, the SfAA mission statement states, "The Society has for its object the promotion of interdisciplinary scientific investigation of the principles controlling the relations of human beings to one another, and the encouragement of the wide application of these principles to practical problems."

Ultimately, through the discussions in this book, we have arrived at three critical issues for the future interaction of the applied social scientist in community-building endeavors: (1) legitimate knowledge is produced not only in the academy but also in the experiences and interpretations of those directly implicated in the research topic; (2) the identification of assets and existing resources in the community is a critical starting point for research but must be linked to a consideration of the various political, economic, and cultural factors that are divisive in all the processes that operate in building and sustaining community; and (3) building upon those resources, the establishment and preservation of relationships between the community and the engaged scholar will generate new roles, methods, theory, and social capacity essential for the community's sustainability in an ever-changing world system. Scholars and practitioners positioned to address these three critical issues will shape the definition of engaged scholarship for the next generation. As we look to a future of increased competition for scarce resources, ethnocentrism, and global structural inequalities, the growing knowledge base on community building can inform and chart new paths for conflict resolution.

References

Ahlstrom, S. E.

1975   *A Religious History of the American People.* 2 vols. Garden City, NY: Image Books.

AIDS Community Research Group

1988   AIDS: Knowledge, Attitudes and Behavior in an Ethnically Mixed Urban Neighborhood. Hartford, CT: Institute for Community Research, Hispanic Health Council, Urban League of Greater Hartford, Hartford Health Department.

Alaedini, P., and P. J. Marcotullio

2002   Urban Implications of Information Technology/New Electronics for Developing Countries. *Journal of Urban Technology* 9(3):89–108.

Alinsky, S. D.

1946   *Reveille for Radicals.* Chicago: University of Chicago Press.

1971   *Rules for Radicals: A Practical Primer for Realistic Radicals.* New York: Vintage.

Al-Kodmany, K.

2001   *Online Tools for Participation.* Chicago: University of Illinois at Chicago.

Allen, T.

1977   *Managing the Flow of Technology.* Cambridge, MA: MIT Press.

Alperson, P., ed.

2002   *Diversity and Community: An Interdisciplinary Reader.* Malden, MA: Blackwell Publishing.

Altman, D. G.

1986   A Framework for Evaluating Community-Based Heart Disease Programs. *Social Science & Medicine* 22(4):479–487

Altman, I., and S. Low

1992   Place Attachment. *Human Behavior and Environment, Volume 8: Advances in Theory and Research.* New York: Plenum.

Amin, A., and N. Thrift

1997   Globalization, Socio-Economics, Territoriality. In *Geographies of Economies,* edited by R. Lee and J. Wills, pp. 147–157. London: Arnold.

REFERENCES

Amit, V.

2002   Reconceptualizing Community. In *Realizing Community: Concepts, Social Relationships and Sentiments,* edited by V. Amit, pp. 1–20. London: Routledge.

Ammerman, N. T., J. W. Carroll, C. S. Dudley, and W. McKinney

1998   *Studying Congregations: A New Handbook.* Nashville, TN: Abingdon Press.

Anderson, N. B.

1998   Levels of Analysis in Health Science. A Framework for Integrating Sociobehavioral and Biomedical Research. *Annals of the New York Academy of Science* 840(May 1):563–576.

Ansley, F., and J. Gaventa

1997   Researching for Democracy and Democratizing Research. *Change* 29(1):46–53.

Arcury, T. A., C. K. Austin, S. A. Quandt, and R. Saavedra

1999   Enhancing Community Participation in Intervention Research: Farm Workers and Agricultural Chemicals in North Carolina. *Health Education and Behavior* 26(4):563–578.

Arcury, T. A., S. A. Quandt, and L. McCauley

2000   Farmworkers and Pesticides: Community-Based Research. *Environmental Health Perspectives* 108(8):787–792.

Arensberg, C. M.

1954   The Community Study Method. *American Journal of Sociology* 60(2):109–124.

1961   The Community As Object and As Sample. *American Anthropologist* 63:241–64.

Arensberg, C. M., and S. T. Kimball

1965   *Culture and Community.* New York: Harcourt, Brace and World.

Baba, M. L.

1988   Two Sides to Every Story: An Ethnohistorical Approach to Organizational Partnerships. *City and Society* 2(20):71–104.

1990   Local Knowledge Systems in Advanced Technology Organizations. In *Organizational Issues in High Technology Management,* edited by L. Gomez-Mejia and M. Lawless, pp. 57–76. Greenwich, CT: JAI Press.

1998a   The Anthropology of Work in the Fortune 1000: A Critical Retrospective. *Anthropology of Work Review* XVIII(4):17–28.

1998b   Anthropologists in Corporate America: Knowledge Management and Ethical Angst. *Chronicle of Higher Education* XLIV(35):B4–B5.

1999   Dangerous Liaisons: Trust, Distrust and Information Technology in American Work Organizations. *Human Organization* 58(3):331–346.

2001   The Globally Distributed Team: Learning to Work in New Ways, for Corporations and Anthropologists Alike. *Practicing Anthropology* 23(4):2–8.

Baba, M. L., J. Gluesing, H. Ratner, and K. Harris Wager
2004   The Contexts of Knowing: Natural History of a Globally Distributed Team. *Journal of Organizational Behavior* 25:1–41.

Baba, M. L., and H. Ratner
2003   Equipos Virtuales Globales: La Ecologia de Desarrollo. In *Nuevas Tecnologias y Cultura*, edited by C. Bueno and M. J. Santos, pp. 149–181. Madrid: Universidad Iberoamerican.

Baker, E. A., and C. A. Brownson
1998   Defining Characteristics of Community-Based Health Promotion Programs. *Journal of Public Health Management and Practice* 4(2):1–9.

Ball, N., and S. Barnes
2000   Mozambique. In *Good Intentions: Pledges of Aid for Postconflict Recovery*, edited by S. Forman and S. Patrick, pp. 159–203. Boulder, CO: Lynne Reinner Publishers.

Banfield, E. C., and L. F. Banfield
1958   *The Moral Basis of a Backward Community.* New York: Free Press.

Barger, K., and E. Reza
1989   Policy and Community-Action Research. In *Making Our Research Useful: Case Studies in the Utilization of Anthropological Knowledge*, edited by J. van Willigen, B. Rylko-Bauer, and A. McElroy, pp. 257–283. Boulder, CO: Westview Press.

Barnsley, J., and D. Ellis
1992   *Research for Change: Participatory Action Research for Community Groups.* Vancouver: The Women's Research Centre.

Bartkowski, J. P., and H. A. Regis
2003   *Charitable Choices: Religion, Race, and Poverty in the Post-Welfare Era.* New York: New York University Press.

Basso, K.
1988   Speaking with Names: Language and Landscape among the Western Apache. *Cultural Anthropology* 3(2):99–130.

Bebbington, D. H., and A. Gomez
2000   Rebuilding Social Capital in Post-Conflict Regions: Women's Village Banking in Ayacucho, Peru and Highland Guatemala. Paper presented at the 2000 Meeting of the Latin American Studies Association, Miami.

Becker, P. E.
1999   *Congregations in Conflict: Cultural Models of Local Religious Life.* New York: Cambridge University Press.

Bell, C., and H. Newby
1971   *Community Studies: An Introduction to the Sociology of the Local Community.* New York: Praeger.

REFERENCES

Bellah, R. N., R. Madsen, W. M. Sullivan, A. Swindler, and S. M. Tipton

1985   *Habits of the Heart: Individualism and Commitment in American Life.* New York: Harper and Row.

Berg, M.

2001a   Are Schools Ready for Children? Paper presented at the Annual Meeting of the American Anthropological Association, Washington, DC.

2001b   Empowering Residents as Partners in Research and Building Capacity of Researchers to Do It. Workshop conducted at the Annie E. Casey Foundation, Local Learning Partners Conference, Baltimore, MD.

Berg, M. J., and J. J. Schensul, eds.

2004   Approaches to Conducting Action Research with Youth. Special issue of *Practicing Anthropology* 26(2).

Bernard, H. R.

1995   *Research Methods in Anthropology: Qualitative and Quantitative Approaches.* Walnut Creek, CA: AltaMira Press.

Biddle, W., and L. Biddle

1965   *The Community Development Process: The Rediscovery of Local Initiative.* New York: Holt, Rinehart and Winston.

Black, J.

1999a   Losing Ground Bit by Bit. BBC News Online. Electronic document, http://news.bbc.co.uk//hi/special_report/1999/10/99information_rich_information_poor/47262.stm (accessed January 25, 2000).

1999b   Plugging in to the Revolution. BBC News Online. Electronic document, http://news/bbc.co.uk/1/hi/special_report/1999/10/99information_rich_information_poor/467899.stm (accessed January 25, 2000).

Bott, E.

1957   *Family and Social Network; Roles, Norms, and External Relationships in Ordinary Urban Families.* London: Tavistock.

Bragg, W. G.

1984   Beyond Development to Transformation. *International Review of Mission* 73(290):153–165.

Brannen, M. Y., J. K. Liker, and W. M. Fruin

1999   Recontextualization and Factory-to-Factory Knowledge Transfer from Japan to the United States. In *Remade in America: Transplanting and Transforming Japanese Management Systems,* edited by J. K. Liker, W. M. Fruin, and P. S. Adler, pp. 117–153. Oxford: Oxford University Press.

Briggs, X., and E. Mueller

1997   *From Neighborhood to Community.* Community Development Research Center. New York: New School for Social Research.

Brokensha, D., and P. Hodge

1969   *Community Development: An Interpretation.* San Francisco: Chandler.

Bronfenbrenner, U.

1986   Recent Advances in Research on the Ecology of Human Development. In *Development as Action in Context: Problem Behavior and Normal Youth Development,* edited by R. K. Silbereisen, K. Eyferth, and G. Rudinger, pp. 286–309. New York: Springer-Verlag.

1989   The Ecology of the Family as a Context for Human Development: Research Perspectives. *Developmental Psychology* 22(6):723–742.

Bronfenbrenner, U., and P. A. Morris

1998   Theoretical Models of Human Development. In *Handbook of Child Psychology,* 5th ed., edited by W. Damon. Vol. I, edited by R. M. Lerner, pp. 993–1028. New York: Wiley and Sons.

Brown, J. S., and P. Duguid

1991   Organizational Learning and Communities-of-Practice: Toward a Unified View of Working, Learning and Innovation. *Organization Science* 2(1):40–57.

Brown, L. D., and R. Tandon

1983   Ideology and Political Economy in Inquiry: Action Research and Participatory Research. *Journal of Applied Behavioral Science* 19(3):277–294.

Brown, S. L., ed.

2002   *Intentional Community: An Anthropological Perspective.* Albany: State University of New York Press.

Brydon-Miller, M.

1997   Participatory Action Research: Psychology and Social Change. *Journal of Social Issues* 53(4):657–666.

Bunker, R., and J. Adair

1959   *The First Look at Strangers.* New Brunswick, NJ: Rutgers University Press.

Carle, R. D.

1997a   Introduction to *Signs of Hope in the City: Ministries of Community Renewal,* edited by R. D. Carle and L. A. DeCaro Jr., pp. 1–9. Valley Forge, PA: Judson Press.

1997b   Seeking the Shalom of the City: New York City Missions in Historical Perspective. In *Signs of Hope in the City: Ministries of Community Renewal,* edited by R. D. Carle and L. A. DeCaro, pp. 11–28. Valley Forge, PA: Judson Press.

Caro, F. D.

1991   Cultural Conservation: The Conference. *Journal of American Folklore* 104(411):85–92.

Castelli, J., and J. McCarthy

1997   Religion-Sponsored Social Service Providers: The Not-So-Independent Sector. Unpublished manuscript, Aspen Institute Nonprofit Sector Research Fund.

Castells, M.

2000   *The Rise of the Network Society.* Malden, MA: Blackwell.

Cavan, S.

1972   *Hippies of the Haight.* St. Louis, MO: New Critics Press.

Center for AIDS Prevention Studies (CAPS)

2001   *Working Together: A Guide to Collaborative Research in Prevention.* San Francisco: AIDS Research Institute, University of California San Francisco.

CDC Urban Research Centers for Applied Research in Public Health

1998   *Public/Private Partnerships: Fact Book.* Atlanta, GA: Centers for Disease Control and Prevention (CDC).

Cernea, M. M.

1997   The Risks and Reconstruction Model for Resettling Displaced Populations. *World Development* 25(10):1569–1588.

Cernea, M. M., and C. McDowell

2000   *Risk and Reconstruction: Experiences of Settlers and Refugees.* Washington, DC: The World Bank.

Chambers, R., A. Pacey, and L. A. Thrupp

1989   *Farmer First: Innovation and Agricultural Research.* London: Intermedia Technology Publications.

Chaskin, R. J., P. Brown, S. Venkatesh, and A. Vidal

2001   *Building Community Capacity.* New York: Aldine de Gruyter.

Chaves, M., M. E. Konieczny, K. Beyerlein, and E. Barman

1999   National Congregations Study: Background, Methods, and Selected Results. *Journal for the Scientific Study of Religion* 38(4):458–476.

Checker, M.

2004   Treading Murky Waters: Day-to-Day Dilemmas in the Construction of a Pluralistic US Environmental Movement. In *Local Actions: Cultural Activism, Power, and Public Life in America,* edited by M. Checker and M. Fishman, pp. 27–50. New York: Columbia University Press.

Chidambaram, L., and R. P. Bostorm

1996   Group Development (I): A Review and Synthesis of Development Models. *Group Decision and Negotiation* 6(2):159–187.

Chrisman, N. J.

2000   Yes, It's Fun, but Do You Have a Future? Paper presented in the Applied Anthropology in Clinical Settings session, Annual Meeting of the Society for Applied Anthropology, San Francisco.

Chrisman, N. J., and T. W. Maretzki, eds.

1982   *Clinically Applied Anthropology*. Dordrecht, The Netherlands: D. Reidel
        Publishers.

Chrisman, N. J., and P. R. Schultz

1997   Transforming Health Care through Cultural Competence Training. In
        Cultural Diversity in Nursing: Issues, Strategies, and Outcomes, edited by
        J. A. Dienemann, pp. 70–79. Washington, DC: American Academy of
        Nursing.

Chrisman, N. J., K. Senturia, G. Tang, and B. Gheisar

2002   Qualitative Process Evaluation of Urban Community Work: A Preliminary
        View. *Health Education and Behavior* 29(2):232–248.

Chrisman, N. J., C. J. Strickland, K. Powell, M. D. Squeochs, and M. Yallup

1999   Community Partnership Research with the Yakama Indian Nation. *Human
        Organization* 58(2):134–141.

Cnaan, R. A., with S. C. Boddie, F. Handy, C. Yancey, and R. Schneider

2002   *The Invisible Caring Hand: American Congregations and the Provision of Welfare*.
        New York: New York University.

Cnaan, R. A., with R. J. Wineburg and S. C. Boddie

1999   *The Newer Deal: Social Work and Religion in Partnership*. New York: Columbia
        University Press.

Cohen, A.

1985   *The Symbolic Construction of Community*. New York: Tavisock Publications.

Coleman, E. G.

2000   High-Tech Guilds in the Era of Global Capital. Paper presented at the
        99th Annual Meeting of the American Anthropological Association, San
        Francisco.

Colson, E.

1971   *The Social Consequences of Resettlement*. Manchester: Manchester University
        Press.

Commission on Religion in Appalachia (CORA)

2004   Website, http://www.geocities.com/appalcora.

COMMIT Research Group

1995a   Community Intervention Trial for Smoking Cessation: I. *American Journal
        of Public Health* 85(3):183–192.

1995b   Community Intervention Trial for Smoking Cessation: II. *American Journal
        of Public Health* 85(3):193–200.

Cook, S. R., and B. Taylor, eds.

2001   Academics, Activism and Place-Based Education in the Appalachian Coal
        Belt. *Practicing Anthropology* 21(2):1–32.

REFERENCES

Cortés, E. Jr.
1993   Reweaving the Fabric: The Iron Rule and the IAF Strategy for Power and Politics. In *Interwoven Destinies: Cities and the Nation*, edited by H. G. Cisneros, pp. 294–319. New York: W.W. Norton and Company.
1996   Community Organization and Social Capital. *National Civic Review* 85(Fall):49–53.

Cowley, S., and J. R. Billings
1999   Resources Revisited: Salutogenesis from a Lay Perspective. *Journal of Advanced Nursing* 29(4):994–1004.

Cox, D., S. E. Hyland, V. Spearman, and C. Sadler
2004   Outcomes, Community Capacity Building and Partnership Growth: The Etiology of a Successful COCP Final Report. US Department of Housing and Urban Development, Washington, DC.

Cramton, C. D.
2001   The Mutual Knowledge Problem and Its Consequences for Dispersed Collaboration. *Organization Science* 12(3):346–371.

Cromley, E. K.
1999   Mapping Spatial Data. Vol. 4 of *Mapping Social Networks, Spatial Data, and Hidden Populations. Ethnographer's Toolkit*, edited by J. J. Schensul, M. D. Le Compte, R. T. Trotter II, E. K. Cromley, and M. Singer, pp. 51–124. Walnut Creek, CA: AltaMira Press.

Darley, J., and E. Berscheid
1967   Increased Liking as a Result of the Anticipation of Personal Contact. *Human Relations* 20:29–39.

Davenport, T. H., and L. Prusak
1998   *Working Knowledge: How Organizations Manage What They Know*. Boston: Harvard Business School Press.

Day, K.
2001   Putting It Together in the African American Churches: Faith, Economic Development, and Civil Rights. In *Religion and Social Policy*, edited by P. D. Nesbitt, pp. 181–195. Walnut Creek, CA: AltaMira Press.

Denner, J., D. Kirby, K. Coyle, and C. Brindis
2001   The Protective Role of Social Capital and Cultural Norms in Latino Communities: A Study of Adolescent Births. *Hispanic Journal of Behavioral Sciences* 23(1):3–21.

Dickens, P.
1998   *Global Shift: Transforming the World Economy*. 3rd ed. London: Paul Chapman.

Dirks, R.
1980   Social Responses during Severe Food Shortages and Famine. *Current Anthropology* 21(1):21–44.

Dollard, J.

1937   *Caste and Class in a Southern Town.* New Haven, CT: Yale University Press.

Dunham, A.

1963   Some Principles of Community Development. *International Review of Community Development* 11:141–151.

Durkheim, E.

1951   *Suicide.* Translated by J. A. Spaulding, and G. Simpson. Glencoe, IL: Free
[1897] Press.

Dushay, R. A., M. Singer, M. R. Weeks, L. Rohena, and R. Gruber

2001   Lowering HIV Risk among Ethnic Minority Drug Users: Comparing Culturally Targeted Intervention to a Standard Intervention. *American Journal of Drug and Alcohol Abuse* 27(3):501–524.

Dyer, C.

2002   Punctuated Entropy as Culture-Induced Change: The Case of the Exxon-Valdez Oil Spill. In *Catastrophe and Culture: The Anthropology of Disaster,* edited by S. Hoffman and A. Oliver-Smith, pp. 159–186. Santa Fe, NM: SAR Press.

Edelman, M.

2001   Social Movements: Changing Paradigms and Forms of Politics. Vol. 30 of *Annual Review Anthropology,* edited by B. J. Siegel, pp. 285–317. Stanford, CA: Stanford University Press.

Eisinger, A., and K. Senturia

2001   Doing Community-Driven Research: A Description of Seattle Partners for Healthy Communities. *Journal of Urban Health* 78(3):519–534.

Eng, E., and E. Parker

1994   Measuring Community Competence in the Mississippi Delta: The Interface between Program Evaluation and Empowerment. *Health Education Quarterly* 21(1):199–230.

Erben, R., P. Franzkowiak, and E. Wenzel

2000   People Empowerment versus Social Capital: From Health Promotion to Social Marketing. *Health Promotion Journal of Australia* 9(3):179–182.

Escobar, A.

1995   *Encountering Development: The Making and Unmaking of the Third World.* Princeton, NJ: Princeton University Press.

2000   Culture Sits in Places: Reflections on Globalism and Subaltern Strategies of Localization. *Political Geography* 20(2):139–174.

Etzioni, A.

1993   *The Spirit of Community: The Reinvention of American Society.* New York: Simon and Schuster.

References

Evans, R. G., and G. L. Stoddart

1990   Producing Health, Consuming Health Care. *Social Science and Medicine* 31(12):1347–1363.

Farney, D.

1989   River of Despair, Along the Rich Banks of the Mississippi Live the Poorest of US Poor. *Wall Street Journal*, 13 October: A1, A16.

Ferguson, R. F., and W. T. Dickens, eds.

1999   *Urban Problems and Community Development.* Washington, DC: Brookings Institution Press.

Festinger, L., S. Schacter, and K. Back

1950   *Social Pressures in Informal Groups.* New York: Harper.

Finks, P. D.

1984   *The Radical Vision of Saul Alinsky.* New York: Paulist Press.

Firth, R.

1959   *Social Change in Tikopia: Restudy of a Polynesian Community after a Generation.* London: Allen and Unwin.

Flaskerud, J. H., and A. M. Nyamathi

2002   New Paradigm for Health Disparities Needed. *Nursing Research* 51(3):139.

Flint, C.

2003   Political Geography: Context and Agency in a Multiscalar Framework. *Progress in Human Geography* 27(5):627–636.

Foley, M. W., J. D. McCarthy, and M. Chaves

2001   Social Capital, Religious Institutions and Poor Communities. In *Social Capital in Poor Communities*, edited by M. R. Warren, S. Saegert, and P. Thompson, pp. 215–245. New York: Russell Sage Foundation.

Fortmann, S. P., and A. M. Varady

2000   Effects of a Communitywide Health Education Program on Cardiovascular Disease Morbidity and Mortality: The Stanford Five-City Project. *American Journal of Epidemiology* 152(4):316–323.

Foster, G.

1962   *Traditional Cultures and the Impact of Technological Change.* New York: Harper and Row.

Foster, G., and R. V. Kemper

1996   Anthropological Fieldwork in Cities. In *Urban Life*, edited by G. Gmelch and W. P. Zenner, pp. 135-150. Prospect Heights, IL: Waveland Press, Inc.

Foucault, M.

1982   Truth, Power, Self. In *Technologies of the Self: A Seminar with Michel Foucault*, edited by L. H. Martin, H. Gutman, and H. Hutton, pp. 9–15. London: Tavistock.

Frank, J. W.

1995   The Determinants of Health: A New Synthesis. *Current Issues in Public Health* 1:233–240.

Franklin, R. M.

1996   "My Soul Says Yes": The Urban Ministry of the Church of God in Christ. In *Churches, Cities, and Human Community: Urban Ministry in the United States 1945–1985*, edited by C. J. Green, pp. 77–96. Grand Rapids, MI: William B. Eerdmans Publishing Company.

Freedman, S. G.

1993   *Upon This Rock: The Miracles of a Black Church.* New York: Harper Collins.

Fried, M.

1963   Grieving for a Lost Home. In *The Urban Condition: People and Policy in the Metropolis*, edited by L. Duhl, pp. 151–171. New York: Basic Books.

Gallaher, Jr., A. and H. Padfield

1980   *The Dying Community.* School of American Research Advanced Seminar Series. Albuquerque: University of New Mexico Press.

Gans, H. J.

1962a   *The Urban Villagers: Group and Class in the Life of Italian Americans.* Glencoe, IL, and New York: The Free Press.

1962b   City Planning and Urban Realities. *Commentary* 30(February):170–175.

1967   *The Levittowners.* New York: Pantheon.

Gaventa, J.

1991   Toward a Knowledge Democracy: Viewpoints on Participatory Action Research in North America. In *Action and Knowledge: Breaking the Monopoly with Participatory Action Research*, edited by O. Fals-Borda and M. A. Rahman, pp. 121–131. New York: Apex Press.

1993   The Powerful, the Powerless, and the Experts: Knowledge Struggles in an Information Age. In *Voices of Change: Participatory Research in the United States and Canada*, edited by P. Park, pp. 21–40. Westport, CT: Bergin & Garvey.

Gearing, F. O.

1960   The Strategy of the Fox Project. In *Documentary History of the Fox Project*, edited by F. Gearing, R. M. Netting, and L. Peattie, pp. 182–222. Chicago: University of Chicago, Department of Anthropology.

1970   *The Face of the Fox.* Chicago: Aldine.

Gersick, C. J. G.

1998   Time and Transition in Work Teams: Toward a New Model of Group Development. *Academy of Management* Journal 31(1):9–41.

Gibbon, M., R. Labonte, and G. Laverack

2002   Evaluating Community Capacity. *Health and Social Care in the Community* 10(6):485–491.

Gibson, C., and S. Cohen, eds.

2003   *Virtual Teams That Work: Creating Conditions for Virtual Team Effectiveness.* San Francisco: Jossey-Bass.

Giddens, A.

1990   *The Consequences of Modernity.* Cambridge: Polity Press.

2001   *The Global Third Way Debate.* Malden, MA: Blackwell.

Gluesing, J.

1995   Fragile Alliances: Negotiating Global Teaming in a Turbulent Environment. Ph.D. dissertation, Wayne State University.

1998   Building Connections and Balancing Power in Global Teams: Toward a Reconceptualization of Culture as Composite. *Anthropology of Work Review* XVIII(2/3):18–30.

Gmelch, G., and W. P. Zenner

1996   *Urban Life.* Prospect Heights, IL: Waveland Press, Inc.

Goldsmith, S.

2002   *Putting Faith in Neighborhoods: Making Cities Work through Grassroots Citizenship.* Noblesville, IN: Hudson Institute Publications.

Gonzalez, R. M.

2000   *Platforms and Terraces: Bridging Participation and GIS in Joint-Learning for Watershed Management with the Ifugaos of the Phillipines* Amsterdam: Wageningen University.

Goodenough, W.

1963   *Cooperation in Change: An Anthropological Approach to Community Development.* New York: Russell Sage Foundation.

1966   *Cooperation in Change.* New York: John Wiley & Sons, Inc.

Gough, D. M.

1995   *Christ Church, Philadelphia: The Nation's Church in a Changing City.* Philadelphia: University of Pennsylvania Press.

Green, C. J.

1996   History in the Service of the Future: Studying Urban Ministry. In *Churches, Cities, and Human Community: Urban Ministry in the United States 1945–1985,* edited by C. J. Green, pp. 1–22. Grand Rapids, MI: William B. Eerdmans Publishing Company.

Greenbaum, S.

2002   Social Capital and Deconcentration: Theoretical and Policy Paradoxes of the HOPE VI Program. *North American Dialogue* 5(1):9–12.

Greer, S.

1965   *Urban Renewal and American Cities.* Indianapolis, IN: Bobbs-Merrill.

Guan, J., and R. A. Dodder

2001   The Impact of Cross-Cultural Contact on Value and Identity: A

Comparative Study of Chinese Students in China and in the U.S.A. *Mankind Quarterly* 41(3):271–288.

Gutkind, P.

1973   Bibliography of Urban Anthropology. In *Urban Anthropology*, edited by A. Southhall, pp. 425-489. London: Oxford University Press.

Halperin, R. H.

1998   *Practicing Community*. Austin, TX: University of Texas Press.

Hannerz, U.

1969   *Soulside*. New York: Columbia University Press.

Hansen, A.

1992   Some Insights on African Refugees. In *CORI: Selected Papers on Refugee Issues*, edited by P. DeVoe, pp. 100–110. Washington, DC: American Anthropological Association.

Harding, S.

2003   Cultural Property and the Limitations of Preservation. *Law and Policy* 25(1):1074–1085.

Harvey, D.

1996   *Justice, Nature and the Geography of Difference*. Oxford: Basil Blackwell.

Hawley, W., and J. H. Svara

1972   *The Study of Community Power*. Santa Barbara, CA: ABC-Clio Publishers.

Hawley, W., and F. M. Wirt

1974   *The Search for Community Power*. Englewood Cliffs, NJ: Prentice Hall.

Healthy People 2010

2000   *Healthy People 2010*. Washington, DC: US Department of Health and Human Services.

Herlihy, P. H., and G. Knapp

2003   Maps of, by and for the Peoples of Latin America. *Human Organization* 62(4):303–314.

Higgins, D. L., and M. Metzler

2001   Implementing Community-Based Participatory Research Centers in Diverse Urban Settings. *Journal of Urban Health* 78(3):488–494.

Hill, J. R., A. Raven, and S. Han

2002   Connections in Web-Based Learning Environments: A Research-Based Model for Community Building. *Quarterly Review of Distance Education* 3(4):383–393.

Himmelgreen, D. A., N. Romero-Daza, M. Singer, M. Weeks, and M. Grier

1994   Lowering the Risk of HIV Infection among Injection Drug Users: The Hartford Needle Exchange Program. Paper presented at the 93rd Annual Meeting of the American Anthropological Association, Atlanta, GA.

References

Hinsdale, M. A., H. M. Lewis, and S. M. Waller
1995   *It Comes from the People: Community Development and Local Theology.* Philadelphia, PA: Temple University Press.

Holmberg, A.
1958   The Research and Development Approach to the Study of Change. *Human Organization* 17(1):12–16.

Hudson, W. S.
1965   *Religion in America: An Historical Account of the Development of American Religious Life.* New York: Charles Scribner's Sons.

Hunter, F.
1953   *Community Power Structure.* Chapel Hill, NC: University of North Carolina Press.

Hustedde, R. J.
1998   On the Soul of Community Development. *Journal of the Community Development Society* 29(2):153–165.

Hutton, W., and A. Giddens, eds.
2000   *Global Capitalism.* New York: New Press.

Hyland, S. E.
1998   Reflections on Maps to Success: An Anthropological Perspective. In *Community Building: A New Way of Doing Business,* edited by S. E. Hyland, pp. 86–97. Memphis, TN: Department of Anthropology, University of Memphis.
2000   Issues in Evaluating Neighborhood Change: Economic Development and Community-Building Indicators. *Cityscape* 5(1):209–217.

Hyland, S., P. Betts, R. Brimhall, T. K. Buchanan, and V. Spearman
2004   HOPE VI Evaluation of College Park Final Report. Memphis Housing Authority, Memphis, TN.

Hyland, S., and T. Collins
1991   Applied Anthropology at Memphis State University. *Practicing Anthropology* (3)13:6–8.

Hyland, S., D. Cox, and C. Martin
1998   Memphis Maps. *Metropolitan Universities* 8(4):65–74

Hyman, J. B.
2002   Exploring Social Capital and Civic Engagement to Create a Framework for Community Building. *Applied Developmental Science* 6(4):196–202.

Independent Sector
2000   America's Religious Congregations: Measuring Their Contribution to Society. Publication p. 228. Electronic document, http://www.indepen dentsector .org/programs/research/ReligiousCong.pdf (accessed March 25, 2005.

Institute of Medicine, Committee for the Study of the Future of Public Health

1988   *The Future of Public Health.* Washington, DC: National Academy Press.

International Center for Research on Women (ICRW)

2004   Program on HIV Prevention. International Center for Research on Women. Electronic document, http://www.icrw.org (accessed July 13, 2004).

International Cooperation Administration (ICA)

1955   *Community Development Review,* no. 3. Washington, DC: International Cooperation Administration.

Israel, B. A., A. J. Schulz, E. A. Parker, and A. B. Becker

1998   Review of Community-Based Research: Assessing Partnership Approaches to Improve Public Health. *Annual Review of Public Health* 19:173–202.

Jacobs, J.

1973   *Fun City: An Ethnographic Study of a Retirement Community.* New York: Holt, Rinehart and Winston, Inc.

Jacobsen, D. A.

2001   *Doing Justice: Congregations and Community Organizing.* Minneapolis, MN: Fortress Press.

Jarvenpaa, S. K., D. Knoll, and E. Leidner

1998   Is Anybody Out There? Antecedents of Trust in Global Virtual Teams. *Journal of Information Management* 14(4):29–64.

Jarvenpaa, S., and E. Leidner

1999   Communication and Trust in Global Virtual Teams. *Organization Science* 10(6):791–815.

Jing, J.

1999   Villages Dammed, Villages Repossessed: A Memorial Movement in Northwest China. *American Ethnologist* 26(2):324–343.

Johnson, S. K.

1971   *Idle Haven.* Berkeley: University of California Press.

Judson, E.

1907   The Church in Its Social Aspect. *The Annals of the American Academy of Political and Social Sciences* 30(3):429–440.

Kehrein, G.

1995   The Local Church and Christian Community Development. In *Restoring At-Risk Communities: Doing It Together and Doing It Right,* edited by J. M. Perkins, pp. 163–180. Grand Rapids, MI: Baker Books.

Keller, S.

2003   *Community: Pursuing the Dream, Living the Reality.* Princeton, NJ: Princeton University Press.

REFERENCES

Kelly, E., J. McFarlane, R. Rodriguez, and J. Fehir
1993   Community Health Organizing: Whom Are We Empowering? *Journal of
          Health Care for the Poor and Underserved* 4(4):358–362.

Key, J., and S. Barlow
1998   The Ghostwriters Project: A New Way of Looking at Inner-City
          Neighborhoods. In *Community Building: A New Way of Doing Business*, edited
          by S. E. Hyland, pp. 102–105. Memphis, TN: University of Memphis.

Kingsley, G. T., C. Coulton, M. Barndt, D. Sawicki, and P. Tatian
1997   *Mapping Your Community: Using Geographic Information to Strengthen
          Community Initiatives.* Washington, DC: US Department of Housing and
          Urban Development.

Kingsley, T., J. McNeely, and J. Gibson
1997   *Community Building Coming of Age.* Washington, DC: The Urban Institute.

Kinne, S., B. Thompson, N. J. Chrisman, and J. R. Hanley
1989   Community Organization to Enhance the Delivery of Preventive Health
          Services. *American Journal of Preventive Medicine* 5(4):225–229.

Kleinman, A., V. Das, and M. Lock, eds.
1997   *Social Suffering.* Berkeley: University of California Press.

Koenig, D.
2001   Toward Local Development and Mitigating Impoverishment in
          Development-Induced Displacement and Resettlement. Final Report
          ESCOR R7644, University of Oxford, Refugee Studies Centre.

**Kone, A., M. Sullivan, K. D. Senturia, N. J. Chrisman, S. J. Ciske, and
J. W. Krieger**
2000   Improving Collaboration between Researchers and Communities. *Public
          Health Reports* 115(2/3):243–248.

Kornblum, W.
1974   *Blue Collar Community.* Chicago: University of Chicago Press.

Kretzmann, J. P.
2001   Building Communities for the 21st Century. Paper presented at a plenary
          session at the Society for Applied Anthropology Annual Meeting, Merida,
          Mexico.

Kretzmann, J. P., and J. L. McKnight
1993   *Building Communities from the Inside Out: A Path toward Finding and
          Mobilizing a Community's Assets.* Chicago: ACTA Publications, Center for
          Urban Affairs and Policy Research, Northwestern University.

Krieger, J., C. Allen, A. Cheadle, S. Ciske, J. Schier, K. Senturia, and M. Sullivan
2002   Using Community-Based Participatory Research to Address Social
          Determinants of Health: Lessons Learned from Seattle Partners for
          Healthy Communities. *Health Education and Behavior* 29(3):361–382.

Kubisch, A., P. Auspos, P. Brown, R. Chaskint, K. Fulbright-Anderson, and R. Hamilton

2002   *Voices from the Field II: Reflections on Comprehensive Community Change.* Washington, DC: The Aspen Institute.

Kunda, G.

1992   *Engineering Culture: Control and Commitment in a High-Tech Corporation.* Philadelphia, PA: Temple University Press.

Kusterer, K. C.

1978   *Know-How on the Job: The Important Working Knowledge of "Unskilled" Workers.* Boulder, CO: Westview Press.

Labonte, R., and G. Laverack

2001 Capacity Building in Health Promotion, Part 1: For Whom? And for What Purpose? *Critical Public Health* 11(2):112–127.

Lave, J.

1991   Situated Learning in Communities of Practice. In *Perspectives on Socially Shared Cognition*, edited by L. B. Resnick, M. Levine, and S. D. Teasley, pp. 63–82. Washington, DC: American Psychological Association.

Leighton, A.

1945   *The Governing of Men: General Principles and Recommendations Based on Experiences at a Japanese Refugee Camp.* Princeton, NJ: Princeton University Press.

Lepofsky, J., and J. C. Fraser

2003   Building Community Citizens: Claiming the Right to Place Making in the City. *Urban Studies* 40(1):127–142.

Lifton, R. J.

1970   *Boundaries: Psychological Man in Revolution.* New York: Vintage Books.

Linthicum, R.

2003   *Transforming Power: Biblical Strategies for Making a Difference in Your Community.* Downers Grove, IL: InterVarsity Press.

Little, K.

1998   Science Education with or for Native Americans? An Analysis of the Native American Science Outreach Network. Ph.D. dissertation, Department of Anthropology, University of Washington, Seattle.

Livezey, L. W., ed.

2000   *Public Religion and Urban Transformation: Faith in the City.* New York: New York University.

Low, S. M.

1996   The Anthropology of Cities: Imagining and Theorizing the City. Vol. 25 of *Annual Review Anthropology*, edited by B. J. Siegel, pp. 383–409. Stanford, CA: Stanford University Press.

1999   *Theorizing the City.* New Brunswick, NJ: Rutgers University Press.

REFERENCES

Luepker, R. V., L. Rastam, P. J. Hannan, D. M. Murray, C. Gray, W. L. Baker, R. Crow, D. R. Jacobs Jr., P. L. Pirie, S. R. Mascioli, M. B. Mittelmark, and H. Blackburn
1996   Community Education for Cardiovascular Disease Prevention. Morbidity and Mortality Results from the Minnesota Heart Health Program. *American Journal of Epidemiology* 144(4):351–362.

Lyon, L.
1989   *The Community in Urban Society.* Lexington, MA: Lexington Books.

Mabe, A.
1994   Taking Care Of People through Culture: Zimbabwe's Tongogara Refugee Camp. In *CORI: Selected Papers on Refugee Issues III*, edited by J. L. MacDonald and A. Zaharlick, pp.78–97. Washington, DC: American Anthropological Association.

Macias, J. M., and G. Calderon Aragon
1994   *Desastre en Guadalajara: Notas Preliminares y Testimonios.* Mexico: Centro de Investigaciones y Estudios Superiores en Antropologia Social (CIESAS).

Macionis, J. J., and V. Parrillo
2003   *Cities and Urban Life.* Upper Saddle River, NJ: Prentice Hall, Inc.

Malinowski, B.
1944   *A Scientific Theory of Culture.* Chapel Hill: University of North Carolina Press.
1945   *The Dynamics of Culture Change: An Inquiry into Race Relations in Africa.* New Haven, CT: Yale University Press.

Malkki, L. H.
1992   National Geographic: Rooting of Peoples and the Territorialization of National Identity among Scholars and Refugees. *Cultural Anthropology* 7(1):24–44.

Mangin, W.
1970   *Peasants in Cities.* Boston: Houghton Mifflin

Marmot, M., and R. G. Wilkinson
1999   *Social Determinants of Health.* New York: Oxford University Press.

Marris, P.
1975   *Loss and Change.* New York: Anchor Books.

Mattessich, P., and B. Monsey
1997   *Community Building: What Makes It Work.* Saint Paul, MN: Amherst H. Wilder Foundation.

Mauro, T.
2002   Helping Organizations Build Community. *Training and Development* 56(2):52–58.

May, R. H. Jr.

1985   The Church and Latin American Community Development. *The Chicago Theological Seminary Register* 75(1):1–11.

Mayfield, L., and M. Hellwig

1999   The Chicago Response to Urban Problems—Building University-Community Collaborations. *American Behavioral Scientist* 42(5):863–875.

Maynard, K. A.

1997   Rebuilding Community: Psychosocial Healing, Reintegration, and Reconciliation at the Grassroots Level. In *Rebuilding Societies after Civil War*, edited by K. Kumar, pp. 203–226. Boulder, CO: Lynne Rienner Publishers.

Maznevski, M. L., and K. M. Chudoba

2000   Bridging Space over Time: Global Virtual Team Dynamics and Effectiveness. *Organization Science* 11(5):473–492.

McCollom, M.

1990   Re-evaluating Group Development: A Critique of the Familiar Models. In *Groups in Context: A New Perspective on Group Dynamics*, edited by J. Gillette and M. McCollom, pp. 133–154. Reading, MA: Addison-Wesley Publishing Co.

McCully, P.

1996   *Silenced Rivers: The Ecology and Politics of Large Dams.* London: Zed Books.

McDougall, H. M.

1993   *Black Baltimore: A New Theory of Community.* Philadelphia, PA: Temple University Press.

McElroy, K. R., B. Norton, M. Kegler, J. Burdine, and C. Sumaya

2003   Community-Based Interventions. *American Journal of Public Health* 93(4): 529–533.

McKnight, J.

1995   *The Careless Society.* New York: Basic Books.

McLeroy, K. R., D. Bibeau, A. Steckler, and K. Glanz

1988   An Ecological Perspective on Health Promotion Programs. *Health Education Quarterly* 15(4):351–377.

McRoberts, O. M.

2001   Black Churches, Community and Development. Shelterforce Online (January/February). Electronic document, http://www.nhi.org/online/issues/115/McRoberts.html (accessed March 25, 2005).

Medoff, P., and H. Sklar

1994   *Streets of Hope: The Fall and Rise of an Urban Neighborhood.* Cambridge, MA: South End Press.

Mezirow, J. D.

1963   *Dynamics of Community Development.* New York: Scarecrow Press.

REFERENCES

Miner, H. M.

1939   *St. Denis: A French-Canadian Parish.* Chicago: The University of Chicago Press.

1949   *Culture and Agriculture: An Anthropological Study of a Corn Belt County.* Ann Arbor: University of Michigan Press.

Minkler, M.

1997   *Community Organizing and Community Building for Health.* New Brunswick, NJ: Rutgers University Press.

Minkler, M., and N. Wallerstein

1997   Improving Health through Community Organizing and Community Building. In *Community Organizing and Community Building for Health,* edited by M. Minkler, pp. 30–53. New Brunswick, NJ: Rutgers University Press.

2003   *Community-Based Participatory Research for Health.* San Francisco: Jossey-Bass.

Monplaisir, L.

1999   Comparison of Intelligent CSCW Architecture for Evaluation of Agile Manufacturing Systems Design. *Human Factors and Ergonomics in Manufacturing* 9(2):1–14.

Moody, G.

2001   *Rebel Code.* Cambridge, MA: Perseus Publishing.

Moore, C. M.

1996   What is Community? *Chronicle of Community* 1(1):28-32.

Murdock, G. P.

1949   *Social Structure.* New York: Macmillan.

National Association of County and City Health Officials

2001   Turning Point: Collaborating for a New Century in Public Health. Electronic document, http://naccho.org/project30.cfm (accessed March 16, 2004).

National Consortium for Community/University Partnerships (NCCUP)

2000   Core Competencies: The Needs of Community and Economic Development Professionals. Committee report at the National Congress for Community Economic Development annual meetings, October, Washington, DC.

Navarro, V.

1999   The Political Economy of the Welfare State in Developed Capitalist Countries. *International Journal of Health Services* 29(1):1–50.

2002   *The Political Economy of Social Inequalities: Consequences for Health and Quality of Life.* Amityville, NY: Baywood.

Newscomb, T.

1956   The Prediction of Interpersonal Attraction. *American Psychologist* 11:575–586.

Nguyen, V. K., and K. Peschard

2003   Anthropology, Inequality and Disease: A Review. *Annual Review of Anthropology* 32(1):447–474.

Nisbet, R.

1966   *The Sociological Tradition.* New York: Basic Books Publishers, Inc.

Nonaka, I.

1994   A Dynamic Theory of Organizational Knowledge Creation. *Organization Science* 5(1):14–37.

Nordstrom, C.

1992   The Backyard Front. In *The Paths to Domination, Resistance and Terror,* edited by C. Nordstrom and J. Martin, pp. 260–276. Berkeley: University of California Press.

Norton, I. M., and S. M. Manson

1996   Research in American Indian and Alaska Native Communities: Navigating the Cultural Universe of Values and Process. *Journal of Consulting and Clinical Psychology* 64(5):856–860.

O'Fallon, L. R., F. L. Tyson, and A. Dearry, eds.

2000   Final Report of the Successful Models of Community-Based Participatory Research Conference, National Institute of Environmental Health Sciences, Bethesda, MD.

O'Hara-Devereaux, M., and R. Johansen

1994   *Global Work.* San Francisco: Jossey-Bass.

Oliver-Smith, A.

1991   Success and Failures in Post-Disaster Resettlement. *Disasters: The Journal of Disaster Studies and Management* 15(1):12–24.

1992   *The Martyred City: Death and Rebirth in the Andes.* 2d ed. Prospect Heights, IL: Waveland Press.

1999   The Brotherhood of Pain: Theoretical and Applied Perspectives on Post-Disaster Social Solidarity. In *The Angry Earth: Disaster in Anthropological Perspective,* edited by A. Oliver-Smith and S. M. Hoffman, pp. 156–172. New York: Routledge.

2001   Displacement, Resistance and the Critique of Development: From the Grass Roots to the Global. Final Report ESCOR R7644, University of Oxford, Refugee Studies Centre.

Oliver-Velez, N., A. H. Finlinson, S. Deren, R. R. Robles, M. Shedlin, J. Andia, and H. Colon

2002   Mapping the Air-Bridge Locations: The Application of Ethnographic Mapping Techniques to a Study of HIV Risk Behavior Determinants in East Harlem, New York, and Bayamon, Puerto Rico. *Human Organization* 61(3):262–276.

Orr, J.

1990   Sharing Knowledge, Celebrating Identity: War Stories and Community Memory in a Service Culture. In *Collective Remembering: Memory in Society,* edited by D. S. Middleton and D. Edwards, pp. 169–189. Beverly Hills, CA: Sage Publishers.

Orr, M.

2000 Baltimoreans United in Leadership Development: Exploring the Role of Governing Nonprofits. In *Nonprofits in Urban America*, edited by R. C. Hula and C. Jackson-Elmoore, pp. 151–167. Westport, CT: Quorum Books.

Owens, M. L.

2000 Black Church-Affiliated Community Development Corporations and the Coproduction of Affordable Housing in New York City. In *Nonprofits in Urban America*, edited by R. C. Hula and C. Jackson-Elmoore, pp. 169–198. Westport, CT: Quorum Books.

Park, R. E.

1952 *Human Communities: The City and Human Ecology.* Glencoe, IL: The Free Press.

Partridge, W. L.

2001 The Population Displaced by Armed Conflict in Colombia. *Social Justice: Anthropology, Peace and Human Rights* 2(1/2):25–46.

Paul, B. D., ed.

1955 *Health, Culture, and Community.* New York: Russell Sage Foundation.

Payne, L.

1998 *Rebuilding Communities in a Refugee Settlement.* Oxford: Oxfam Publications.

Pearce, W. B.

2001 Community-Building in the 21st Century through Public Dialogue. Paper presented at the Michael M. Osborn Lecture, March 6, Department of Communications, University of Memphis, Memphis, TN.

Pelto, P. J.

2002 Building Social Sciences and Health Research: A Decade of Technical Assistance in South Asia. *Human Organization* 61(3):189–195.

Pelto, P. J., and G. H. Pelto

1978 *Anthropological Research: The Structure of Inquiry.* 2d ed. Cambridge: Cambridge University Press.

Perella, F. J. Jr.

1996 Roman Catholic Approaches to Urban Ministry, 1945–1980. In *Churches, Cities, and Human Community: Urban Ministry in the United States 1945–1985*, edited by C. J. Green, pp. 179–211. Grand Rapids, MI: William B. Eerdmans Publishing Company.

Perkins, J. M.

1993 *Beyond Charity: The Call to Christian Community Development.* Grand Rapids, MI: Baker Books.

1995 What Is Christian Community Development? In *Restoring At-Risk Communities: Doing It Together and Doing It Right*, edited by J. M. Perkins, pp. 17–26. Grand Rapids, MI: Baker Books.

Pilcher, W.

1972   *The Portland Longshoremen.* New York: Holt, Rinehart & Co.

Popkin, S. J., V. E. Gwiasda, L. M. Olson, D. P. Rosenbaum, and L. Buron

2000   *The Hidden War: Crime and the Tragedy of Public Housing in Chicago.* New Brunswick, NJ: Rutgers University Press.

Popkin, S., B. Katz, M. K. Cunningham, K. D. Brown, J. Gustafson, and M. A. Turner

2004   *A Decade of HOPE VI: Research Findings and Policy Challenges.* Washington, DC: The Urban Institute

Poplin, D. E.

1979   *Communities: A Survey of Theories and Methods of Research.* 2d ed. New York: Macmillan.

Poppendieck, J.

1998   *Sweet Charity: Emergency Food and the End of Entitlement.* New York: Penguin Books.

Putnam, R.

1993   The Prosperous Community: Social Capital and Public Life. *The American Prospect* 4(13):35–42.

2000   *Bowling Alone: The Collapse and Revival of American Community.* New York: Simon and Schuster.

Rajan, S. R.

1999   Bhopal: Vulnerability, Routinization and the Chronic Disaster. In *The Angry Earth: Disaster in Anthropological Perspective,* edited by A. Oliver-Smith and S. M. Hoffman, pp. 257– 277. New York: Routledge.

2002   Missing Expertise, Categorical Politics and Chronic Disasters: The Case of Bhopal. In *Catastrophe and Culture: The Anthropology of Disaster,* edited by S. Hoffman and A. Oliver-Smith, pp. 237–360. Santa Fe, NM: SAR Press.

Rambaldi, G., and J. Callosa-Tarr

2000   Exploring the Synergies of GIS and Participatory 3-D Modeling to Increase Local Communication Capacity. Paper presented at the fifth seminar on GIS and Developing Countries, GISDECO 2000, IRRI, Los Banos, Philippines.

Rankin, K. N.

2003   Anthropologies and Geographies of Globalization. *Progress in Human Geography* 27(6):708–734.

Rauschenbusch, W.

1991   *Christianity and the Social Crisis.* Louisville, KY: Westminster/John Knox
[1907]   Press.

1997   *A Theology for the Social Gospel.* Louisville, KY: Westminster/John Knox
[1917]   Press.

REFERENCES

Redfield, R.

1955   *The Little Community: Viewpoints for the Study of a Human Whole.* Chicago: University of Chicago Press.

1960   *The Little Community and Peasant Society and Culture.* Chicago: University of Chicago Press.

Reed, P.

1995   Toward a Theology of Christian Community Development. In *Restoring At-Risk Communities: Doing It Together and Doing It Right,* edited by J. M. Perkins, pp. 27–46. Grand Rapids, MI: Baker Books.

ReliefWeb

2004   Zimbabwe Camp Sows Seeds for Sustainable Farming. Electronic document, http://www.reliefweb.int/w/rwb/nsf/0/c21b529b619ca73149256 ede001adc35?OpenDocum (accessed April 15, 2004).

Rheingold, H.

2002   *Smart Mobs: The Next Social Revolution.* New York: Perseus Publishing.

Rifkin, S. B., F. Muller, and W. Bichmann

1988   Primary Health Care: On Measuring Participation. *Social Science and Medicine* 26(9):931–940.

Roberts, B.

1978   *Cities of Peasants.* Beverly Hills, CA: Sage Publications.

Rodman, M. C.

1992   Empowering Place: Multilocality and Multivocality. *American Anthropologist* 94(3):640–656.

Roethlisberger, F. J., and W. J. Dickson

1939   *Management and the Worker.* Cambridge, MA: Harvard University Press.

Rogers, M. B.

1990   *Cold Anger: A Story of Faith and Power Politics.* Denton: University of North Texas Press.

Rogoff, B.

1990   Cognition as a Collaborative Process. In *Handbook of Child Psychology,* vol. 2, *Cognition, Perception, and Language,* edited by D. Kuhn and R. S. Siegler, pp. 679–744. New York: John Wiley.

Rooney, J.

1995   *Organizing the South Bronx.* Albany: State University of New York Press.

Rothman, J.

1995   Approaches to Community Intervention. In *Strategies of Community Intervention,* edited by J. Rothman, J. L. Erlich, J. E. Tropman, and F. M. Cox, pp. 26–63. Itasca, IL: F.E. Peacock Publishers.

Rubin, H. J.

2000   *Renewing Hope within Neighborhoods of Despair: The Community-Based Development Model.* Albany: State University of New York Press.

Saegert, S., J. P. Thompson, and M. R. Warren, eds.

2001   *Social Capital and Poor Communities.* New York: Russell Sage Foundation.

Sanjek, R.

1990   Urban Anthropology in the 1980s: A World View. Vol. 29 of *Annual Anthropological Review*, edited by B. J. Siegel, pp. 151–186. Stanford, CA: Stanford University Press.

Sassen, S.

1991   *The Global City.* Princeton, NJ: Princeton University Press.

Sawicki, D. S., and W. J. Craig

1996   The Democratization of Data: Bridging the Gap for Community Groups. *Journal of the American Planning Association* 62(4):512–523.

Schaller, L. E.

1965   *Planning for Protestantism in Urban America.* New York: Abingdon Press.

Schensul, J. J.

1985   Systems Consistency in Field Research, Dissemination, and Social Change. *American Behavioral Scientist* 29(2):186–204.

1994   *The Development and Maintenance of Community Action Research Partnerships.* Hartford, CT: The Institute for Community Research.

2000   Sites and Settings: Older Adults and HIV Risk. Paper presented at the NIA Conference on AIDS and Older Adults, Bethesda, MD.

2001   Strengthening Communities through Action Research. Paper presented at the Annual Meeting of the Society for Applied Anthropology, Merida, Yucatan.

2002   Democratizing Science through Social Science Research Partnerships. *Bulletin of Science, Technology and Society* 22(3):190–202.

in press   Sustainability in HIV Prevention Research. In *Context, Culture, and Collaboration in AIDS Interventions: Ecological Ideas for Enhancing Community Impact*, edited by E. Trickett and W. Pequenot. New York: Oxford University Press.

Schensul, J. J., and M. Berg

2004   Youth Participatory Action Research: A Transformative Approach to Service Learning. *Michigan Journal of Community Service Learning* (special issue on anthropology and service learning) 10(3):76–88.

Schensul, J. J., and M. D. LeCompte

1999   *Ethnographer's Toolkit.* Walnut Creek, CA: AltaMira Press.

Schensul, J. J., J. A. Levy, and W. B. Disch

2003   Individual, Contextual, and Social Network Factors Affecting Exposure to HIV/AIDS Risk among Older Residents Living in Low-Income Senior Housing Complexes. *JAIDS: Journal of Acquired Immune Deficiency Syndromes* 33(2):S138–S152.

Schensul, J. J., J. Robison, C. Reyes, K. Radda, S. Gaztambide, and W. Disch
in press   Building Interdisciplinary and Intersectoral Research Partnerships for
            Community-Based Research: Research on Depression and Barriers to Care
            with Older Minority Adults. *Journal of Community Psychology*, vol. 35.

Schensul, J. J., and S. L. Schensul
1992   Collaborative Research: Methods of Inquiry for Social Change. In *The
       Handbook of Qualitative Research in Education*, edited by M. D. LeCompte,
       W. L. Millroy, and J. Preissle, pp. 161–200. New York: Academic Press.

Schensul, J. J., M. R. Weeks, and M. Singer
1999   Building Research Partnerships. In *Researcher Roles and Research
       Partnerships*, edited by M. D. LeCompte, J. J. Schensul, M. R. Weeks, and
       M. Singer, vol. 6, pp. 85–164. Walnut Creek, CA: AltaMira Press.

Schensul, S. L.
1974   Skills Needed in Applied Anthropology: Lessons from El Centro de la
       Causa. *Human Organization* 33(2):203–208.

Schensul, S. L., and M. Borrero
1982   Introduction to the Hispanic Health Council. *Urban Anthropology*
       11(1):1–8.

Schensul, S. L., and J. J. Schensul
1978   Advocacy and Applied Anthropology. In *Social Scientists as Advocates: Views
       from the Applied Disciplines*, edited by G. H. Weber and G. J. McCall, pp.
       121–165. Newbury Park, CA: Sage Publications.

Schwartz, N.
1978   Community Development and Cultural Change in Latin America. *Annual
       Review of Anthropology* 7:235–261.

Scotch, N. A.
1963   Medical Anthropology. In *Biennial Review of Anthropology*, edited by
       B. J. Siegel, pp. 30–68. Stanford, CA: Stanford University Press.

Scudder, T.
1973   The Human Ecology of Big Projects: River Basic Development and
       Resettlement. *Annual Review of Anthropology* 2:45–61.

Sherman, A. L.
2002   *Reinvigorating Faith in Communities*. Fishers, IN: Hudson Institute.

Shirley, D.
2002   *Valley Interfaith and School Reform: Organizing for Power in South Texas*. Austin:
       University of Texas Press.

Siegel, J., V. Dubrovsky, S. Kiesler, and T. McGuire
1986   Group Process in Computer-Mediated Communication. *Organizational
       Behavior and Human Decision Processes* 37(2):157–187.

Simonelli, J., and B. Roberts
2003   Editor's Choice: Cultures within Cultures: Practicing Anthropology in the
       U.S. *Practicing Anthropology* 25(4):2.

Singer, M.

1994   *The Hartford Needle Exchange Evaluation Project: Final Report.* Hartford, CT: Hispanic Health Council.

Singer, M., N. Romero-Daza, M. R. Weeks, and P. Pelia

1995   Ethnography and the Evaluation of Needle Exchange in the Prevention of HIV Transmission. In *Qualitative Methods in Drug Abuse and HIV Research,* edited by E. Y. Lambert, R. S. Ashery, and R. H. Needle, pp. 231–253. NIDA Research Monograph Series no. 157. Bethesda, MD: National Institutes of Health.

Smidt, C., ed.

2003   *Religion as Social Capital: Producing the Common Good.* Waco, TX: Baylor University Press.

Smith, D. A.

2003   Participatory Mapping of Community Lands and Hunting Yields among the Bugle of Western Panama. *Human Organization* 62(4):332–343.

Sohng, S. S. L.

1995   Participatory Research and Community Organizing. Paper presented at the New Social Movement and Community Organizing Conference, University of Washington, Seattle.

Southall, A.

1973   *Urban Anthropology.* London: Oxford University Press.

Sphere Project

2000   *Humanitarian Charter and Minimum Standards in Response.* Oxford: Oxfam Publishing.

Spicer, E. H.

1970   Patrons of the Poor. *Human Organization* 29(1):12–19.

Spicer, E. H., ed.

1952   *Human Problems in Technological Change.* New York: Russell Sage Foundation.

Sproull, L., and S. Kiesler

1986   Reducing Social Context Cues: Electronic Mail in Organizational Communication. *Management Science* 32(11):1492–1512.

Stafford, P. B.

2001   When Community Planning Becomes Community Building: Place-Based Activism and the Creation of Good Places to Grow Old. In *Empowering Frail Elderly People: Opportunities and Impediments in Housing, Health, and Support Service Delivery,* edited by L. F. Heumann and M. E. McCall, pp. 137–152. Westport, CT: Praeger.

Stansbury, J. P., R. Barrios, R. Palencia, C. Rojas, and M. T. Medina

2001   After the Hurricane: Nutritional Status of Under-Five Children in Three Hurricane-Affected Areas of Honduras. *Nutritional Anthropology* 24(1):3–7.

Steckler, A., B. Israel, L. Dawson, and E. Eng

1993   Community Health Development: An Anthology of the Works of Guy Steuart. *Health Education Quarterly* supplement 1:S1–S153.

Stevens, P. E., and J. M. Hall

1998   Participatory Action Research for Sustaining Individual and Community Change: A Model of HIV Prevention Education. *AIDS Education and Prevention* 10(5):387–402.

Stevenson, H. C.

1998   Raising Safe Villages: Cultural-Ecological Factors That Influence the Emotional Adjustment of Adolescents. *Journal of Black Psychology* 24(1):44–59.

Stocks, A.

2003   Mapping Dreams in Nicaragua's Bosawas Reserve. *Human Organization* 62(4):344–356.

Stone, L.

1992   Cultural Influences in Community Participation in Health. *Social Science and Medicine* 35(4):409–417.

Sullivan, M., A. Kone, K. D. Senturia, N. J. Chrisman, S. J. Ciske, and J. W. Krieger

2001   Researcher and Researched-Community Perspectives: Toward Bridging the Gap. *Health Education and Behavior* 28(2):130–149.

Suttles, G. D.

1968   *The Social Order of the Slum: Ethnicity and Territory in the Inner City.* Chicago: University of Chicago Press.

Taplin, D. H., S. Scheld, and S. Low

2002   Rapid Ethnographic Assessment in Urban Parks: A Case Study of Independence National Historical Park. *Human Organization* 61(1):80–93.

Tax, S.

1958   The Fox Project. *Human Organization* 17(1):17–19.

Tilley, C.

1994   *A Phenomenology of Landscape: Places, Paths and Monuments.* Oxford: Berg.

Todd, G.

1996   Presbyterian Ministry in Urban America, 1945–80. In *Churches, Cities, and Human Community: Urban Ministry in the United States 1945–1985*, edited by C. J. Green, pp. 151–178. Grand Rapids, MI: William B. Eerdmans Publishing Company.

Tönnies, F.

1963   *Community and Society.* New York: Harper and Row.
[1887]

Trostle, J. A., and J. Sommerfeld

1996   Medical Anthropology and Epidemiology. *American Review of Anthropology* 25:253–274.

Trotter, R. T. III

1999   Friends, Relatives, and Relevant Others: Conducting Ethnographic Network Studies. Vol. 4 of *Mapping Social Networks, Spatial Data, and Hidden Populations*. Ethnographer's Toolkit, edited by J. J. Schensul, M. D. LeCompte, R. T. Trotter II, E. K. Cromley, and M. Singer, pp. 1–50. Walnut Creek, CA: AltaMira Press.

Tuckman, B. W.

1965   Developmental Sequence in Small Groups. *Psychological Bulletin* 63(6):384–399.

United States Commerce Department National Telecommunications and Information Administration

1999   Falling through the Net. Electronic document, http://www.ntia.doc.gov/ntiahome/digitaldivide/index.html (accessed February 3, 2000).

United Nations High Commission on Refugees (UNHCR)

2004   UNHCR Global Appeal (Southern Africa). Electronic document, http://www.sahims.net/doclibrary/2004/03_March/17_Wed/Regional/UNHCR%20Southern%20Africa.pdf (accessed March 25, 2005).

Van Maanen, J., and S. Barley

1984   Occupational Communities: Culture and Control in Organizations. *Research in Organizational Behavior* 6:287–365.

van Willigen, J.

1973   Concrete Means and Abstract Goals: Papago Experiences in the Application of Development Resources. *Human Organization* 32(1):1–8.

1989   *Getting Some Age on Me: Social Organization of Older People in a Rural American Community*. Lexington: University Press of Kentucky.

1993   *Applied Anthropology: An Introduction*. 2d ed. Westport, CT: Bergin & Garvey.

2002   *Applied Anthropology: An Introduction*. 3d ed. Westport, CT: Bergin & Garvey.

van Willigen, J., and N. K. Chadha

1999   *Social Aging in a Delhi Neighborhood*. Westport, CT: Bergin & Garvey.

van Willigen, J., B. Rylko-Bauer, and A. McElroy, eds.

1989   *Making Our Research Useful: Case Studies in the Utilization of Anthropological Knowledge*. Boulder, CO: Westview Press.

Vélez-Ibáñez, C., and J. Greenberg

1992   Formation and Transformation of Funds of Knowledge among US Mexican Households. *Anthropology and Education Quarterly* 23(4):313–335.

Venkatesh, S. A.

2000   *American Project: The Rise and Fall of a Modern Ghetto*. Cambridge, MA: Harvard University Press.

References

Verma, R., P. Pelto, S. L. Schensul, and A. Joshi, eds.

2004   *Sexuality in the Time of AIDS.* New Delhi: Sage Publications.

Vidal, A. C.

2001   Faith-Based Organizations in Community Development. Report prepared for the US Department of Housing and Community Development, Office of Policy Development and Research. Electronic document, http://www.huduser.org/publications/pdf/faithbased_1.pdf (accessed March 25, 2005).

Waldkoenig, G. A. C., and W. O. Avery

1999   Mission at the Eastward, Maine. In *Cooperating Congregations: Portraits of Mission Strategies,* edited by G. A. C. Waldkoenig and W. O. Avery, pp. 152–186. Bethesda, MD: Alban Institute.

Wallace, A. F. C.

1957   Mazeway Disintegration: The Individual's Perception of Sociocultural Disorganization. *Human Organization* 16(2):23–27.

Warren, M. R.

2001   *Dry Bones Rattling: Community Building to Revitalize American Democracy.* Princeton, NJ: Princeton University Press.

Warren, M. R., and R. L. Wood

2001   *Faith-Based Community Organizing: The State of the Field.* Jericho, NY: Interfaith Funders.

Warren, R.

2004   Older and Newer Approaches to the Community. In *Urban Community,* edited by A. W. Martin, pp. 54-71. Upper Saddle River, NJ: Pearson Education, Inc.

Washington State Department of Health

1994   Public Health Improvement Plan. Government document. Olympia, WA: Washington State Department of Health.

Watson, N.

1997   Why We Argue about Virtual Community: A Case Study of the Phish.Net Fan Community. In *Virtual Culture: Identity and Community in Cybersociety,* edited by S. Jones, pp. 102–132. London: Sage.

Weeks, M. R.

1991   *Community Outreach Prevention Effort: Designs in Culturally Appropriate AIDS Intervention.* Intervention manual for Project COPE. Hartford, CT: Institute for Community Research.

1999   Linking People through Places: Drug User Social Networks and Connections to Drug-Use Sites. Paper presented at the 98th Annual Meeting of the American Anthropological Association, Chicago.

2002   The Risk Avoidance Partnership: Peer-Led HIV Prevention with Drug-Using Networks in High-Risk Settings. Paper presented at the Annual Meeting of the Society for Applied Anthropology, Atlanta, GA.

Weeks, M. R., M. Grier, K. Radda, and D. McKinley

1999   AIDS and Social Relations of Power: Urban African-American Women's Discourse on the Contexts of Risk and Prevention. In *Power in the Blood: A Handbook on AIDS, Politics, and Communication*, edited by W. N. Elwood, pp. 181–197. Mahwah, NJ: Lawrence Erlbaum Press.

Weeks, M. R., M. Grier, N. Romero-Daza, M. J. Puglisi-Basquez, and M. Singer

1998   Streets, Drugs, and the Economy of Sex in the Age of AIDS. In *Women, Drug Use and HIV Infection*, edited by S. J. Stevens, S. Tortu, and S. L. Coyle, pp. 205–229. Binghamton, NY: Hawthorn Press.

Weeks, M. R., M. Singer, D. A. Himmelgreen, P. Richmond, and N. Romero-Daza

1998   Drug Use Patterns of Substance-Abusing Women: Gender and Ethnic Differences in an AIDS Prevention Program. *Drugs and Society* 13(1/2):37–64.

Weeks, M. R., L. B. Sylla, M. Abbott, B. Valdes, R. Martinez, M. Prince

2002   Microbicide Acceptability to Prevent HIV in High-Risk Women. Paper presented at the 3rd CIRA Science Day Conference, New Haven, CT.

Weinberger, D.

2002   *Small Pieces Loosely Joined: A Unified Theory of the Web.* New York: Perseus Publishing.

White, A. J.

1967   The Churches and Community Development. *The Lutheran Quarterly* 19(4):371–384.

Whyte, W. F.

1943   *Street Corner Society: The Social Structure of an Italian Slum.* Chicago: University of Chicago Press.

Whyte, W. F., ed.

1991   *Participatory Action Research.* Newbury Park, CA: Sage Publications.

Williamson, K. M.

2003   Race, Power, and Participatory Action Research. Paper presented at the Annual Meeting of the Society for Applied Anthropology, Portland, OR.

Williamson, K. M., M. J. Berg, K. Brown, M. Caez, and K. Mathis

2003   Making Connections, Building Healthy Communities, and Making Change. Panel presentations given at the Child Welfare League of America Building Communities for 21st-Century Child Welfare Conference, Albany, NY.

Williamson, L., J. Brecher, R. Glasser, and J. J. Schensul

1999   Using Ethnography to Influence Public Programming. In *Using Ethnographic Data: Interventions, Public Programming and Public Policy*, edited by J. J. Schensul, M. D. LeCompte, G. A. Hess Jr., B. K. Nastasi, M. J. Berg, L. Williamson, J. Brecher, and R. Glasser, vol. 7, pp. 115–178. Walnut Creek, CA: AltaMira Press.

REFERENCES

Winston, D.

1999   *Red-Hot and Righteous: The Urban Religion of the Salvation Army.* Cambridge, MA: Harvard University Press.

Winter, T.

2002   *Making Men, Making Class: The YMCA and Workingmen, 1877–1920.* Chicago: University of Chicago Press.

Woolever, C., and D. Bruce

2002   *A Field Guide to US Congregations.* Louisville, KY: Westminster/John Knox Press.

Index

School of American Research Advanced Seminar Series

PUBLISHED BY SAR PRESS

URUK MESOPOTAMIA & ITS NEIGHBORS:
CROSS-CULTURAL INTERACTIONS IN THE
ERA OF STATE FORMATION
  Mitchell S. Rothman, ed.

TIKAL: DYNASTIES, FOREIGNERS,
& AFFAIRS OF STATE: ADVANCING
MAYA ARCHAEOLOGY
  Jeremy A. Sabloff, ed.

REMAKING LIFE & DEATH: TOWARD AN
ANTHROPOLOGY OF THE BIOSCIENCES
  Sarah Franklin & Margaret Lock, eds.

GRAY AREAS: ETHNOGRAPHIC
ENCOUNTERS WITH NURSING HOME
CULTURE
  Philip B. Stafford, ed.

AMERICAN ARRIVALS: ANTHROPOLOGY
ENGAGES THE NEW IMMIGRATION
  Nancy Foner, ed.

VIOLENCE
  Neil L. Whitehead, ed.

LAW & EMPIRE IN THE PACIFIC:
FIJI AND HAWAI'I
  Sally Engle Merry &
  Donald Brenneis, eds.

ANTHROPOLOGY IN THE MARGINS
OF THE STATE
  Veena Das & Deborah Poole, eds.

PLURALIZING ETHNOGRAPHY:
COMPARISON AND REPRESENTATION IN
MAYA CULTURES, HISTORIES, AND
IDENTITIES
  John M. Watanabe & Edward F. Fischer,
  eds.

THE ARCHAEOLOGY OF COLONIAL
ENCOUNTERS: COMPARATIVE
PERSPECTIVES
  Gil J. Stein, ed.

COPÁN: THE HISTORY OF AN ANCIENT
MAYA KINGDOM
  E. Wyllys Andrews and
  William L. Fash, eds.

REGIONAL PERSPECTIVES ON THE OLMEC
  Robert J. Sharer & David C. Grove, eds.

THE CHEMISTRY OF PREHISTORIC
HUMAN BONE
  T. Douglas Price, ed.

THE EMERGENCE OF MODERN HUMANS:
BIOCULTURAL ADAPTATIONS IN THE
LATER PLEISTOCENE
  Erik Trinkaus, ed.

THE ANTHROPOLOGY OF WAR
  Jonathan Haas, ed.

THE EVOLUTION OF POLITICAL SYSTEMS
  Steadman Upham, ed.

CLASSIC MAYA POLITICAL HISTORY:
HIEROGLYPHIC AND ARCHAEOLOGICAL
EVIDENCE
  T. Patrick Culbert, ed.

TURKO-PERSIA IN HISTORICAL
PERSPECTIVE
  Robert L. Canfield, ed.

CHIEFDOMS: POWER, ECONOMY, AND
IDEOLOGY
  Timothy Earle, ed.

RECONSTRUCTING PREHISTORIC PUEBLO
SOCIETIES
  William A. Longacre, ed.

WRITING CULTURE: THE POETICS
AND POLITICS OF ETHNOGRAPHY
  James Clifford &
  George E. Marcus, eds.

Participants in the School of American Research Contemporary
Issues seminar "Community Building in the Twenty First Century,"
Santa Fe, New Mexico, July 21–22, 2000.
Standing from left: Jean J. Schensul, Noel J. Chrisman,
Marietta L. Baba, Stanley E. Hyland, Anthony Oliver-Smith,
Francisco Fernandez Repetto, John van Willigen.